P[illegible]

SEVENTY . . . [illegible]

Shobhaa Dé's books include [illegible] *Evenings*, *Starry Nights* and *Superstar India*. [illegible] columnist in leading publications, she is known for [illegible] outspoken views, making her one of India's most respected opinion shapers. She lives in Mumbai with her family.

Seventy...
and to hell with it!

SHOBHAA DÉ

PENGUIN BOOKS
An imprint of Penguin Random House

PENGUIN BOOKS

USA | Canada | UK | Ireland | Australia
New Zealand | India | South Africa | China

Penguin Books is part of the Penguin Random House group of companies
whose addresses can be found at global.penguinrandomhouse.com

Published by Penguin Random House India Pvt. Ltd
7th Floor, Infinity Tower C, DLF Cyber City,
Gurgaon 122 002, Haryana, India

First published in Penguin Books by Penguin Random House India 2017

10 9 8 7 6 5 4 3 2 1

ISBN 9780143414247

Typeset in Sabon by Manipal Digital Systems, Manipal
Printed at Thomson Press India Ltd, New Delhi

www.penguin.co.in

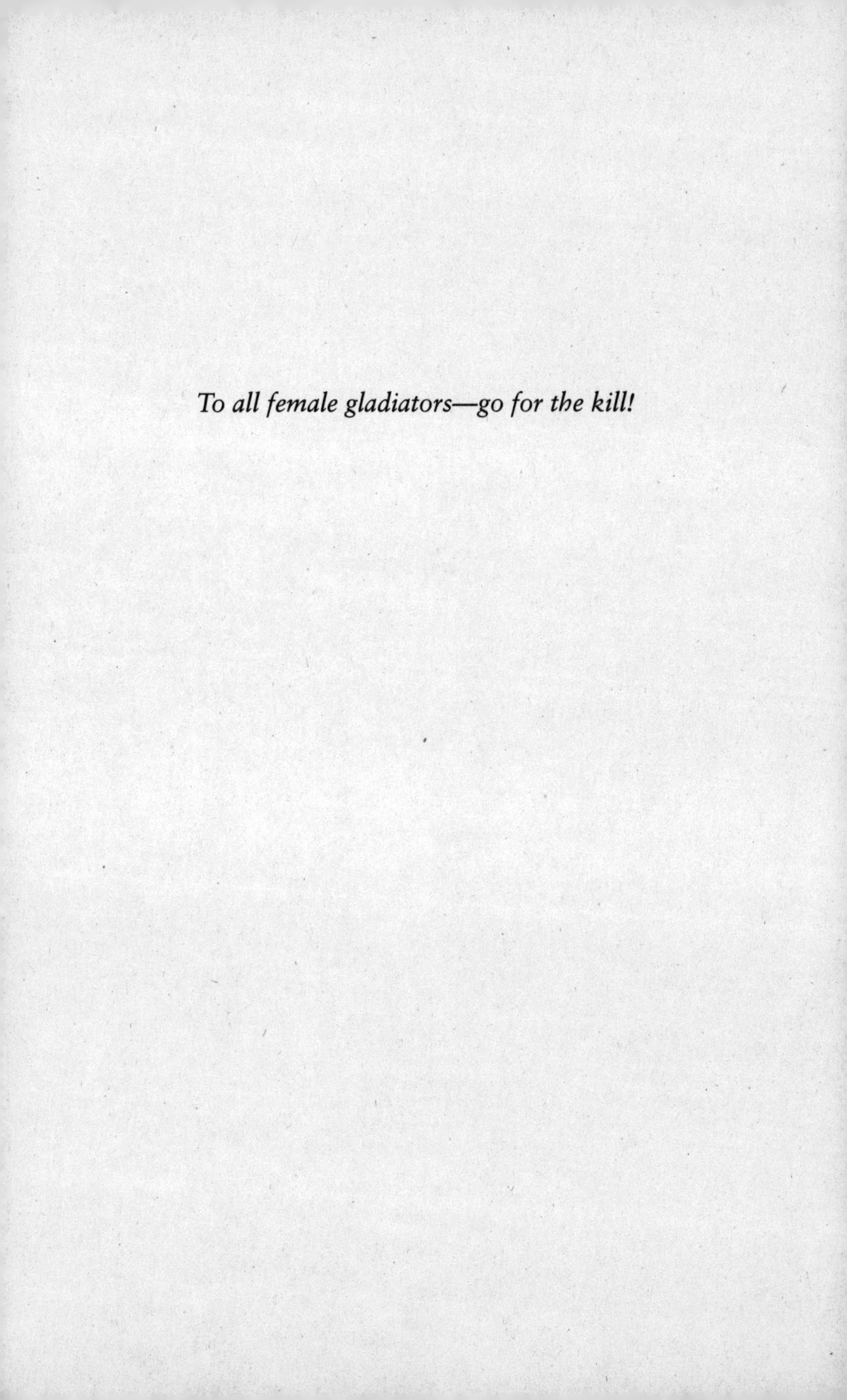

To all female gladiators—go for the kill!

Aaj phir jeeney ki tamanna hai . . .
Aaj phir marney ka iraada hai . . .

—*Guide* (1965)

Haravaley teh gavasley ka . . .
Gavasley teh, haravaley ka . . .

Have you lost something precious, and found it again?
Or have you found something precious, and lost it again?

—Sung by Lata Mangeshkar, lyrics by P. Savalaram

Between what is said and not meant, and what is meant and not said, most of love is lost.

—Khalil Gibran

Preface

Zara sa jhoom loon main
Arrey na re na re na . . .
Main chali banke hawa

I have been writing this book for seventy years. It's up to you to decide what you make of these seventy years! If you ask me, I'd say I've had lots of fun. Real, unalloyed fun. For me, that has been enough. You are allowed to ask, 'Then why write a book? Keep having fun!' Let me attempt an answer. More than fifty out of those seventy years have been filled with writing. Not just filled . . . flooded! Torrents of unstoppable writing have been at the centre of all the fun. Of my world. Of my life. Therefore, this book.

All writers are narcissists. All. Even when you are writing about someone else's life, you're really writing about yourself. Ultimately it is about you. Think about it. Since I am no exception, here's me, *jaisey bhi, waisey bhi*. All writers are selfish too. Some disguise it better, that's all. I am selfish. When I am writing, nothing else matters. Nobody else matters. This book is a birthday present from me to me. 'Do you write for posterity?' I am asked. What nonsense! Who does that? I write for the moment. This very moment. I write because it hurts not to. I write because I am hooked—I am an addict. I feel so lucky that writing chose me. And to all aspiring writers reading this, I want to say: Stay hungry, stay insecure, stay curious, write, write, write, write . . . write in your sleep, write when you are talking to people, write with your ears and nose and tongue and skin. Write till you bleed. Become that beast.

Through writing, I meet extraordinary people. People are my narcotic. I am an avid collector of moments and memories. There isn't a single person on earth who does not interest me. They may not interest themselves, but they definitely interest me.

But this book is not about those wonderful people. It is about me. And I am admitting it gleefully. Finally, I have started liking myself. Let's call it the Dinosaur Syndrome. When you have been around long enough, you become used to 'you'—however you are. It's you. And you have lived with this person, known this person, more intimately than any other creature, living or dead. Better to like than dislike, na? Then there is the question of timing. This book felt right for this time. It asked to be written. Books have their own birth charts and horoscopes. I believe that. Books also possess a *taqdeer* which may or may not be linked to the author's. A book has an independent existence and destiny. Some books take off, and you wonder—Why? How? Others remain stuck and you again wonder the same thing—Why? How? Then comes a book that is written 'just' like that. Simbly! Like this one. It makes the book very special because there is zero *aagey-peechey* to it.

I felt like treating myself, revisiting bits and pieces of my own life. And writing coquettishly about—me! Not in the boastful 'I did this . . . I did that . . . I met this VVIP . . . I interacted with that amazing person . . . I won this award . . . I ate here . . . I drank there . . . I travelled to the North Pole . . . I suffered . . . I sacrificed . . . I survived . . . aren't I amazing?' manner. No, no, no. But hey, at seventy you do feel you have earned those bragging rights. Uff, the temptation to boast is just overwhelming. 'What have I to lose? If not now, then when?' you say, and start showing off. I admit I had to restrain myself several times from becoming entirely insufferable, self-absorbed and nauseating. But that's what good editors are for—they know how to deal tactfully with dinosaurs.

If you are expecting words of wisdom, well, look hard. You may find them. Profound truths? I have lived them! But please, this is not a chronological account of my seventy years or even a comprehensive one, with nary a detail skipped. If you want a standardized, sanitized bio, check the hopelessly inaccurate info available on the web. I never google myself, but some fools do. They ask me to verify really bizarre stuff about my life, saying plaintively, 'But it's on Wikipedia!' Okay then, stick to Wikipedia if that version appeals to you—I have not bothered to correct/edit any of it—and skip this book, I tell them.

The only worthwhile reason for writing *Seventy . . . and to Hell with It* was my desire to connect, and laugh and love. Mine has been a life defined by irresistible, if way too many, 'why nots'. I wanted to share my 'why not' moments with you. Don't worry, there is no heavy-duty gyan here but plenty of josh. I wrote the book in an uninterrupted burst of pure energy. I sat back languidly and let it flow. Halfway through, I was pretty exhilarated! Where was all this going? Perhaps nowhere. But for me, it was a deep recognition of my much younger, truer self—the girl with wild passions and reckless dreams. I touched those insane passions all over again. I thought they had died years earlier! It was such a delirious discovery. I never want to let go of that original person.

I refuse to give up and become a harmless old lady. I still want to dance naked under the stars. I want to go to Buenos Aires and learn how to tango with a tall, graceful, ponytailed stranger. I want to eat figs in Tuscany. And wade into moonlit waters in Goa, Andrea Bocelli singing just for me. I want to wear jasmine in my hair and watch apsaras dance at Konarak. There are so many things still left to do, taste, experience.

To live a lot, you have to die many times. The *khushboo* of life is the world's most expensive perfume. I wish I could bottle it. I have trained my senses to enjoy its fragrance any time, anywhere. I have identified it, given it a name. For years, I felt embarrassed to acknowledge its existence because I thought it made me look like a sentimental loser. But now that I have freed myself from myself, I can say it without cringing: My special khushboo is love. This was the single biggest discovery while remembering, forgetting, remembering, rewinding. I kept asking myself as I sifted through seven decades of memories—What is it that stays? What is important? What nourishes you? What completes you? The answer surprised me. And when that four-letter word—love—refused to go away, I meekly surrendered to its presence and power.

So, my dear readers, here it is, my simple philosophy of life—and don't laugh—inspired by a cheesy Bollywood cabaret song featuring Rekha in the hit movie *Janbaaz* (1985): '*Pyaar do. Pyaar lo.*' Give love. Get love. Nothing more is needed!

A space of my own

At seventy, you have nothing to lose. Finally, you are *befikre*!

Nails. Would you believe it? Everything comes down to nails. Toenails. I am writing this soon after celebrating my sixty-seventh birthday with the family. As always, they had made it extraordinarily special for me. I felt a little guilty. Poor children and considerate husband—how much longer will they have to keep coming up with birthday surprises for me? Thoughtful, hand-picked gifts, sweet notes, an unexplored venue, candles and flowers. Year after year, my family has taken enormous trouble to make my birthday amazing—to make me feel amazing. This year, perhaps for the first time, I asked myself—do I deserve their love? The question depressed me. I came home in an uncharacteristically pensive mood. The mellow white wine we had consumed contributed to the introspection. Don't get soppy and sentimental, I told myself. Don't feel martyred. Feel happy, not guilty. Rejoice. Sixty-seven today, sixty-eight next year, sixty-nine the year after, seventy after that, life goes on.

The next morning, for the first time in my life, as I bent over to clip my toenails, I recoiled in shock. Those couldn't possibly belong to me. These were the toenails of a really old person! I reached for my reading glasses and looked closely. My toenails had aged. Which meant the rest of me had aged too. But this drastically? Toenails never lie. Look at your own. Check what they are saying. Toenails tell you the sort of bald truths your face doesn't. Perhaps it has something to do with being taken for granted. I had never thought about my toenails till that defining moment, the morning after my birthday. It was as if I was looking at them for the very first time in my life. And at that precise moment, I felt like I was staring at my mother's feet. Those were her toenails when she was in her seventies.

It's not about pedicures or caring enough for your feet. Nails cannot be fooled or pampered. Those damn toenails remind you to take a clear-eyed look at yourself—other body parts that are giving up, slowly but surely. Like the ropelike veins on the back of your hands, the loose skin under your chin and so many other telltale signs of physical deterioration. Since that day, I have started to examine my toenails every morning after my bath. I have scrupulously applied foot cream for years, but mechanically, without paying the slightest attention to the nails. Now that the toenails have become my main focus, I examine them somewhat obsessively. My toenails have started talking to me!

Old people's nails thicken and are exceedingly hard to clip. They also get discoloured and ridged on the surface. By this point, chances of the toes getting misshapen are pretty high. Feet tend to flatten and broaden with advancing years. When that happens, toenails become brittle and crack vertically, which is very painful. The surrounding skin gets sore, leading to ingrown nails. Jagged edges appear, and get caught in bedclothes. You wake up in the middle of the night wincing in pain. It's dark. You can't find your spectacles. You grope on the bedside table, knock over a water jug. Switch on the light. Forget where you've stored the nail clipper. Wake up the husband and ask for help. The toenail-fixing operation gets under way. With eyes full of sleep, you nick yourself. There's blood on the bed sheets. You need ice. You stagger to the kitchen. Wake up the dog. Wake up others. Slip on something squishy. Keel over. Fall. But not badly. Your old training as a sportsperson helps you break the fall. But there will be a bruise tomorrow morning. Ice cubes in hand, you make it back to the bedroom in one piece. Dawn is breaking. And your toenail still hasn't been fixed. You finally feel old. Yes, *old*!

It took my toenails to remind me of my biological age. In my head and heart, I am stuck at thirty-four—possibly the best year of my life. That was a long time ago. But so what? What a year it was, tumultuous and life-altering. I decide there and then that no matter what my toenails are telling me, I will treat them as toenails, not as time bombs ticking away, warning me to be cautious, slow down, retire, find my inner calm, change. Sixty-seven is not all that terrible an age to be. If I continue to feel thirty-four, it doesn't really matter.

That unexpected encounter with the toenails brought me face-to-face with the sixty-seven-year-old me. And forced me to shift my gaze upwards and look more closely into the mirror. All of a sudden, I took note of the deepening lines around the mouth, the additional crow's feet at the corners of my eyes. The extra strands of grey framing my face, the slackening of the skin on the neck, the slight discoloration of the lips. My reflection was a revelation. How had I not noticed these changes earlier? Had I not looked hard enough? That's not possible. I am as vain as the next person. I had looked but I hadn't seen. Such a big difference between looking and seeing. Just as I was fretting over a deep furrow between the brows, I happened to catch a glimpse of my ears. Here's a confession: I like my ears. And to my great satisfaction and utter relief, the ears looked just the same. The ears could have belonged to a thirty-four-year-old. And that was my big thrill. Why focus on the negatives (discoloured toenails) when there are positives (pretty ears) to cheer you up?

It's important to be realistic and self-critical in life. But it's equally important to remain upbeat and positive about the inevitable. Age is one of them. From now on, it's going to be ears over toenails.

I am not going to put on a fake jaunty attitude and declare: Seventy is the new fifty! Because seventy is seventy. And no matter how 'young' you feel, you can neither look it nor hack it as anyone but a (hopefully) well-preserved septuagenarian. Life definitely does not begin at seventy—but neither does it have to end. I don't believe in milestones. Hitting seventy is not an achievement. And it is certainly not a milestone. It is merely a biological fact of life. I have survived my seventh decade. That's about all it says to me.

Why focus on the negatives (discoloured toenails) when there are positives (pretty ears) to cheer you up?

This book started off as a philosophical look at the space I have travelled over seven decades. Our life is made up of the spaces we constantly negotiate. Some we revisit. Some we love. Some we never want to be reminded of. The space in our hearts is supposed to be limitless. It is believed that, as one grows older, this space expands and accommodates more and more of everything—people, experiences, heartaches, sorrow, loss, death, disappointment, despair. But the one thing the heart never loses is hope, no matter how terrible life is.

As I write these words, I am watching a delicate tulsi plant on the ledge of my balcony. It is struggling to survive the lashings of the Mumbai rains. It has been a particularly harsh monsoon this year. And the tulsi plant is tenaciously hanging in there, much like the people of this great metropolis. Nobody gives up hope in Mumbai. I am so proud to possessively claim it as 'my city'. Even at my lowest, something about Mumbai's much-touted 'spirit' always pulls me back from the edge and stops me from giving up. Mumbai keeps me going. Mumbai keeps me afloat. I owe Mumbai the 'space' within, the space I alone own.

I hated the idea of space when I was a child. Space meant separation. At that point, space meant separation from just one person—my mother. I didn't trust space—physical or emotional. I still don't.

The first space in life is created the moment you are born, the umbilical cord is cut and you are separated from your mother. How you negotiate that particular 'away from the security of a warm womb' space for the rest of your life colours just about everything else.

The most important space in the world is the one you subsequently snatch, appropriate and occupy. This is the space you create for yourself. After years of living in this space, perhaps you can find the courage to ask yourself the single most important question: How happy am I in my own space?

This is really the starting point for living the life that suits you. The awareness leads you to many other places and spaces. Awareness is a privilege. A child may possess it at age ten. And you—at thirty, forty, fifty, sixty, seventy, eighty—may not! If and when you sadly discover 'your space' is not providing the quality and level of happiness you seek, you have to ask yourself why that is so. Are you letting yourself down? Do you feel you are not loved? Not respected? Not appreciated? Do you focus on the many negatives and take the few positives for granted? The painful realization that you are not loved, have never been loved, is perhaps the most crushing truth of all. An unloved life! What a tragedy.

I am somewhat oversensitive about space—both my own and other people's. I see this as a major liability. I am forever analysing and reanalysing simple conversations and gestures, looking for hidden meanings, imagining agendas. I drive myself and my family nuts with all the 'conclusions' that I draw. They tell me I have an overheated imagination. Perhaps that's true. But it is this same imagination that has saved me time and time again.

There is no such thing as 'good space' and 'bad space' in a close relationship. I used to get mildly irritated when young marrieds complained about one partner not giving the other 'space'. 'Stop it!' I would want to yell. 'Stop whining. This is the time in your life to close those spaces that threaten to become chasms, not widen them.' I would also raise my eyebrows when a movie star boasted, 'Our relationship works great because we give each other a lot of space.' I used to think this 'space business' was just another way of covering up for basic indifference and the lack of an emotional connection. How can two people in love want space? I would extend the argument further and wonder, 'Can a mother actively crave for space from her children?

Why would she want it?' The word 'space' itself had started to irritate me.

That was till I found the answer. I realized I was afraid of that feeling. I was afraid of space. I was nervous I would have more space in my life than I wanted. I had equated space with a lack of commitment, an absence of love and responsibility. I had convinced myself that there was no space for space in my life. It took me six decades to value my own space. And to respect other people's space equally. Today, I have freed myself from the guilt of enjoying my own special space. And this space is not physical or emotional, nor is it discernible to others. I have found it within. I can retreat into my private haven without moving an inch away from the familiar—my home, my family, my friends.

This fairly recent awareness has liberated me from old fears. It has, in fact, been my most significant self-discovery and my most valuable gift to myself. Therefore, this book.

~

Risk: A four-letter word

Here I am, looking back on seven decades of a life that has been pretty exhilarating. Yes, of course I have messed up. But even those mess-ups have taught me vital lessons—in survival, coping, collapsing, undoing, rejoicing. Most of these lessons have come from allowing myself to be open to everything life is throwing my way—good stuff, bad stuff, indifferent stuff. This is what I frequently tell my children when they are despairing. If you remain yourself and stay receptive to what's happening around you, you will pick up signals that will provide most of the answers you seek. Perhaps not instantly, but the answers will come.

When I was a teenager, I used to take every aspect of my life for granted, without questioning what was going on around me. In a way, this attitude protected me and spurred me on to take crazy chances, often with my life. I thought nothing of jumping in and out of rapidly moving local trains which I took to and from school. Of course, I was showing off my daredevilry, since there was always a crowd at Churchgate station. But those adrenaline-fuelled seconds when I tried to make it inside the compartment without losing my footing gave me such a rush it made that lunatic risk very attractive. Today, I can ask myself, 'What on earth were you thinking? Or proving?' I still don't have an answer that satisfies me. Perhaps I was testing myself. All I know is, danger and dangerous situations still attract me. I have never opted for 'safe' when there was 'risky' staring at me. It's a personality trait, or a character flaw. God knows. Show me two scenarios, one that is controlled and the other that's insane, and I'll instinctively opt for the latter. This worries my husband and children, but deep within, even I know half of this is nothing more than posturing. Confronting fear is just a part of it.

I am in the process of identifying my biggest fears as I key this in. What do most human beings fear the most? I'd say it is loss. Loss of a loved one, loss of face, loss of security, loss of health, loss of identity, loss of mental and physical faculties. Loss of one's own life. From this abbreviated list, I would say, for a wife and mother, there can be no greater loss than the loss of a child and spouse. Nothing prepares you for it. Nothing can. Sages advise us to start gearing ourselves up for such an eventuality from the time marriage vows are taken to that dreaded moment you are forced to come face-to-face with tragedy. Meditate, they tell you. Pray. Ask God to provide succour. Does any of this help you to deal with a wound that can never be healed? I don't know. I hope I am never tested. But it is this fear of losing a beloved that is at the root of all other fears. As a child, you fear losing your parents. As a grown-up, you fear losing your child. Conquering this fundamental fear is what drives us to face other fears.

When I think of all those reckless stunts I performed in school and college (most of which were unknown to my trusting parents), did I stop to think what the repercussions would have been on so many lives had something terrible happened to me as I hung out of a fast train, tempting fate every second day? I continued to ride racing bikes down crowded roads, clinging on to the handle of a public transport bus for additional speed. I crashed cars that didn't belong to me when I was grossly underage, after persuading the children of the owners to steal the car keys. I lied about my adventures in local trains (ticketless travel being the more innocent one) to my mother, who believed I was at a school picnic when I was actually bunking school and loitering on distant beaches. What if any of these silly jaunts had backfired? Point is, they didn't. I was fortunate.

Risk-taking is something I enjoy immensely. It comes naturally to me. I like stepping into the unknown and seeing where those steps take me. This is true whether it involves love and romance in my youth or professional choices later in life. My decisions were mainly impetuous ('immature' is how my father described them) and spontaneous. Where did this behaviour pattern come from? Certainly not from my home environment, which was conservative, conformist and solidly, comfortingly middle class. I appreciated anarchy and chaos far more than control and comfort. This troubled my parents a great deal, and I must have given them countless sleepless nights during those restless years when I couldn't wait to get out into the big, wicked world, the one beyond my traditional Maharashtrian home, and taste the myriad exotic flavours waiting to consume me, in Turkey, Brazil, Japan, just about anywhere. But where was I stuck? At home!

I thought about this feeling of being trapped, my desire to flee, when I was in Chandigarh recently. It was early winter and the weather was wonderful. My husband and I were with a good friend, going to a formal function, when news came that it had snowed in Shimla. I turned to our friend and asked excitedly how many hours it would take to drive to Shimla. Approximately four, he said, provided the roads weren't blocked. 'Let's go after the function!' I beseeched. There was a full moon rising over the Kasauli Hills in the far distance. We had a flight to catch the next afternoon.

'We can do it! Let's just go!' I kept pleading. The men looked at each other and I knew the answer. It wasn't going to happen. I tried another tack, 'Look! This moment is never going to come back! Don't give me that boring old lie, "we can plan it better and come back". That won't happen. Besides, it won't be the same. We can drive through the night. Have breakfast at the Cecil, and drive straight to the airport. It can be done.' Of course, it didn't happen. I went through not one but two 'official' functions, with my mind on the powdery snow falling gently over Kufri. In my heart, I was there, enjoying every magical moment, laughing at the sky and catching snowflakes on my tongue. But in reality, I was making a speech to a hall full of enthusiastic folks.

Now here's the dilemma: Should I have ignored a promise, not given a damn about commitments made months ago and simply followed my heart which was urging me to break all the rules and rush to Shimla? My younger self would have done just that. Alas, I did the sensible, boring thing and behaved myself. Not only did I make the speech, I also smiled at total strangers, made meaningless conversation and performed my assigned role. Nobody was disappointed. Except me!

Nobody wants to risk a darn thing. Nobody actively courts risk. Only the foolish do. I guess I am very foolish. 'At my age', to use that phrase, some of the recent risks I have taken have been totally nuts. Why did I bother? Here's one example. I was to take a conveniently timed flight to Dehradun for a lit fest. As it happened, I didn't read the ticket correctly. Result? I smartly reached the counter only to be told the flight had left an hour earlier. It was not the first time. My faithful driver, Choudhary, has been given permanent instructions not to leave the airport till I call and inform him that I have made it to the flight. This particular goof-up was doubly embarrassing. An event had been carefully curated and structured around my presence. There were more than a hundred invitees, not to mention a press conference and dinner. And I was going to be a no-show? Because I can't read airline tickets?

I was ashamed and close to tears. There were zero flights to Dehradun at that hour. I called the organizers to declare, 'I am a complete ass.' They didn't disagree. One bright spark told me if I tried really hard, I could catch the last flight to Delhi and then drive up to Dehradun. Without asking about the logistics involved, and out of a deep sense of shame, I foolishly agreed. Landing in Delhi, I was met by a scruffy fellow who shuffled up to say he was the assigned driver and could we please leave before it got too dark and too dangerous? Dangerous? How many hours will it take? I asked him. He looked up at the sky for answers and shrugged. 'Six, eight, nine—depends on the traffic.'

I calculated I could have gone to London in the same time. Too late. I was in his smelly, run-down car and we were on our way. A smart army colonel I had met at the airport had told me it was a risky drive. 'Ma'am, I suggest you go back to Mumbai.' Any sensible person would have done just that. I am anything but sensible. I had not dared inform my husband. He was under the impression I was already at my event in Dehradun. I phoned a friend in Delhi, who was aghast. 'I know that road, and it is not safe.' The worried friend kept tracking me on the mobile phone, but frankly, that was not helping. 'Oh God! You haven't crossed Meerut? Call me when you get to Muzaffarnagar. Tell the driver to avoid Khatauli—there are no lights on that stretch and it is most dangerous. Don't stop on the way, no matter what.'

It was close to midnight when I finally arrived at the Dehradun hotel. It was cold. And all I could feel was relief.

It brought back memories of an even more terrifying late-night ride in Lahore, getting into a dodgy-looking car at 3 a.m. with an unknown driver, speeding along unlit back roads and taking deserted shortcuts. This was after landing at that unearthly time, no thanks to a delayed flight from Dubai. At that hour, what choice did I have? My phone was jammed. For all practical purposes, I was cut off from the world. The man behind the wheel could have been anyone, even an ISIS agent. Maybe I was being kidnapped. All these thoughts were racing through my sleep-deprived brain, but it felt more like I was going over a racy movie script that had nothing to do with me. Instead of my heart pounding with fear and apprehension, I was calmly staring at the countryside, looking for signposts—were we even on the road to Lahore? Or driving out to some unknown destination? Would armed/masked captors stop the car and order me to kneel in the nearby field before videotaping my beheading? I was thinking of Daniel Pearl instead of focusing on myself. It was almost surreal, like I was not in the picture at all.

Worst of all, I was travelling with my daughter Avantikka, who had left two little babies at home to join her mother on this crazy trip—her first, and possibly last, to Pakistan. It all ended wonderfully well, I am happy to report, give or take some major unpleasantness at the airport when we were departing. Do I still want to go back? In a flash! I have wonderful friends in Karachi and Lahore. Friends who extended the warmest, most lavish hospitality, and have since become like my extended family members. Their homes and hearts were generously thrown open on each visit. One day I would love to reciprocate their love when they come to Mumbai.

I still harbour tremendous hope that during my lifetime, the two countries will see sense and become better neighbours.

A few years later, when I recreate that harrowing ride in my mind, I ask myself incredulously, 'What were you thinking? Or weren't you thinking at all?' Even now, I am not sure what it is that goes through my head in such situations. Is it a self-protective detachment that acts like a filter and keeps me from panicking? Or do I go into instant denial and tell myself, 'This is not happening to me. Ignore it and it will go away.' When I discuss similar situations with other women (most of whom proclaim dramatically that they are relieved never to have been in such insane situations in the first place), they stare incredulously at me, before asking in sepulchral tones, 'Surely you must think of your family! Children, husband? It's only natural for a woman in a similar crisis to first worry about what will happen to them.' We are brainwashed into believing every mother places herself last. I am no exception. I do the same, mostly. But in self-created crises, another self takes over. That self is a strange creature.

Danger has always fascinated me. In the sense that I always wonder how I would react when faced with a potentially life-threatening situation. What would my immediate response be? Are my reflexes good enough? What about my survival skills? Do I know how to think on my feet? Will I freeze or act? It's a test I give myself. It has nothing to do with anybody else. Not husband and not children, since they are not part of that scenario. I am generally alone, dealing with a mess of my own doing. Saving my skin under challenging circumstances may not be my biggest strength. Despite knowing that, I tend to push the limits. Why? I search within for some mysterious inner

Danger has always fascinated me. In the sense that I always wonder how I would react when faced with a potentially life-threatening situation. What would my immediate response be? Are my reflexes good enough? What about my survival skills? Do I know how to think on my feet? Will I freeze or act?

source to provide answers and solutions. Somehow, so far, at least, I have managed to find that special something when I have most needed it. I have found courage. A little voice yells from inside my head and heart, 'Don't look away. Don't back off! Don't blink! Keep going!'

I swear that little voice has saved my butt countless times, especially when I have had to deal with political goons. I have had my share of run-ins with Mumbai's lumpen. Well-meaning advisers would say, 'What's the point of taking on these hooligans? You'll end up hurting yourself.' And then, the ultimate 'warning' issued to stubborn women: 'Think of your family.' Yes, I do think of my family. A lot. But when faced with nameless, faceless fellows using muscle power to intimidate me, I think of myself. And I know by standing up to them I am doing the right thing. Giving in to bullies, negotiating with them, meekly going along with strong-arm tactics, backing off from threats and ultimatums, is simply not an option in my book. You surrender once and you surrender for all time.

~

The umbilical cord

The premier space is created at childbirth, the moment the umbilical cord is cut. From a single entity, suddenly there are two. A lot of mothers find this hard to accept, as they hold a squirming newborn in their arms and coo lovingly. Is this what was inside me for nine months, they silently ask. Some like the tiny creature they are holding but a surprising number don't. Mothers are not allowed to articulate their true feelings, unless those feelings are positive and loving.

But there is no such thing as 'instant love', even between a mother and her baby.

As I write this, one of my daughters is expecting her first child. She has mixed feelings about the pregnancy. I tell her it's okay. Perhaps she isn't psychologically ready for this life-altering development. Even as I tell her it's okay to feel what she does, a part of me is saying, 'You are dealing with this a little oddly.' But as her mother, I realize I have to bolster her confidence all the time, tell her motherhood is the most beautiful emotion on earth. Make her believe in the miracle of life. Motivate her to bond with the unborn baby. I do that too. But in my heart of hearts, I also understand her feelings of uncertainty, doubt, fear. Her space is not 100 per cent her own any more. She has already started to share it with her unborn baby. Their heartbeats are connected. This can be disconcerting and confusing. She has to drink, eat and rest for two. The feeling is alien and confusing.

Some women instantly accept the major change within—and without—while others take more time. Perhaps, a couple of months later, my daughter will experience the magical maternal bond, when she is fully geared for the major development. Right now, she is concerned with other issues—a new job, maintaining her trim, toned body, her life as a wife. All of these are legitimate concerns. She is being upfront and honest. If she feels squeamish about the stirrings within, she is entitled to feel that way. If she wonders about her own ability to deal with the new entrant, she should be allowed to do so, without anybody making her feel guilty. And yet, when we meet, I feel it is my 'duty' to lecture her and make light of her anxieties. I think, for a change, I am being the sensible, conventional, wise mother, whose job it is to provide instant pep talks and dole out advice. This is the predictable role I have never been comfortable with. But my daughter is more conventional than I. And I am tuning into her emotional requirements this time.

I instinctively know that if I were to be candid at this point and say, 'Hey, it's okay to feel resentful, it's okay not to feel mushy, it's okay to focus on a new job,' it is she who would be confused. She will most likely remind me that her friends' mothers would never say that, and that she wants me to be more like them. I am really not like those wonderful ladies. Wouldn't know where to begin. Once or twice I have hit back and asked, 'Are any of them like me?' And heard her mutter, 'Thankfully not!'

Most children want their own mothers to be like everybody else's mothers. Frankly, I didn't feel that way about mine. She was who she was. I didn't want her to be any different. We understood each other instinctively. She was deceptively simple to look at. Neatly dressed in fine, cotton sarees, her hair pinned in a nape bun, a red bindi in the middle of her broad forehead, a girlish voice and the seeking, curious, bright eyes of a child. Aie was a no-nonsense person who spoke her mind without a trace of apology. She was also remarkably intuitive. Our relationship remained on an even keel till the day she passed away. I must have annoyed and frustrated her a great deal. But I honestly cannot recall a single major flare-up. I never walked out of the house in rage. I didn't slam the door on her. I didn't yell back. That was simply not the pattern of our relationship. And yet, I have had to deal with my daughters' tantrums and accusations at different times. I have had to tiredly concede that this is by far the most complex of all intimate relationships. The mother–daughter equation has not been given its rightful due in any popular medium. We focus far more on the mother–son relationship. But in today's charged times, when roles have become so diffused and mothers are no longer the cookie-cutter variety of yore, it is important to acknowledge and address problem areas that come up between us and grown-up daughters who have their own complicated lives to cope with.

I ask myself, 'How controlling a mother are you? Or how remote?' Both extremes come with their own problems. At different times in my daughters' lives, I am sure I have swung from one end of the spectrum to the other. Especially when I may have been dealing with stressful situations of my own. The key aspect in any relationship is the strength of the basic bond between protagonists. How strong or fragile is it? Ask yourself that question when you are moping and blaming somebody else. A strong bond can overcome a crisis, even a series of crises. A rebellious daughter who constantly challenges her mother's views is, in fact, telling her mother something important. She is demanding attention. Are you giving it? Not any kind of attention, but specifically what she is seeking from you. Have you put yourself in her shoes? Empathized with her?

I ask myself, 'How controlling a mother are you? Or how remote?' Both extremes come with their own problems. At different times in my daughters' lives, I am sure I have swung from one end of the spectrum to the other. Especially when I may have been dealing with stressful situations of my own.

Do you constantly judge and correct her, thinking you are performing your motherly duty? Are you overcritical? Do you get her world at all? Or are you secretly hoping she becomes you? One more photocopy to flatter your ego?

I have had my share of mother–daughter run-ins and emotionally unsettling conflicts. When I look back I realize I was using a familiar, tried-and-tested yardstick to 'help' and 'sort out' issues. There is no such thing as a uniform mom code. Each individual is unique. Emotional demands are unique. It isn't a case of 'one size fits all'. Parents frequently make that mistake and argue, 'But this is how I was with her sister/brother. If that tactic worked wonderfully then, why isn't it working now?' The answer is obvious. No two children are the same. In fact, your children may not be like you at all—physically, mentally and emotionally. Is that too tough to accept? Do you sometimes wonder, 'Where did this one come from?' We are always looking for ourselves in our children.

I have watched some of my friends struggle to hang on to their dignity as their children go on a rampage. Some were dealing with drug abuse, others with teenage alcoholism, still others with personality disorders. While I was spared most of this, I had to confront quite a few challenging situations for which I wasn't entirely prepared. I mean, who can 'prepare' you to deal effectively and intelligently with modern-day emergencies which didn't exist ten or twenty years ago? Drugs and our kids? No way! We were in denial. And because we hid from the truth, we couldn't help our children.

I have seen some of my contemporaries watch helplessly as their children moved away from them, lost in a hallucinatory world which nobody could access. Why were we such cowards? So many young adults could have been saved, brought back from the brink. But we failed them, and in the process, hurt ourselves. We lacked the courage to say, 'Look—there is a problem. My child needs help.' Some of us were so busy safeguarding our own precious egos, our image, our standing, our status, our position, we quite forgot this wasn't about us—it was about our children who were suffering and sick and lonely and desperate and isolated.

It is never too late to reach out. Some parents feel desolate and defeated. They believe their children are rejecting them . . . spurning their love. So what? You are still the parent! Behave like one. Take charge of a child's tattered life. Don't give up. I have seen both parents and children come back from the brink. So many children these days are caught in a reversal of roles. They watch the lives of their own parents, and those of friends of parents, spiral downwards into a hellhole, fuelled by drugs, adultery and alcohol. I have read extraordinary stories of teenagers suddenly thrown into dramatic situations in which they become the saviours and assume responsibility of their parents. These are tragic, everyday realities of our times. We have to face them.

Seeking help is step number one. Gradually, we are moving towards a more rational approach towards mental health. So many families are admitting they cannot cope with issues like domestic violence, sexual abuse, depression, withdrawal, bipolar conditions, anxiety and chronic fatigue, which afflict millions. With aggressive campaigns talking about these problems more openly, doors are opening up and families are going in for much-needed counselling.

This is a positive development, the first big step in the right direction.

How does a relationship change when abuse of any kind, and on any level, enters the picture? Bluntly speaking, it changes radically and possibly forever. The main solution lies in better communication. If you can sense a difference in your child's behaviour, don't ignore it. Don't fool yourself that it will go away on its own. Pay attention to the smallest indicators. Monitor the child's eating and sleeping patterns closely. Make sure the child doesn't feel abandoned. If possible, don't let a disturbed child spend hours on his/her own. Try to persuade the child to leave the bathroom/bedroom door open—spending a major portion of the day inside a locked room can be extremely worrisome, dangerous and lead to terrible consequences. If you feel you are unable to deal with the situation, seek professional intervention immediately.

~

My space vs yours

This is the thing about negotiating spaces. In reality, your own space is often the most neglected one. You become your own last priority. You start enjoying feelings of martyrdom and denial. You think you are being 'dutiful' even as you seethe with resentment from within. You discover that not everybody out there stands at a respectable distance and says, 'We understand you want to be left alone right now.' Most intrude roughly and rudely, at a time that you may hold personal and precious. A time to call your own. How do you handle it? Do you voice your annoyance? Display irritation? Keep quiet and play along?

Most times, I play along. It's easier, quicker and comparatively painless. Sometimes, I snap. And people around me get visibly distressed. It is almost as if I have somehow let them down. It's a cruel shot: 'How dare she want time for herself? What about us?' I can overhear whispers: 'What's with her? Why is she being so weird?' It's a conditioned response to a pattern of behaviour I have created. A pattern that is now so entrenched in emotional transactions I don't know how to break it. And when I do, the repercussions tend to be pretty harsh. It's as if it is my priorities vs yours. My space vs yours. Who wins?

On a recent week-long vacation with family and friends, I found myself on a short fuse more than once. I snapped and snarled several times over silly stuff I would have ignored had I been in my own space. Aha! There's the answer. I was feeling displaced. And I was feeling responsible for the others in our group. It was a holiday I had initiated. I had got everybody on board. I had worked on a programme keeping the group's collective interests and sensibilities in mind. Yes, it had been a strain. But hey, nobody had thrust any of this on me. I had undertaken this ambitious expedition entirely on my own. And now, I was feeling oppressed? Taken for granted? Crotchety? I was feeling all that and more. Worse, I was showing it.

Travelling can be a great litmus test that often reveals more than you wish to show about yourself to your travel companions. I know I can regain my equilibrium if I can take half an hour off to connect with that inner space I cherish. This half hour has to be uninterrupted, undisturbed.

I need to physically shut myself down, lie down, close my eyes and open the door to my secret room—the space that belongs exclusively to me. Give me that, grant me this small indulgence to withdraw, and I am fine.

We all have that magic room (physical or imaginary) to hide in when the day is done, a day crammed with activity and people. We are entitled to that half hour locked up within ourselves. Often, we don't get it because our need to withdraw does not suit others. Try to remember when it happened to you. What did you do? How did you respond? Did you grit your teeth, mutter inaudibly and join in? Were you physically present and mentally absent? I had hoped to master it by now, but I fail a bit too often these days. As I did on that holiday.

I know I can regain my equilibrium if I can take half an hour off to connect with that inner space I cherish. This half hour has to be uninterrupted, undisturbed.

Reviewing your own behaviour and writing notes to yourself, can be therapeutic. On my return from the trip, I sorely missed the easy camaraderie and laughter. All of us had made the effort to carve out precious time to be together. I was with people who mean the world to me. I actively enjoy their company. And yet, I had slipped on more than one occasion, and hurt feelings. Why? Lack of sleep? Fatigue? Age? Perhaps it was a combination of all three. But everybody else had suffered the same conditions. They were fine. But I wasn't. I couldn't cope. Had I taken on too much? Was the presence of so many people 24/7 getting to me? Equally, was I getting on their nerves?

I came back and started writing about it in the diary I maintain. I identified the source of my impatience. I had unresolved issues. And those had surfaced during the holiday. Not directly, but in small, sharp exchanges that spoilt the mood for the others, those who were unaware of the tricky equation between us in my mind. I should have risen above my anger and behaved with grace. It was not a question of whether my feelings were 'justified'. They were just horribly misplaced on a holiday we were meant to enjoy.

How would I handle it now? What would I do differently?

As I stand back and think of the brief holiday, I realize my unfortunate behaviour had a history. A long history. It wasn't just a momentary annoyance. No single incident had sparked the unnecessary sharpness. It was something deeper, and it was corrosive. I was ready to acknowledge it. Perhaps I had been ready to do so for years. But that was my need. I needed to purge whatever it was, from the past. Often, our misunderstandings fester and become toxic over time, because we lack the courage to confront the real issues. Sometimes, we get emotionally intimidated. At other times, we are emotionally lazy. It's when we give up and say, 'What's the point? Nothing is ever going to change!' that we surrender to forces that stop us from moving forward.

How does one tackle toxic relationships? My self-protective response is to move away from the person. I just disconnect and tell myself to focus on other issues. Most times, this approach works and saves both parties from uttering words that are potentially wounding. I dislike confrontations and find them unaesthetic. This may not be an ideal solution, but over time, it has worked for me.

No matter how damaging the relationship, the mere act of creating a distance—a space—reduces the trauma. Years go by. Soon, the person stops affecting you altogether. There is no discomfort. No hate. No anger. You are free.

This is what I advise my daughters when they are dealing with people who hurt them—serial 'hurt givers'. Move away! I implore. The hurt will heal if you leave it alone. Don't revisit it. Don't demand apologies or explanations. Look carefully and truthfully at your own impulses while you are busy blaming the other. Get rid of your own toxicity. Step outside yourself, and watch. Block out nasty memories of who said what and who did what. There is so much beauty all around us. When things look desperate, hopeless and ugly, walk away. Look beyond the fight, beyond the argument, and tell yourself there are no winners in such situations. Nobody is one up or one down.

Young people are fragile and troubled. They need to be nurtured like the tender roots of a delicate plant struggling against the elements. Sometimes, just a wordless hug can elevate the mood, but if there is nobody around to provide the hug, look out of the nearest window. Look with your heart, not just your eyes. If you look hard enough, you will see what you may have ignored earlier—a street scene, a raucous crow, new leaves shimmering on the peepul tree, a young dad cradling his newborn. So often, we shut ourselves up and shut ourselves out. Dive into a useless, energy-draining exercise. Self-absorption takes a heavy toll eventually. By the time you shake yourself out of that mode, so much has passed you by. You have neglected nobody as much as you have neglected yourself.

I spend a few minutes (at least!) every day, sitting on a low armchair near the balcony that overlooks the sea. I watch the water as it moves. It never moves in the exact same way. I watch the sky that changes by the second. I look at the egrets perched on treetops. The beautiful birds seem to be exchanging notes, gossiping. I can hear the neighbour's dog barking at a stray cat. These are all considered 'useless', 'non-productive' activities.

I am joined by Gong Li, my beautiful white Pekinese beauty, who jumps on to my lap and settles down for her teatime snack. Sometimes, one of my children walks in and sees me by the window. A chair is pulled up, coffee and popcorn arrive minutes later, and we fall into an easy pattern of light conversation. Sparrows come and drink from the earthen bowl on the ledge. They seem to be swapping *gup shup*, same as we are. It's always a mellow moment. We need to make that quiet time for such moments, at least once during a hectic day. You can always choose yours. Some people prefer early mornings, when the rest of the family is yet to awaken. I like the 'in-between time' before dusk settles in. It is a good time to review the day, and the people you have connected to in that period.

~

'Relative' reality

People ask me whether it is easy to make friends after a certain age. I answer that it is never easy to make friends, at any age. At this point in my life, I am not looking for new friends. I simply do not have the time and energy to invest in friendships. I don't use the word 'friendship' lightly. For me, it is a weighty word. I see that this attitude has affected my children's idea of friendship as well, which may not be such a bad thing given the fragile nature of friendship itself. Initially, my children would accuse me of cynicism, saying, 'You don't allow outsiders into your space. You don't trust people easily. That is not nice!' I was never looking for 'nice'. Yes, there is a fair bit of cynicism in my attitude, but in the long run, I believe it has saved me a great deal of useless bother.

Take relationships with relatives. Cousins, uncles and aunts. Blood ties that can't be changed or challenged. But does that mean we have to fake love? Pretend we like and understand each other despite major personality differences? I have tried and failed. Friends, as is often pointed out, can be chosen. But you are stuck with relatives. It's better to come 'unstuck' if the relationship doesn't work than constantly crib about the person. I hear so many awful comments about this cousin and that uncle, which makes me wonder why the two parties bother to keep up appearances at all. Who cares? Why do they visit one another? Talk on a daily basis? Start a family group on WhatsApp? Why do I have to listen to their regular bitching? I also wonder what they are saying about me behind my back.

In earlier times, when the joint family system was the strongest social unit, these ties were relevant and needed. A joint family represented strength, even power. Generations lived

Take relationships with relatives. Cousins, uncles and aunts. Blood ties that can't be changed or challenged. But does that mean we have to fake love?

together, helped one another, aided a weaker family member when required and therefore survived. This system does not exist in our cities these days. Extended family members are virtual strangers, often living in far-flung cities across the world. 'Keeping in touch' becomes a burden, an obligation. Nobody has the time or inclination to maintain a record of births and deaths as they take place around the globe, or even in different cities across India. Where has that nosy aunt disappeared? The one who kept records better than a computer? She can be found running her own business, an NGO, a factory. Without a self-appointed record keeper, family members are adrift and pretty lost. Yes, it is a bit of a shame. But I think it's still better than getting embroiled in nasty family gossip and ugly intrigues involving a relative with the all-important 'blood ties'.

Family feuds can be exceedingly corrosive. Sometimes, they cross generations and this horrible legacy carries on. Why get into it in the first place? I admit I have been a 'bad' relative and not participated in too many extended-family gatherings. The few I have attended over the years left me disheartened and sad. I couldn't really see much joy. The conversations were superficial, forced and empty. There was bickering and, at times, an angry exchange of words. Then came the accusations and insults. It was not for me. Now, of course, I am rarely invited to join any function hosted by my parents' relatives. There are a few young cousins and nephews I admire and like. I have no idea whether they reciprocate my feelings.

These are spaces that require enormous tact. Possibly, I lack the attribute. My loss. I encourage my children to reach out and stay friends with relatives they enjoy as people, and not just as relatives. Fortunately, my children have accepted relatives as friends; rather, these are people they consider friends first and relatives later. How does one maintain a healthy balance on the relatives front? It needs work. There will always be that conscientious person who never fails to call and wish you on your birthday, wedding anniversary, children's birthdays, spouse's birthday. God help you if you don't reciprocate and remember. But hey—I didn't ask you to maintain my family's logbook and call me! I find such 'thoughtfulness' oppressive and fake. I dread the 'thank you' ritual. I hate protocol. I feel like telling these well-meaning folks to leave me alone. Ignore me but please don't burden me with empty politeness.

I wonder: Does this person maintain records and files like in a government office? What purpose does that two-minute call serve? Greetings are robotically exchanged. 'How sweet of you to remember! Thank you soooooo much for calling. Yes, we have plans for the night. Nothing specific as of now. Yes! I received lovely gifts. Oh, you want to know what those were?' Frankly, it's a pain. Because then, the ball is in my court—will I forget the caller's birthday four months down the line? Chances are I will. Finished. It will confirm the worst about the 'sort of woman' I am—selfish, egotistical, full of herself, indifferent. I'm fine with it! Really.

Then there are those dreary 'duty' outings—lunches and dinners 'to stay in touch'. Stay in touch with what? Why? I overhear conversations about similar social events that drive everybody crazy, and yet, nobody dares to break the pattern. 'It's a family tradition . . .' goes the chorus. Correction: It is an imposition. It used to be a family tradition when families lived, celebrated and mourned together. Where is that cohesive, well-knit unit today? If it does not exist—bury it! Why keep it alive on a ventilator, when the plug needed to be pulled years ago?

If this sounds horrible, the reality is much worse. I have watched family functions disintegrate into terrifying wars, because someone has downed one too many and brought up a long-forgotten scandal. There is rarely a happy ending to these artificial family get-togethers. If you can't avoid them and are forced to participate, mark your presence, greet everybody politely, and run! Of course, you will be torn to shreds for being arrogant and rude. But at least you would have spared yourself the trauma brought on by being around to witness one more family meltdown.

Maintaining a 'good relationship' with distant family needs a special skill set. My idea of balancing family responsibilities with hanging on to my sanity involves keeping a safe distance, and not indulging in overfamiliarity. Being respectful towards one and all is a given. But being chummy is an option I like to exercise. I am there when needed. I will always stand by family. But I will not indulge in a hypocritical show of 'devotion'. I don't expect family members to bend over backwards for me either. It should be understood we will be loyal and will protect one another. We don't have to put on a production to prove it. Extended family relationships are taxing and time-consuming. It's important to define parameters and stick to them.

I don't like to stay with relatives when I am travelling. Nor do I encourage relatives to stay with us. I have seen far too many family fights brought on as a result of this. And yet, I have also seen genuinely close-knit joint families with several branches. Families living pretty harmoniously through decades of ups and downs, with three generations sharing the same roof. They are not putting on an act. Invariably, such families are led by a shrewd matriarch or a patriarch, determined to protect the family's legacy. And the family wealth, of course. As it happens across the world, the break-up begins with the third generation. When you see that coming, and if you are a part of the crumbling set-up, move away as swiftly as you can. Too much proximity can get destructive and claustrophobic. Relatives have their place in your life, but you get to choose the role you play in theirs.

Class divides can divide families. Strange conversations take place about those who 'belong' and those who clearly don't. We judge, judge, judge on the basis of superficial, telltale signs that reflect 'upbringing'. These rules change constantly and annoyingly. But there is no escape from instant conclusions based on nothing more significant than, say, a suitor turning up for a first date, with a shabby, unwashed handkerchief that he constantly blows his nose into. Or a loud, young person making non-stop references to possessions ('My dad's Merc . . . my mom's Beemer . . . my uncle's Rolls'). I know of one potential romance that was murdered when the young lady kept referring to her 'business class' travels. I also know of another relationship that died prematurely when the girlfriend heard the

Class divides can divide families. Strange conversations take place about those who 'belong' and those who clearly don't. We judge, judge, judge on the basis of superficial, telltale signs that reflect 'upbringing'.

boyfriend abuse his driver and throw the car keys at him in a fit of rage. Whereas there is much to learn from those who conduct themselves with modesty and grace despite being born into enormous wealth. A fifth-generation super wealthy family in Mumbai makes sure each guest is personally greeted and escorted to the porch when they are entertaining at their mansion. Nobody is made to feel lesser or greater depending on their social importance. By contrast, I attended a splashy, extravagant wedding in the national capital, at which three separate areas had been created for guests belonging to different categories. The VVIP section had even hired bouncers to keep lesser beings out! And I was immensely saddened to see the indifference demonstrated by the hosts towards people who had travelled long distances to bless the couple. Every guest is a god, so say our shastras. Even if that is a huge exaggeration, every guest is certainly an equal. If children grow up watching their parents discriminating in such an insensitive way, they will metamorphose into social monsters who think it is fine to disrespect invitees by placing them in demarcated ghettos.

Yes, we are hopelessly, incurably, horribly class-conscious. Colour-conscious. Money-conscious. Everything-conscious! I have long chats with friends who also have daughters of a 'certain' (read: marriageable) age. We discuss prospective grooms from the available pool, and invariably the talk gets more focused and one of the ladies quickly gets to the point: Is the boy well off? Once his financial status is established, the next query is still more direct: Fair or dark? How fair? How dark? Examples are sought from people one knows. As fair as so-and-so? Darker than that distant cousin . . . ? Then comes the most important piece of information: Where does the family live? In town? Or in the suburbs? Armed with this basic info, several conclusions are reached: The prospective suitor is declared 'suitable' or 'unsuitable' based on key data that has nothing to do with any important personal attributes—his qualifications, qualities or future prospects.

I used to hope the younger generation was differently sensitized and had discarded such stereotyping. But no! I hear the same old conversations revolving around flashy acquisitions—not genuine ambitions. Chest thumping in place of a lively exchange of ideas.

~

Friends for life?

Years and years ago, when I was fresh out of college and desperately searching for myself, I was introduced to a group of self-styled intellectuals—some seriously wealthy, others just wealthy. There was an air of entitlement about them that I found strangely attractive. All this came back to me on a recent holiday when my sister made several references to my 'rich and famous' life. I actively resented her comment and told her so, somewhat testily. She was equally irritated and reminded me about those very days, before asking a pertinent question: 'You gravitated towards that set, or they gravitated towards you. The point is, you didn't choose the other, less privileged people from your age group, and they didn't pick you!'

I am still not sure whether this was an accusation or an observation, nearly five decades later. But her comment forced me to go back to those distant days and recall a few defining moments. One of them involves a chicken dish—coq au vin, to be specific. At the time, I had never tasted 'vin' and the 'coq' we had at our home was generally tandoori chicken brought in from Delhi Darbar. This was no ordinary coq au vin, let me tell you. It was the speciality of a very gracious, very beautiful princess, who was in love with a dashing prince. But the prince didn't fancy her back and she felt the only way to his heart was to cook his favourite dish for him. Considering the lady had at least ten handmaidens on call, it was understood she wouldn't do any of the stirring, chopping, cleaning or serving. She would elegantly supervise the proceedings from a safe distance, making sure her head remained demurely covered with the *pallu* of her French chiffon saree at all times. Her devotion was touching and genuine. His indifference to her, heartless and mean. And yet, each time I was invited to the carefully orchestrated 'coq au vin' dinner parties at her sprawling apartment, I would happily go—to feast on the pantomime as much as on the chicken drowning in expensive red wine.

It was through this set of 'friends' that I started to read J. Krishnamurti and attend his discourses, held in the compound of the J.J. School of Art. I have no idea why the princess would want to rub shoulders with the unwashed at that stage. She must have been a genuine seeker. I went along as I was curious. The first few times I pretended to be terribly interested and impressed. All around me, there were people of varying ages with one thing in common—their expression. They were clearly mesmerized. And I was clearly not. This worried me initially. Why was I not overawed like everybody else? I figured it was because I wasn't intelligent enough to get what the beautiful man in unbleached silk was saying, his proud head like a Roman emperor's, his voice well-modulated and supremely refined. From time to time, he'd pause, survey the crowd and ask impatiently, 'Are you with me? Do you understand?'

The princess would nod her head eagerly, as would the others, and the great philosopher would carry on for another hour or so, before wafting towards a waiting Mercedes and heading out to dinner with a more exclusive gathering of diehard, well-heeled devotees. This was such a fascinating phase of my own 'self-development' plan. Even if it did make me feel totally inadequate on so many levels. The great thinker–philosopher was referred to as 'J' by the core group, and after every discourse, there would be a lively if intensely self-conscious discussion on it . . . I had my views, but lacked the confidence required to participate.

So I kept mum and tried to melt into the shadows as different ways to 'still the chattering of the mind' as per the Guru's instructions were tried out by the noisy group. Of course, he was never to be called a 'Guru'—he was vehemently opposed to such a tag. But . . . but . . . he did encourage followers . . . they were devoted to him . . . yet, they didn't call themselves his 'disciples'. Then what were they? I found the whole thing a bit of a farce, even though 'J' had a powerful presence that made me go back for more. I actually enjoyed looking at him—the many vanities on parade. I would stare at his carefully groomed silver mane, framing the face of a saint or a king, the aristocratic curl of his upper lip almost a sneer. 'J' was a god. Yes, he was—god of beauty and beyond.

I would notice his pampered, pedicured feet, neatly manicured hands, the radiant glow on his face, his silken attire, the nonchalant air that is bred by a highly privileged existence. I would watch his fawning admirers as they formed a possessive, proprietorial ring around him, making sure his immediate environment stayed free of people 'pollution'. This was a rarefied world which belonged to the intellectual/moneyed elite of the city. And they were not about to surrender even an inch of this fiercely guarded turf to anybody. He would be hastily swept off to a grand home on Pedder Road, and the discourse would continue—this time for the chosen few alone. I did make it to one or two such sessions, but didn't enjoy the subtext of exclusion. The public discourses were meant for the *janata*—which may be why he chose to talk down. These were closed-door sessions for the inner circle, and he was a different man in this setting. I was welcomed—but cautiously. Which was fine by me. I could never have been converted into a fawning sycophant, and the group realized that quickly. I remained an interested outsider, a vigilant observer, and that trait has never left me.

Which is why when my youngest daughter asked me recently, 'Were you always this aloof?' I was a little taken aback that she, not any of the older children, had guessed my secret! I laughed and wondered aloud, 'Why aloof? You really think I am aloof?' It was her turn to stare at me quizzically and retort, 'You may fool the world. But you don't fool me!' I was never trying to fool the world! I was merely being true to my own fears. I like to stay away from hostile situations that I know will lead nowhere. Yes, I don't trust easily, and that again has to do with a fear of betrayal. I tell my children the same thing: 'Don't be cynical. But for God's sake, don't be gullible either!'

Friendships are created on several levels. At different times in your life, you automatically shift gears, just as your friends do the same. In a highly romanticized notion of 'friendship' people believe it lasts forever. It doesn't, and nor does it have to. So long as it is sublime while it lasts, be happy. I know people who cling to relationships that are clearly over. Once upon a time, the same relationships were intimate and close. Well, it's a different scenario now. Deal with it! But how?

> Yes, I don't trust easily, and that again has to do with a fear of betrayal. I tell my children the same thing: 'Don't be cynical. But for God's sake, don't be gullible either!'

Last year, I found myself spending hours with a girlfriend I have known for thirty years. She was lamenting the end of another close friendship and feeling really upset by what she considered a 'betrayal'. Was it really that? Or had the other person outgrown my friend? Possibly, the spouses weren't compatible. Or they had both moved miles away from what had once been the main area of common passions. It happens and when it does, step away and acknowledge it. Once you recognize the reason for the crack in the friendship, it's much easier to accept the new reality.

I asked my friend to figure out what exactly it was that she missed. Companionship? The two hardly met any more. A confidante? Their lives had changed dramatically, and so had the emotional equation between them. A mentor? Possibly. But if my friend needed a new one, there wasn't a dearth of mentors to choose from in her field. After several hours and a great deal of tears, I finally figured what it was that she was seeking: approval. When the friendship ended on a sour note, my friend experienced a level of rejection she was unable to handle. Her ego was bruised. She felt deflated, as if her friend was saying, 'Sorry, you are no longer the same woman. We have nothing in common today. You are not good enough for me.' That stung!

My friend asked, 'Am I really that unworthy? That boring?' Of course not! But had her friend said so? Or was she presuming too much? What had led to the betrayal? An incident? A breach of trust? It turned out to be both. Tough after so many years of closeness, but there it was. Now what? My friend was a broken woman, weepy and depressed. It's always hard to deconstruct an intimate relationship dispassionately and ask yourself where you had failed. That is an important first step. I advised her to stop pushing all the blame on the other person and spend time introspecting. Did she want to go back and start again? Was she expecting an apology? If not, there was no point in digging up the past. Instead, she would be better off remembering their wonderful times together—all those lovely holidays they'd taken, the laughter and crazy moments getting drunk, dancing in the rain, watching world cinema, reciting poetry, eating home-cooked biryani. This is what makes life richer, more bearable.

When any relationship dies—a slow death or a cardiac arrest, death is death—it's best to mentally organize a decent funeral for it. And continue living. Continue seeking. Friendships, even intense ones, are replaceable. Most people find that hard to stomach. Friends are like precious jewels. One has to place enormous value on them. Preserve them well. Look after them. But they can't be locked up inside a vault. That's when suffocation happens.

Friendships must be shared. Don't get proprietorial and possessive about those you love. Be confident enough to introduce your beloveds to other beloveds. You lose nothing by doing so. If anything, you are enriching your life and several others'. There is a great deal of joy in getting like-minded people together. Be open and large-hearted—the more you share, the greater the pleasure.

I love hosting evenings at home for visiting writers. The other guests are friends who may or may not know one another. Within the first hour, I can sense new bonds developing, numbers and addresses being exchanged, and it makes me feel genuinely happy to play a 'facilitator'. Sometimes, a casual encounter at home leads to an unexpected romance—even marriage! That's the icing on the cake. Other times, people drift away, and we meet years later. So what? At least for those short hours we shared a wonderful time, laughter, goodwill and sparkling conversation. Shouldn't that be enough?

Why do friendships have to shift and change?

I received a distress call from an old friend. She had just finished reading one of my columns where I had made oblique references to friendships that sour. Clearly, I had hit a raw nerve. She wanted us to meet immediately. There was much to share. But mainly she wanted to discuss two long-standing friendships that had crumbled virtually overnight. Over a glass or two or three of chilled Chilean white, we talked late into the night. At the end of her narration, I said something pretty obvious and simple. 'From what you just told me, these two women were never your friends!' It hadn't occurred to her that the ladies with whom she had holidayed frequently, met regularly, confided in and invested so much of herself, over a forty-year period, had no feelings for her. If they had been on holidays together, it was only because it suited them! If they spent Sunday afternoons with her, it was because they were equally at a loose end. If they unfailingly attended one another's dinner parties, it was because they belonged to the same social circle.

So what changed that stable equation?

For one, my friend felt deeply hurt and let down during a sickness, when the two women displayed indifference to her condition and were almost heartless. For another, they had started to take her generosity—moneywise, timewise and emotion-wise—entirely for granted. Conceded, she was the wealthiest of the trio. But the other two were not exactly paupers! There were repeated acts of meanness . . . and soon, my friend started to feel excluded. Like she was the intruder. Then, as frequently happens when friendships get a bit claustrophobic, jealousy entered the picture. Sniping started. Fortunately, my wise and sensitive friend picked up the vibes and retreated. That's the sensible thing to do when things start to get toxic. I asked why she didn't confront the two. And she said it would have been pointless. I agree. Often, things of this kind are best left alone. Otherwise, one 'frank' discussion leads to the opening of a Pandora's box. Nothing good ever comes out of 'upfront' conversations that are supposed to clear the air. Nothing gets cleared. The pollution levels increase, you end up choking and gasping, hating yourself for opening your mouth.

I prefer to stay away from people who have hurt me. I have no desire to nail their lies. No desire to ask for explanations. I just can't bear to be in their presence. And when that point is reached, there is often no return. Very rarely, and after years of maintaining a distance, does it happen that I accept such a person back in my life. But I do so cautiously, safeguarding my own emotions. Often, the relationship limps along self-consciously—no reference to the past, no 'you said, I said'. Just a heavy, oppressive feeling of 'Do I really need this—again?' I hate self-conscious 'friendships'. Either you can be totally naked in front of a friend, or that person is no better than an acquaintance. The moment there is calculation and stiffness in the picture—like Johnnie Walker ads advise: Keep walking!

> I prefer to stay away from people who have hurt me. I have no desire to nail their lies. No desire to ask for explanations. I just can't bear to be in their presence. And when that point is reached, there is often no return.

I remember this one time when I was dead beat. Looking like something dragged in by a stray dog. It had been a long, long day. And I was dressing to go out. My husband asked, 'Why are you bothering? If you are tired—don't go! It's not even as if you like this person.' Was he right? Should I have begged off? Did I really dislike the birthday girl? As I lashed on last-minute mascara, I did a quick rethink. There was still time. I could say, 'Forget it!' and wash my face, get into a kaftan and stay home. But I didn't. I continued applying mascara and thought about the party thrower. It was her birthday. She genuinely liked me. It mattered to her that I attend her party. Yes, she had invited over two hundred people. Even so, I wanted her to know I cared enough to show up.

As I drove to the venue, I thought about the birthday girl. There was a time when she was by far the biggest vamp in town. Rightly or wrongly, she had acquired a terrible reputation as a homewrecker. Shunned by most, she had fled from the barbs and waited it out. Despite her best efforts, she remained a social pariah. I was aware of all this. But not bothered by it. I figured she had made her decisions based on her own judgements. In the process she had hurt a few people and been hurt herself. I wasn't about to take sides or judge her. Did I like her? An unambiguous 'yes'. She was spunky, bright, sharp and sassy. I had never been offended by her on any level. She was consistently warm, well mannered and generous. In fact, I liked her a whole lot more than many other 'good' girls. Each time we met, we spent time chatting about our lives in a meaningful way. I kept her confidence and she clearly trusted me. That was enough.

We all have our ways of figuring out that 'enough'. Why get greedy? Maybe we invest too much time and energy in analysing friends to death. Why not accept them for what they are? Some are superficial, some are complex, some are hateful, some are enriching. The minute we allow another person into our emotional space, a relationship gets established. It has nothing to do with permanence or intensity. Some relationships are fleeting and perfect. They fill a specific need in a specific context. Others take time to develop. Do we have the patience to allow that to happen? We fast-track everything—relationships included. Unable to cope with the multiple demands on our time, we first look for reasons to cut a potentially wonderful friendship by finding a hundred reasons for it not to work! When I find myself attracted to a new individual these days, I distract myself by finding flaws. The faults invariably win over the good points. It is as if I am determined to stall the attraction from moving ahead, because I am already preparing myself for disillusionment. How sad! Earlier, I would be the excited, happy puppy eagerly exploring possibilities. I approached relationships with enormous optimism. Today, I take ten steps back before taking that one step forward. I continue to make new 'friends', but I redefine my expectations first. It is enough to enjoy an evening with a person whose mind is engaging and whose presence is positive. If that evening leads to more evenings, it's fine. If not, that's fine too. The experience is complete.

We hunger too much. For love, attention, reassurance. We demand 'proof'! What proof? During the throes of teenage passion, we used to be impressed if the gangly, unworthy fellow from the neighbourhood cut his finger and signed a love note with his blood. That was 'proof'. Later, the 'proofs' we craved became more materialistic. A ring, a wedding band, a mangalsutra. Such nonsense! As if that bit of metal guaranteed everlasting happiness. Proof is for those who live with insecurity. The whole point of a solid, confident relationship is to do away with proof. Either you believe, or you don't. Without unconditional trust, there is nothing but unhappiness. Often, it takes decades to figure out a simple fact of life—friends change. So do we.

How boring life would be if all of us stayed constant! When you start off liking someone instinctively, suspend all other reservations. Just like! Don't try to pry or find out too much. That ruins discovery. Let the friendship unfold gently, organically, painlessly. If it is meant to bloom, it will. If not, so what? I remain open to newness. I enjoy meeting young people. They bring so much to the table with their wicked views and irreverence. I see my younger, cheekier self and chuckle. Was I this irritating? I must have been. I got away with a lot. And so should my young friends. Sometimes, they are stumped as to how they should address me. They start off haltingly with a 'ma'am'. Then it gets changed to 'Shobhaaji'. Finally, when I can't stand the stiffness and formality, I raise my hand and say, 'Stop! Call me by my name. It is Shobhaa. Just Shobhaa. Call me Shobhaa . . .' They look a bit embarrassed. They stare questioningly at one another. The first one who dares to say 'Shobhaa' out loud gets a high five from the others. Some push their luck and call me 'Shobes'. Excuse me? Once the breakthrough is achieved, it's all good.

We should actively aim for that elusive 'all good' feeling.

~

Officially yours

Work relationships require a different code. I have always preferred to maintain some distance and a level of formality with people I have met only because we have a common professional platform. I have seen my children and their friends struggling to maintain a balance between intimacy and aloofness with their colleagues. This is never easy. Today's generation communicates differently; the language is more colloquial and racy. The use of slang is not discouraged even in semi-official emails. This leads to serious missteps, especially if the boss is from another generation and he/she mistakes a certain relaxed exchange for something else.

Office flirtations are a strict no-no and I have rarely seen anything good come out of them. Yet, when you are spending long hours together, how stiff can the upper lip be, and for how long? A beer or two after work may be considered de rigueur and mean nothing, but when those beers start multiplying and become a regular routine, even the most disciplined colleague with high standards of correct office behaviour sometimes slips—and that's when problems escalate. Why get into such a potentially messy situation? By all means be friendly, helpful and polite. But that's about it.

Office trips sound like amazing fun—which they are! I hear about all the team building taking place at an exotic venue, and chuckle to myself. I wonder how exactly a beach volleyball contest contributes to the company's bottom line. All I can tell from the exuberant FB posts is a bunch of people having a great time by day and getting piss drunk at night. Perhaps buried deeply in all this frenzied activity, there is earth-shattering progress being made. But I have spent far too many hours consoling friends who have returned from 'bonding' with mates and regretted the changed dynamics to recommend this strategy blindly. Especially so in our predominantly conservative corporate culture, which, despite claims to the contrary, still clings to old-fashioned, deeply hierarchical roles.

Learn to traipse lightly over rough terrain in the workplace. You don't have to be cold or distant with colleagues. But neither should you be in a zone that is intrusive. Sharing personal information beyond a point is counterproductive and can lead to embarrassing situations. Imagine a scenario in which a husband/wife gets introduced to a stranger, who exclaims: 'Oh! So you are the person who messed up on that amazing trip to Istanbul by missing the flight home!' Not cool.

Know where to draw the line. Know how much to share. Ask yourself why you are sharing it in the first place. Does it add to the other person's knowledge base in a positive way? Or are you doing it to look good, to show off? Never discuss a colleague behind his/her back, or post jokes about the boss on social media. None of this makes your position stronger. If anything, chatty-flirty exchanges can come back and bite you hard. So can 'harmless' dates with colleagues. Take a look at the number of victims whose careers have been irreversibly ruined because of office indiscretions.

> Learn to traipse lightly over rough terrain in the workplace. You don't have to be cold or distant with colleagues. But neither should you be in a zone that is intrusive.

Then comes the question of inviting the boss home. This is a delicate one, and varies from company to company, boss to boss. I would suggest broad guidelines: Let the boss define social behaviour. If the boss invites juniors home, it is a strong signal that he/she is keen to get to know employees better outside the office environment. Should you wish to reciprocate, it is more appropriate to start by thanking the boss for the hospitality by sending flowers and an appreciative, personalized note—perhaps praising some item of food or the choice of wine. After a decent interval, and if there is a celebration in your life to which you have invited several people, then it is acceptable to include the boss. But at no stage should it become a pressure to attend.

Nor should you ask for an explanation if there is a no-show. This puts the boss in an embarrassing situation and works against you.

Inviting colleagues over is another difficult call. By all means do it, if you enjoy entertaining people you spend most of your waking hours with. Don't do it as an obligation or a duty—that always shows. Keep the evening short rather than long. Indicate a time frame. Stick to it. Don't allow it to drag on and on because one person wants the bar to remain open. Any guest behaving inappropriately should be firmly dealt with. This is your space. Guests who do not respect its sanctity should be struck off your guest list forever. Letting one's hair down is one thing. Being obnoxious, quite another.

We have had incidents at our home with guests who tried to misbehave with other invitees. The boors who had offended our friends were promptly asked to apologize and leave our residence. Needless to add, they were struck out of our lives permanently. Yes, it isn't easy to deal with ill-mannered colleagues—they can present a completely devilish side to their personality in a social gathering, especially if the drinks are flowing. Use your skills to control the party from degenerating into a disgusting brawl.

I often tell my children to err on the side of caution rather than regret an office relationship that sours later. I myself have made monumental mistakes in the past. I talked too much, allowed strangers into my life without a single filter in place. I revealed too much, heard too much, got intricately involved in their lives and didn't succeed in extricating myself from an emotional tangle in time. This led to major misunderstandings, which could have been avoided had I maintained a distance.

I was young, over-communicative, reckless and, I suppose, a bit of a show-off. Each morning, I'd waltz in cheerfully and share all that happened the previous evening—a fight with a potential boyfriend, an argument with my sister, any trivial, silly little thing—there was a compulsion to immediately share it. I still don't know why I did it. Was I looking for approval that desperately? Did I want to belong at whatever cost? The attention I received while I blabbed on must have been flattering too. But I do realize it was a mistake on my part. Not everybody is on the same wavelength, or the same page. Some snigger behind your back, others remain indifferent. Still others throw your words back at you later. It was very childish and impulsive on my part to confide in strangers. I learnt my lesson soon enough.

My daughters are wiser than I ever was at their age. Their office relationships are friendly but formal. They leave office affairs back in the office when they come home. Yes, they do socialize once in a while, but, by and large, they keep a healthy distance. This is the space where modern careerists often trip up, unable to define the limits of social–official intercourse. I would say sending flowers to the boss on a birthday/wedding anniversary is fine. Taking a bottle of wine with you if there is a party at a colleague's home is also fine. But anything more intimate—regular weekend binge drinking, for example—is just not on.

Sleeping casually with colleagues? Call me a prude, but there have to be better options out there. Office 'affairs' are the worst affairs. I have rarely seen them end happily ever after. The aftermath invariably gets messy, and one or the other loses the job—gets sacked, has to resign, leave town, demand a transfer, consult a lawyer, cough up court charges, get blackmailed. Why bother?

~

Dangerous social media games

Then comes the other age-related issue: social media and Facebook. It's primarily my age group that still believes it's a great way to 'stay in touch' and 'find old friends'. Others, far younger, have long moved on to different, sexier, hipper platforms. Since I have always maintained privacy settings on FB, I have fewer than 150 'friends' I share stuff with on a regular basis. I like it this way. It's more manageable, and I like to think of it as 'quality control'. I have not the slightest desire to 'reconnect' with people I knew at school. If we have not been in touch for fifty years, why ask for trouble at this stage? Our lives have changed. We have changed. There is no real love lost. Why bother? But there are some deliciously wicked FB friends I have known, respected and loved for decades. We never really lost touch. Some have children the same age as mine, who in turn are close friends too. I deeply value our fun exchange on a daily basis, especially since we are all photo-obsessed. There are also a few very young people whose minds and views are terrific. We may have met once, twice, ten times. But over FB it's a special bond and it's wonderful to get a fresh perspective on life through these individuals.

There is also the troubling question of 'unfriending' people. And getting 'unfriended'. I don't care a jot about being 'unfriended'—often it's a relief. But I do feel apologetic when I unfriend someone. I don't do that often, but when I do, it's with good reason. I see FB as an interesting platform to share some of our joys and celebrations with people who appear to care for one another—albeit virtually. If that sounds naive and self-delusionary, it is! Most of my FB friends are on the same side of the political spectrum so there is a certain comfort level in expressing views that are not in line with the establishment. I also post my columns, and read other people's posted on my timeline. This creates a small community of people with compatible mindsets, speaking freely in a world that is increasingly bigoted and illiberal.

My children assure me nothing but nothing is private any more, least of all what is posted on FB. Somehow, that doesn't deter or daunt me. It's comforting to say something one is feeling strongly about, and have comments coming in that suggest we are on the same page on that particular issue. Those I unfriend are either aggressively selling something, promoting themselves shamelessly, pushing an agenda too blatantly or have nothing of consequence to share. Of course, there are the pests who bother strangers they have 'met' on your timeline and claim 'friendship'. And then the worst offenders—those who use crude language and post abusive, offensive material. Out!

I am not on FB to peddle anything. That's the way I like it. I once accepted a friend request from a really senior journalist whose columns I used to appreciate, only to read his boasts about hitting 5000 'friends'. I asked him directly why on earth he would even want so many friends. How can there be a meaningful dialogue with so many strangers?

He replied testily that he was proud of the number, and it made him feel important. He also added, the number of his 'contacts' across the world had dramatically gone up, thanks to FB.

FB posts create odd situations, even with those who know you well. Like when I talked about being depressed after watching a particularly depressing film. I received solicitous messages from people I thought would get the comment in the right perspective, expressing their concern: 'Are you okay? Did something happen? I can't imagine you being depressed. You are a bright, happy, luminous star. Why are you feeling depressed? We don't know you to be like this! Please just get back to your usual, positive, upbeat self.' I was affected by a powerful film. Am I not entitled to feel low? Did my mood affect them so much because they can't handle emotional swings themselves? Was it personal? Or was it about me? I am still not sure. If Mark Zuckerberg's Twitter account was hacked—who are we? Take it for granted your accounts are far from secure. Assume there is zero privacy. Remind yourself that whatever you put out there is going to be accessed. That has been my ground rule from the time I became active on social media. Most of my contemporaries find it hard to decode the unwritten rules of social media. There are specific but not stated procedures in place that

If Mark Zuckerberg's Twitter account was hacked—who are we? Take it for granted your accounts are far from secure. Assume there is zero privacy. Remind yourself that whatever you put out there is going to be accessed.

the young understand instinctively. Social media protocol doesn't come with a rule book. You have to figure it out as you go along. I have made a few blunders myself, despite the caution.

Today, I follow a few basic dos and don'ts. Rule number one: There is no such thing as a Facebook relationship. I have very few friends on FB. These are all people I know, respect and admire. I do not accept requests from strangers. I don't hit 'share' if there is a negative or insulting post. I generally let the person know I am sharing something. And thank them for posting it. Even when it comes to my children, I seek their permission before posting their pictures. I have been hollered at in the past for displaying unseemly haste. I now know better.

It's different with old friends—some of whom I have 're-met', albeit virtually, after a gap of forty or more years. It's lovely to connect as oldies today and share memories. With younger, newer acquaintances, I have a simple reasoning—if they are clever, witty, non-judgemental, creative, we start an FB dialogue. If not, well, it's a bit harsh, I realize, but after a decent trial run, I unfriend them, no hard feelings. I also do that with nosy people, or those who focus on negativity in their posts. God knows our lives are tough enough, who needs to read nasty comments? Then there are the professional snoops who trawl through accounts looking for media stories. They think nothing of shamelessly lifting personal pictures and posts and making an item out of them for their columns. Not realizing, of course, that if these were meant for public consumption, they'd be in a public space.

I also don't quite get sending FB greetings to dead people. Or writing deeply personal letters to a spouse, child, grandpa, grandma and cousins on a birthday or a death anniversary. It's embarrassing and ridiculous. I read cringeworthy posts by intelligent people and wonder why they can't communicate those sentiments directly to the person. Why should strangers read all that stuff about 'You are my life . . . you are my breath . . . you are my heartbeat . . . I love you to death, my adorable munchkin'? And worse! Declarations of undying love need to be made face-to-face. Anything that goes public gets instantly devalued. Unless you are a famous movie star/ rock star and your PR team generates such stuff for you. For the rest of us struggling with more mundane issues, FB should really be restricted to having a bit of harmless fun, exchanging information and hopefully, learning something from one another—recipes, travel tips, good reads. That's it.

~

Twitter is far more lethal. What you commit to in 140 characters is going to follow you to your grave. For me, it's an occupational hazard. I have an uneasy relationship with Twitter. But I have also made my peace with its destructive aspects. I never read reactions to a tweet. Which automatically means I have zero idea what the trolls are saying. This self-protective strategy works for me. Nothing good comes out of getting into a slanging

I have an uneasy relationship with Twitter. But I have also made my peace with its destructive aspects. I never read reactions to a tweet. Which automatically means I have zero idea what the trolls are saying.

match with toxic, anonymous creatures spewing hate. Some of my journalist colleagues have gone off Twitter completely when trolls started abusing and targeting their families. I wouldn't take that route. This is the nature of the beast. This is what trolls do. Often, there is a huge mechanism backing the nasty, humiliating and obscene tweets. The most frustrating thing for trolls to digest is to be systematically ignored. That is the worst snub of all. The minute you get riled up and react, it is a huge victory for the trolls. From there on, it only gets worse. Some high-profile showbiz celebrities have made a second career out of Twitter storms. You need to be brazen and thick-skinned to get into this territory. I have no stomach for it. I just say what I have to say and leave it at that.

Negotiating this terrain can be pretty strenuous and horribly time-consuming. Those notifications and comments really cut into my workday and distract me. I want to check into rehab just to break this nasty addiction. I want to sign up for a phone-detox programme. But then again, I convince myself it's a harmless indulgence, like I convince myself a glass or two of white wine on a Friday night is the same. I realize I'm conning myself. But having fun!

I see how differently the younger generation uses social media. I'm not sure it enhances their life, all I know is they are fantastically well informed and well connected. I taunt my youngest daughter constantly about her mobile phone usage. Secretly, I am jealous of all the time she spends with her phone. I want her company. I want eye contact, not a glazed, distracted look. I want to chat and laugh and gossip. But she is preoccupied and absorbed. This is her space. And that space is sacred to her. It doesn't belong to me. I am the intruder. It's the same as my wanting to barge into her room when she prefers to be left alone, and demanding her attention when she is not ready to give it. Is it fair? No, it isn't. If I demand and get time to myself when I need it, I must understand her requirement—which is to be on the phone. It is never switched off. She routinely wakes up in the middle of the night to check it. What is it she wants to know that can't wait till morning? 'You won't understand,' she sighs before going back to her beloved—the phone.

I have spoken to several parents struggling with the same problem—how to get their children's undivided attention, even for a brief two minutes. It's a challenge. But I like challenges. I realize that to wean her away from that nifty gadget, I have to make myself more interesting than my rival. I try to come up with innovative tricks to impress her. I bring up topics are of zero interest to me, but could perhaps interest her. I try to sound young, hip and cool. I talk about fashion trends, Bollywood/Hollywood break-ups, music videos, what's trending, what's gone viral, sports stars and their glamorous lives, exotic foods, new restaurants, pop-ups—just about anything I overhear her discussing with friends. Sometimes, I surprise her and myself. She looks up from her phone to ask, 'How do you know about that?' I don't state the obvious—I have a smartphone too!

~

Curating our lives?

I was amused and then a little annoyed when Facebook decided to remind me of the year gone by. If I wanted to chronicle the year, I would have picked far better pictures and used catchier music. That apart, I felt there was a great deal of deception on social media—and I was a part of it. I played along. I participated in deceiving and being deceived. When I posted pictures of my many travels, my outings, my dinners, my life on various levels, I was indulging in something not terribly high-minded! I was play-acting and projecting too many illusions and half-truths. I was creating a parody of my precious life. Why? Why did I have to 'share'? Or keep checking my notifications to see how many likes a post had garnered. Why did I look out obsessively for comments? Why did I need the validation in the first place? Did it matter what I said during a seminar? Was . . . I that thrilled when my outfits at some lit fests received compliments? And disappointed when nobody reacted to certain posts? When I scrutinized other people's FB and Instagram posts, what exactly was I looking for? The vicarious pleasure I had started to feed on was finally getting to me. But I lacked the courage to quit the space. I had become a FB junkie, a pathetic addict, like countless others.

I reviewed my recent posts. They weren't obviously boastful—wait a minute, they were pretty boastful! Just better camouflaged. I had turned into an unattractive show-off, preening and strutting five times a day (minimum), hungry for responses and waiting for pats on the back from strangers. Well . . . my FB account is meant for people I know. It is not a public account. To be fair, I am now in touch with a group of interesting people—mainly other writers. Plus a few really, really old friends I had completely lost touch with. I tell myself, truthfully, that the real reason I am hooked has to do with a certain loneliness. A specific kind of loneliness. FB fills the need to reach out to like-minded people and connect instantly. Learn from their lives, share articles and music and ideas, without having to meet or converse. It is so damn convenient! All this is possible on my own time. Strong bonds get established once such communication channels open up. A sense of community keeps me interested. I don't have to leave home, dress up, smile or create time to interact with 'friends'. I have noticed how rapidly my original 'friends' have established relationships with strangers they've met on my page. This is how it works. But has it worked for me? My children tell me FB is strictly for over-the-hill folks with too much time on their hands. I protest vehemently. No, it's not!

I am not sure whether I want to withdraw from FB or not. How is it done? A surgical strike? Or a more gentle phaseout? Does one write a 'goodbye' post? And stick to it? Making a dramatic announcement seems like a cheap way to get off the FB treadmill. I am still figuring out a good exit. Meanwhile, questions about FB's role in my life remain unanswered. I am telling myself not to despair in advance. Then again, I rationalize: What's so wrong about showing off from time to time? It's harmless. It can also be comforting. When I am feeling low, I look for a good image to share. I then write a short text to match the image. Depending on how low I am feeling, I embellish and dress up the story to enhance the image. That's the fun part. It's like writing a really short short story. Generally with a happy ending. Let's call it creative escapism.

I am going to take a crack at posting searingly 'honest' stuff soon. Dark and gloomy, 'The end is near' posts. I wonder what the response will be. When I was a FB novice, I had absently posted a mildly moody something. Alarm bells clanged! I got personal emails from people who should have known better asking me what had happened. Was I okay? Could they help? Hello? What was going on? I was not allowed a moody post? Clearly not! I was pretty late getting into the FB 'friend' zone. Compared to my real-world friends and contemporaries, this was surreal. But once I got the hang of it, I got hooked—like most FB fans do. Cynicism was kept on hold. Yes, we were all liars on FB. So what? These were harmless little lies. Or were they? I started to notice patterns in other people's posts, and my own, of course. There was a lady, a fine writer, who only posted pictures of children. She didn't have any of her own. But she had several nephews and nieces. Her own pics were also of her as a toddler. When we met, I gingerly asked her why there were zero adult pics. Her smile vanished and she turned away without answering. Perhaps she liked her childhood a whole lot more than her present life? Maybe she cherished stronger memories of that golden period? Then there were the standard, professional boasters who used FB for shameless self-promotion. I got sick of reading about their hourly triumphs. I was also not interested in friends who spoke exclusively about their pets—and nothing else. There were other 'intellectuals' who shared obscure articles from rare sources—never boring, mind you. But so impersonal! If I needed information on bleak environmental issues, or wanted to know the exact status of endangered rainforests, I could

Yes, we were all liars on FB. So what? These were harmless little lies. Or were they? I started to notice patterns in other people's posts, and my own, of course.

seek it on my own! Narcissists posted Photoshopped selfies, non-stop. Groupies couldn't get enough of flashing celeb connections—the grand parties, receptions and soirées they'd attended, the famous people they'd met. There were all sorts out there—and I was one of them. Also bragging and preening. Had I not been me looking at me on my page, what would I have felt? Well, I would have thought, here's someone who is playing games. Some of her games are amusing. She is wicked and occasionally witty. She is clever. She shows off without it appearing in-your-face. She travels a lot. Leads an interesting enough life. Looks reasonably attractive 'for her age'. Is inoffensive towards her FB friends. Likes her dog more than people. Likes herself. Blahhhhhh! Get over yourself already!

With these 'safe' perceptions in place, why change a thing? Why, indeed? Yet, the sense of unease persists. I am only contributing to more lies, more illusions. FB does not encourage the use of mirrors. It prefers filters. We all strive to present versions of our true selves, hoping to fool the rest. Since the pantomime is effortless and in most cases harmless, we carry on and on, our free hours consumed by an activity that is essentially hollow and futile. How depressingly middle-aged!

FB does not encourage the use of mirrors. It prefers filters. We all strive to present versions of our true selves, hoping to fool the rest. Since the pantomime is effortless and in most cases harmless, we carry on and on, our free hours consumed by an activity that is essentially hollow and futile.

There are FB users who do share their demons. I had one or two 'friends' who terrified me. They confessed to feeling suicidal—even homicidal. And I shuddered at the sort of unfair responsibility being thrust on me—and on other unwary people. What was I expected to do? Call the cops? Call mutual friends? Call the person directly and plead, 'Don't do it . . . why do you want to kill yourself . . . or someone else? All our lives are pretty awful. I will help you cope . . . here, hold my hand. You're going to be fine, okay? Promise me you won't do anything . . . promise!' But these 'friends' are exceptions. My FB buddies are like me—which is why we are on the same page, as it were. We play pretend. And we try to do so stylishly, using reference points that are far from 'inclusive'. The idea is to exclude those who don't 'get it' in the first place. Our chats are 'smart' and filled with in-jokes—the nudge nudge kind. We lavish praise on one another's meticulously framed images. We sigh over a poignant poem about loss and remembrance, we coo over baby pictures and share culinary tips. We project a 'cool' we may not possess. For anything else would make us look shabby and uninformed. In these constructed poses from our mixed-up, messed-up lives, some good stuff does emerge. We make small and big discoveries that in turn lead us to other wonders. That's what keeps us hooked. We cease to care where truth ends and fantasy begins. We become our manufactured 'profile'.

~

Toddlers and energy fields

Even toddlers today are sensitive to protecting their spaces. They are picky about the people who can invade their little area—the bed, for instance. Adults who think babies don't really care as long as they have a comfortable place to sleep are wrong. Babies too register reactions when strangers push themselves on to them. I have seen four- and five-year-olds getting pretty upset when people they aren't fond of those who invade their precious little space

My advice is to leave babies and toddlers alone. Let them choose you. It's not difficult to figure out when you aren't wanted. Kids are the most undiplomatic people in the world! You can neither fool them nor win them over all that easily. If you leave them alone and watch their body language, they let it be known—pretty unambiguously at that—whether they are receptive to you or not. I wait for a child to smile at me spontaneously before I initiate any move. Even after that smile, I wait for the next signal—it could be a tiny hand reaching out for a quick touch, or arms extended to say, 'Come and pick me up!' When that happens, I grab! Not too tightly or aggressively but enthusiastically and firmly enough for the child to feel secure. One more thing: Please resist the temptation to baby-talk. Most kids get confused and don't particularly enjoy it. They really prefer direct, adult communication. Try to see the difference. It is a whole lot more respectful as well. Though I was pretty disarmed by a young mother who told me candidly, 'It's only now when my daughter is still a toddler that I can speak to her in this ridiculous lingo. Why not enjoy it while it lasts?'

My advice is to leave babies and toddlers alone. Let them choose you. It's not difficult to figure out when you aren't wanted. Kids are the most undiplomatic people in the world!

It's good to remind yourself that even very young children listen attentively when you are talking—to anybody, not just them. It could be a phone conversation with an old friend.

While you imagine the child is busy playing and carry on a personal chat, which may refer to familiar people, all the while thinking the kid isn't really interested, believe me—kids hang on to every word. Years later, a long-forgotten comment is brought up and you don't know where to hide. Children absorb it all—even if they don't understand the words or the context, they definitely get the tone. They know when adults are fighting, even if they appear to be playing video games.

Children are very sensitive to nuances and signals. I was shaken recently, when a young adult I was talking to mentioned a conversation he had overheard when he was six or seven years old. It was at a difficult time in his parents' marriage. There was a wedding in the family, and his mother was busy getting dressed. He was playing in the room when the father walked in and a heated exchange followed. He recalls the exact moment when his mother turned to his father and said calmly, 'I will be leaving you right after this wedding is over.' It's a memory he had blocked off for thirty years. But it was the single most defining moment of his tender life. He fled the room and sought out his grandparents. He didn't tell them a thing. He simply withdrew, and decided to protect himself emotionally the only way he knew—by creating a safe distance from his warring parents. He figured he was better off with the grandparents—who then became his primary caretakers. So many years later, his eyes well up with the tears he didn't shed at the time.

So, you see, we can never take the presence of children for granted. They are the little people who understand a lot. They may not articulate it—ever! But everything has registered. And those memories remain for life. Not all memories are this depressing, of course! But if you think about it, our major relationships are memory-driven. Positive memories reinforce feelings of love and loyalty. Negative ones fester and create alienation. As adults, we train ourselves to rationalize a lot of the 'bad stuff', take it in our stride and move on. We have to! Or else we get stuck in a negative past that doesn't allow us to forge healthy bonds with people we interact with. It leads to a lack of trust and unresolved hatred. When I meet people who, without really doing or saying anything, make me recoil for no logical reason, I put it down to our energy fields clashing. God knows there's no rational explanation for this reaction.

As soon as you sense something that's like an early warning system, stay away. The trick is not to show your antipathy. In most cases, the feelings are mutual. In some cases, they can be reversible too. But that's pretty rare. The social survival kit tells you how to deal with such individuals. Let me share a few of my basic rules: I am wary of people who come on too strongly minutes after being introduced. My first question to myself is: What does he/she want? Yes. It is a cynical response. But experience is the best teacher, as they say. In the past, I would extend a pretty long rope and give the person the benefit of the doubt. No more. I have neither the time nor the energy to invest. Flattery can be pretty irresistible, depending on the skills of the flatterer. But if you are honest with yourself, you will know the difference between a genuine compliment and a fake gush.

~

Dulhanji, adjust karo

Within the conservative framework of extended families, it's important for the new entrant to pick up clues without being constantly prompted. Young brides of today don't want to be patronized or spoken down to. There is a great deal of mutual adjustment involved. This takes skill, time and patience. I always tell the brides (if they ask me!) to put their sensitive egos aside during the first few weeks and learn, observe, file. Don't worry at this stage about 'asserting' yourself. Life in a new family is hard—not just for the bride, but for the groom as well. Accept that you are the 'outsider' who needs to put in that little bit of an extra effort as an 'investment'.

> I know how hard it is for a young bride to suddenly start feeling 'love' for the strangers who surround her. There's no need to fake that love. It will come—if it comes—when it has to. What counts is effort. Genuine effort.

Showing respect to family elders should be the basic rule for both sides. Finding your own space in the new set-up may take years—you are warned. But if you start claiming it from day one, you will find it isolates not just you, but your spouse as well. The first six months should be spent in understanding the rhythm of both families. Clearly, it isn't the same. You have your own specific beat, which needs to harmonize with that of the others—'*Taal se taal milao*'—as the lovely old song suggests. Silence is power. Silence is wisdom. If something upsets you, resolve it with your partner privately. Table your concerns, but only after thinking about them calmly. Running to your mummy's home each time you face a mini crisis displays your personal insecurity. Pick your battles with care. Stand up for what you believe in—but do so while maintaining your dignity.

I know how hard it is for a young bride to suddenly start feeling 'love' for the strangers who surround her. There's no need to fake that love. It will come—if it comes—when it has to. What counts is effort. Genuine effort. This is definitely a two-way process. But often effort is missing from one side or the other. The pressure on the bride is far greater, since it is she who will be under a scanner 24/7. She will be the one being judged, scrutinized. For starters, it's useful to memorize names. Brides who address long-lost uncles, cousins, aunts and distant relatives by name are appreciated a little more! Ditto for the groom who shows interest in getting to know his new wife's folks by name. You may think this is a minor aspect of 'adjustment'. You'd be surprised how touchy people are about names getting mangled or forgotten.

Family equations are the most baffling, complex and confounding equations of all. Tomes are written on 'managing' a mother-in-law. This has given the poor woman a really bad reputation. Today's mother-in-law is a different animal. I'm not sure which one is worse—the stereotype from yesteryears, or the 'cool' mother-in-law of today who wants to go clubbing with the kids (did I just describe myself?) It's an important and delicate balance that requires fine-tuning. One of my closest friends is a great mother-in-law. I watch her keenly and marvel at how seamlessly she manages to stay involved and yet distance herself, as required. When her young and impetuous daughter hit a huge obstacle in her marriage, I was wondering what my friend would do. Advise her to pack her bags and rush home? Or to stay put and suffer, hoping it will all blow over? There was much at stake—the usual—children, money, home. My friend was remarkably calm. She placed multiple options in front of the daughter and asked her to identify the one that would work in the long term. She did not panic. And she didn't call her son-in-law vile names. Nor did she plan a family summit to confront the wayward husband in the presence of his parents. As she put it, 'I am only concerned with the welfare of my daughter and the grandchildren. I have to think of their interests—financial and emotional. The rest is unimportant.'

What she did tell her daughter was this: 'You always have a place to stay at our home. You and the children are free to move in tomorrow . . . tonight. But will that solve your problem?' Perhaps a lot of daughters need to hear just those words: 'You always have a home . . .' Most parents are reluctant to say that in our society. Too often, rash, hasty decisions are taken by a distressed spouse because all doors appear closed.

The issue got resolved to the satisfaction of both parties, mainly because tact and sensitivity were deployed, keeping in mind various practical factors involving the children's education. It's been a struggle. The transition was hard on everyone. But it could have been a lot worse had my friend encouraged her daughter to go to war and to hell with the broader consequences. It is to the credit of the man's parents that they too thought of the children and counselled their son in a sensible manner. Who is to say whether this is the only route to 'save' a floundering marriage? Every case is unique and cannot be compared. But when I run into my friend's daughter with her family these days, it certainly makes me believe in the power of reconciliation and healing.

I recall the words of a girlfriend who is my age and has been through a lot in her forty-year marriage, which has faced unusual challenges given her precarious health. After a recent scare, she was back in town and we got talking. She was in a candid mood and looking back at her early years as a newly married girl, full of hope and expectations. Considering her education and background, I was stunned when she told me what her mother had said to her when she was leaving her maternal home to go to her new one. 'The only time you will leave your husband's home is when they bring your body out for the funeral. The doors of this home are closed to you forever—make no mistake. Your place is in your husband's home from this moment on.'

I couldn't believe what I had heard. My friend was crying at the memory. She added, 'My mother was not being harsh or cruel. This is the way it was! My friends at college had been told the same thing. We never doubted for a minute that our mothers meant it.' That told me so much about my friend and her stoic acceptance of all that transpired in her marriage. After her emotional outburst had waned, she grinned, 'I have now reached the point when I have made my peace with my life the way it is. If my husband is playing around behind my back—I don't want to know.' Cowardly, practical, cold-blooded, calculating or resigned?

The evening ended on a jaunty note. We made plans to meet in New York. She was busy working on an exciting new project. Her children were well settled. Her husband was steadily moving up the corporate ladder, going from one glorious assignment to the next. They had been ardent lovers once. Today, they were supportive companions. She wasn't complaining. I guess he had never had much to complain about. It was all good.

Handling troubled marriages is a skill few possess. If that troubled marriage happens to be your own—God help you! At that point all one can see is darkness with no glimmer of light at the end of the tunnel. Fortunately, things have changed a lot in cities, and professional counselling is readily available. Most marriage counsellors are pretty competent and handle couples with the required sensitivity. Marriage courts too have changed their old, inflexible positions ('Go back to your marital home. ADJUST!') and are more receptive to at least giving a fair hearing to the battling couple before passing judgement. Modern marriage requires a modern approach. One can't automatically assume everything will be tickety-boo once the couple is publicly shamed and reprimanded (twenty years ago, it was that or nothing). Today, the judges themselves are more sympathetic. If they advise couples to try and make a go of it, they also offer practical solutions. It is not unusual to hear a judge say, 'Try for an out-of-court settlement. Do it amicably.'

This is the same advice caring parents should offer children if the couple is struggling to deal with common marriage issues. Unless, of course, there is cruelty, abuse or worse involved. Society continues to be pretty hard on couples on the verge of splitting. Taking sides becomes mandatory if both parties have common friends. This is when mothers and mothers-in-law can play a key role in cushioning the trauma. I always request mothers to take a deep, deep breath when a child announces his/her intention to file for divorce. 'Do not slap your forehead and start cursing your fate!' I tell them, adding, 'This is not about you and your fate. Your daughter/son needs your support—just give it! Do it unconditionally.' Sometimes, the child wants to just talk, get things off his/her chest. Let it flow—the words, the tears, the blame. Listen with empathy without jumping in with advice—'In your place I would not have said this, or done that'.

If it's a daughter with young children, offer to keep the kids with you for a while. Take them all on a short holiday. Keep her mind distracted. Most importantly, *feed her*! We forget the róle food plays in our lives. A sad person often forgets to eat. Sometimes even to sip water. Dehydration and hunger play games with the mind. Endless cups of coffee or glasses of wine don't help at all. They add to the all-consuming depression. But comfort food, like piping hot dal chawal, pizza or khichdi, reach spots that hours of sage advice can't. When in doubt—eat!

Men are more reluctant to share their woes with family and friends. They mistakenly believe they can 'handle it'. Perhaps a father needs to step in at some point and have a man-to-man talk with the son. This can be extremely awkward given that even modern-day dads are a bit nervous around their sons and vice versa. Men are self-conscious about showing their emotions to start with. If those emotions are sensitive and negative, most men withdraw into the cave and stay there, hoping the dark clouds will roll away on their own. Since they are reluctant to share deeper emotions, it is important to read their body language and respond with sensitivity. Slouched shoulders are the first indication something is wrong.

I thought about this during a recent family wedding, when the focus was almost exclusively on the women and how they were dealing with the many demands of a traditional Indian shaadi. The men were left to their own devices and not really consulted unless the issue involved money. I thought it was a bit unfair. Then again, did the men really want to participate in matters like 'Which is the best place to order fresh haldi–chandan for the bride?' I couldn't see them trudging along for trousseau shopping either. Did they feel left out? Nobody asked! Culturally, we are brainwashed to exclude menfolk from such expeditions, with reasons such as 'men find shopping boring'. I know men who are very keen shoppers and happy to accompany ladies to the market. Often, we assume too much, too soon.

During wedding preps, we imagine the bridegroom is doing just fine. What does he have to worry about? Everything is being done for him by his adoring relatives. True. But that's the stuff one can see—clothes, accessories. What about the man's emotional landscape? Bridegrooms have panic attacks too. Marriage is as monumental a change for the groom as it is for the bride. We rarely reassure the groom that it's okay to feel nervous. All the fussing is reserved for the bride. The groom is supposed to get drunk and stay drunk. But what if he is a teetotaller? That is never an option!

Culturally, we are brainwashed to exclude menfolk from such expeditions, with reasons such as 'men find shopping boring'. I know men who are very keen shoppers and happy to accompany ladies to the market. Often, we assume too much, too soon.

Ditto for warring young couples. Those involved in the battle automatically assume it's the wife who needs cosseting.

And the husband is left to his own devices, even by his own family. 'He's a man. He can take it.' He's also a human being, just like the wife. Both of them are experiencing pain. Perhaps the intensity of the pain differs. But this is not a 'pain contest'. Pain is pain. Since the frequency of early divorce (within the first five years of marriage) has shot up dramatically, it's important for both sets of parents to get together and counsel their children jointly. At least try it, for starters. Face-to-face meetings often bring prickly issues out into the open. And since both sides are equally represented, the feelings of rage and revenge can be better absorbed, even dealt with there and then. Parents should not duck this important responsibility, even if they feel most uncomfortable. Children need guidance—no matter the age and stage. They may not ask for a summit, but it is worth initiating. If things have turned so acrimonious that both parties feel the marriage has reached a point of no return, it is still worth giving that joint meeting a shot. It may last for two minutes, or two days! But it will definitely lead to a better understanding of what led to the breakdown.

If such a meeting does happen, it's crucial to follow a few basic civilities, before the tirade begins. Keep young children out of it completely. Meet at a neutral venue. A family elder, known and trusted by the two sets, always acts as a sobering influence and can be appealed to equally by both to arbitrate at the right point. Keeping one's cool is not easy. Emotions are volatile and can get out of control. If the young couple gets into a 'You did this, you said that' conversation, don't intervene and stop them. Often, it is just the means of catharsis they both need. Let them shout, scream and cry. Once the fury subsides, take a short break, drink lots of water. Eat a snack. Never argue on an empty stomach!

It usually gets ugly and spiteful. What saves time is lists. Eventually, it's about 'You took this . . . you took that . . . just return everything!' If there is a list in place with all transactions clearly stated, it is quicker to table it at this meeting (you may not get another chance!) and get everyone present to sign. Sounds horrible. But who says divorce is pretty? I have witnessed parents of the couple fighting over two zari sarees and six silver *katori*s, even though they were both millionaires many times over! Ideally, distribute CDs with images of all the disputed items. These can be scrutinized at leisure and decisions reached as to who gets to keep what.

Avoid lawyers.

It's best to sit down together and figure out mutually acceptable terms, if divorce is inevitable. Suggest a 'cooling-off' period of two months. Encourage the couple to talk to one another and keep communication lines open. So much can be resolved if people are sensible and treat this traumatic development with more sensitivity. Friends wonder: 'Can divorced couples stay friends?' The unambiguous answer is 'yes'. But let me qualify. They cannot become casual hi–bye buddies/lovers on an easy-come-easy-go basis. It is a waste of time to try this. But they needn't turn

It's best to sit down together and figure out mutually acceptable terms, if divorce is inevitable. Suggest a 'cooling-off' period of two months. Encourage the couple to talk to one another and keep communication lines open.

into sworn enemies either. Respect each other's identity as individuals. And move on in a dignified manner. It is possible. Washing dirty linen in public only adds to your laundry bills. Serves zero purpose too. Refrain! No matter how much you have consumed at the friendly neighbourhood bar! Once you split—that's it. You are no longer a 'couple'. Accept that. And other mundane details will fall into place after some time. Acknowledge each other in public. There is no reason why you shouldn't. You have shared a bed (and bathroom!) once. It's the decent thing to do. If both have new partners, make the effort to greet the person. It won't kill you.

~

Toxic is as toxic does

Young people often ask me, 'How difficult is it to conceal one's negative feelings? Should one hide or express them?' That depends on the specifics, doesn't it? You may detest your boss or the husband/wife of a colleague. It happens all the time. Why show your animosity? Is it worth the backlash that is sure to follow? Then comes the question of hypocrisy. Should one play-act all the time? It's a lot of strain, let me tell you. My own experiences have been largely positive, except for a few times. The fact that the memory still stings so many years later means I must have been pretty hurt back then.

I was young, immature and inexperienced. I thought speaking my mind was a birthright. It was my first job. I was sincere but a bit too impetuous. I also talked a great deal more than was needed. When I was assigned to work with a far more senior colleague, I plunged in cheerfully, with the sort of enthusiasm that must have annoyed the jaded, cynical man. I didn't pick up on the vibe, and for the longest time I couldn't understand his hostility and coldness towards me. I was a newbie. He could have been kinder, a little more patient. He wasn't. After a while, his attitude got to me—I became surly and short when he asked me questions about the assignment. I thought he was belittling me, often in the presence of other colleagues. I couldn't keep my own resentment under wraps. The entire atmosphere became charged and ugly. One fine day, I walked into the managing partner's office to say I was quitting. Fortunately, this person was much more mature in his handling of the situation. Without getting into the nitty-gritty of my issues with the other man, he promptly and smoothly offered me another assignment.

Decades later I am still asking myself how I could have salvaged the situation without compromising my principles. Was my conduct offensive? I don't think so. Did I display 'attitude'? Nope. Then what? Perhaps it was merely a matter of mismatched personalities. Today, I can sense a potential disaster walking up to me, and quickly take a detour. Back then, I was gauche and bewildered. I felt wronged—which I probably was. It happens. Had I swiftly read the guy's annoyance right at the start, and just done my job efficiently without getting into childish chatter and petulant remarks, I would not have had to consider quitting. Often, it takes a bad experience early in life to learn a trick or two about managing one's own shortcomings a little better.

Social situations are a little more complicated. A lousy job can always be swapped for a less stressful one. But what does one do if the relationship is a more intimate one? How does one walk away? I have done it a few times—you can do it too. One of my daughters said to me a little sadly, 'The thing is, not everybody is strong, not everybody can take tough calls and move on.' True. But even the strongest individual hides a few chinks in their armour. It is important to identify those chinks and work on fixing them.

A recent visitor sat across from me and the first thing I noticed were the chinks she was trying so desperately to conceal. I knew a little about her personal tragedy (she'd lost her husband a few years earlier and never quite recovered). The person in front of me was running away from the trauma a bit too obviously. She was ashamed of her grief. Scared that her deeply morose state would put people off. She was feigning a cheer that wasn't fooling anybody. Her life had been tough to start with. It had become tougher still after his sudden death. Left with two young sons and little money, she had managed somehow with the insurance payout the family received. But this was not even the real problem. It was her sisters she couldn't handle. She, being the youngest and financially the weakest of the three, was made to feel like an incompetent idiot by the other two, overachieving career women, who talked down to her and started most conversations with a hurtful, 'The trouble with you is . . .'

Knowing this lady's high IQ, I was surprised she took it all without once telling her siblings off. She sighed and said, 'It goes back to our childhood. We are carrying forward an old, established pattern. I don't have the courage to break it.' I asked why not. Then came a familiar story of deep-seated feelings of inadequacy stemming from being the less successful, less good-looking, less loved one. My question to her was pretty direct: Now that she had identified the root cause of the ongoing strife, how did she propose to tackle it?

Her answer pleasantly surprised me, 'I have decided to respect myself more . . . respect my personal space . . . and not allow intrusions. This baggage has to be dropped . . . all of us have been carrying it around for way too long. I will not seek their approval, neither will I express my disapproval of their lives. With time, we will arrive at a fresh equation. But even if we don't, I will not fret and drive myself into a tizzy.' Attagirl!

When she left, I experienced a sense of relief. In her own way, she had helped me resolve an ongoing conflict about my own relationships. I felt freed of several self-imposed guilty feelings which had been bogging me down for no good reason. For years I had tried my best to please a few family members who were disinclined towards accepting and acknowledging key aspects of my life. Suddenly, it became obvious why it had been so. Regardless of their reasons, I was not answerable to them. Nor did I require their so-called 'support' during a crisis. I was perfectly capable of handling my own affairs. Looking back, I realized they had never been by my side, neither during the good times nor during the bad. When they had turned up for any function, they'd behaved like guests, not close family members. Forget offering help or assistance, they had demanded extra-special treatment and attention. When they didn't receive it, they withdrew, criticized me openly and sulked.

These incidents used to bother me a great deal. I would confess my disappointment to my children who were equally puzzled by this behaviour. They advised me to switch off and ignore the barbs. But how could I? It was when I started behaving uncharacteristically that I figured it was time to give myself a break. I merely withdrew. No more daily phone calls. No more solicitous conversations. No more pretending there was any intimacy or warmth left in the relationship. I like to think it was a relief both ways. Today, I no longer torment myself over the lack of communication. I don't wish anybody ill, nor do I mope about how it could have been, should have been, but wasn't to be. I'm done.

~

A war veteran's manual

At my age, I qualify as a war veteran in every sense of the word. Or should I call myself a war survivor? You win some, you lose some. We all pick our battles—sometimes wisely, most times not. The important question is this: What sort of a battle is worth staking a friendship or relationship for? How do you extricate yourself once it's over? Who apologizes? How? What are the stakes? How well defined are the issues? Who plays referee? Should there be a cooling-off period? Can a broken relationship ever be mended? Do you hold grudges? Do you find it hard to eat crow, saying, 'I was wrong'?

At my age, I qualify as a war veteran in every sense of the word. Or should I call myself a war survivor? You win some, you lose some. We all pick our battles—sometimes wisely, most times not.

Does ego play a huge role in your fights? Are you a poor loser? Too many uncomfortable questions.

I subject myself to 'rational' reviews after each major fight—normally with one of my children or my husband. I also pride myself on my clinical post-mortems. I tend to analyse everything to death—fights included. Sometimes it's better to let things go. Even though, this is what I realize and know deep down, I tend to make the same mistakes over and over again. I guess we all have what are called 'anger patterns' or 'anger fields'. We can see an argument brewing. We can sense it will lead to an ugly exchange of words, but we still go headlong into a nasty 'you said this, which is why I did that' exchange.

No matter what your age and maturity level, there is generally a set format to how one conducts verbal confrontations. My first impulse is to walk away. But I don't! How much ugliness I would have spared myself (and the other person) had I done just that—walked away from an impending fight. I also plug my ears during a particularly loud and aggressive slanging match. Is that a smart thing to do? I think not. It frustrates the person who is yelling, generally making things worse and escalating the conflict. Voice levels rise and facial expressions begin to indicate an imminent meltdown. If at all possible, this is the right time to exit—in a quietly dignified manner. If that option isn't available, the next best thing to do is to mentally disconnect. Trust me, that's the hardest—you have to channel your inner Buddha, and not all of us are fortunate enough to possess this gift. People say it's a matter of training. Anger management is a technique that can be developed. It is also said that as you get older, it gets easier to control emotions, anger included. It is not true, at least not in my case. Forget mellowing and becoming more accepting of oneself and those around me, I am most annoyed at myself! An open display of anger is one of the biggest turn-offs for me. I can put up with almost any other failing, but I find a bad temper hard to condone. I also find it very unattractive. In the midst of a fight, I am generally studying the other person's altered state—the face contorted with unbridled rage, the body language, dramatically different from the one in peaceful times, eyes bulging, veins throbbing. Please take a look at yourself, I say silently, and let's stop.

I walk towards the nearest mirror (if there is one) and stare at my own reflection. It is so terrible, I turn my eyes away. I don't want to acknowledge this alien creature. I hate what I am looking at. The eyes are cold, the mouth twisted and the vein on my forehead is throbbing. My hands are shaking, my entire body is stiffened by the strong waves of negativity I am experiencing. I look seriously ugly, and that depresses me. Anger is by far the most harmful emotion. It affects every single part of the body. When my heart starts pounding, I am aware that my blood pressure is shooting up rapidly and dangerously. I have read up enough on the subject to realize I could be struck down by a stroke or suffer cardiac arrest. And yet, I am helpless. I do nothing. I can't.

Chanting in a group has helped many of my friends of the same vintage as I. We all agree we could do with being quieter, calmer, more at peace. We seem to be dealing with similar problems of heightened irritability and poor management of emotions. Friends who admit they have a quick temper also confess their inability to deal with outbursts. I have thought about it. I have considered therapy as well. But I have not taken that first important step towards either option so far. Age works both ways—as you hit your sixties and seventies, society expects you to miraculously undergo a transformation and become a different person. You are told it is time to look inward, modify your conduct, behave in a manner that is 'appropriate'. People demand a kinder, softer, more tameable version of you. This is difficult to achieve for someone like me. I am the original 'peacenik'—I believe making love is far, far more important than making war. But 'tameable'? No chance! I am the person I am, and I am okay with most aspects of me. I do find fights abhorrent, but I like to think I fight fair.

There are a few ground rules worth adhering to during fights.

Rule number one: Pick someone your own size. Never attack a person who cannot hit back, is weaker, more vulnerable, defenceless.

Rule number two: Don't hit below the belt. I know what that feels like. And I have done it a few times myself.

It is real intimacy that is often the biggest enemy of two people going to war—they know far too much about each other. They are well-armed. There are no secrets between them and that's the real problem. They can throw things at one another that nobody else is aware of, and that hurts. But we all do it. The worst aspect of a no-holds-barred fight is what comes tumbling out when you least expect it. Accusations fly, buried hurts surface, well-aimed arrows find the right target, vulnerabilities are exposed. Then what? Who takes care of the aftermath? Who clears the debris?

There are theories galore about cold wars being less harmful than hot wars. I am not so sure. An explosion hurts as much as an implosion. Explosions lead to heart attacks, implosions to ulcers. Either way, there is indescribable pain. A hurt that scars and rarely heals. What does one do to prevent war—hot or cold? I wish I had answers. But experience has taught me a few lessons—expensive ones at that.

When I was much younger, I would withdraw completely and remain withdrawn for weeks, perhaps months, till the cold rage dissipated, or I came to terms with the nagging issue somehow. I could not get myself to exchange a word with the person I was angry with. I could barely make eye contact. My wound would fester, often heedlessly, my appetite would disappear almost entirely (come on, how can anybody eat or enjoy a meal with bile rising in the mouth?), I would lose weight noticeably, my face would appear drawn and pinched, my voice would alter, and my entire body would convey my rejection of the person emphatically. This was my slightly foolish way of insulating myself. But as we all know, there is really no protection against wrath—your own or someone else's. You can meditate. Do yoga. Escape to another room, city or country. But the anger will follow you regardless. It is corrosive. It is destructive. It is worse than a vicious dog bite. It is the single most toxic emotion. Murders happen because of anger. A few nasty words are enough to break old relationships permanently. Does anybody possess the magic potion that instantly dissolves anger?

How does one make up after a blowout? It's a subject worthy of an entire book. My own way is to wait it out. Be patient, even with yourself. With time, the issues begin to look less critical and more manageable. If you lead a busy life, domestic problems, big and small, intervene, distract and distance. The stand-off becomes inconvenient, then unimportant. Finally, it is rendered irrelevant.

I strongly recommend a cooling-off period. This can be any length of time between a single day and a year. It's important not to cheat. You can't fool yourself, so why fool someone else? It is only after the volcano within has stopped erupting, and you are sure you won't spew venom, that the process of remorse and reconciliation can begin. I am not a sucker for flowers or flowery words of apology. I can tell if the other person is genuinely sorry, just like I know in my heart of hearts that I am ready to forget and move on.

If these two moments are in sync, it is a huge relief. Ten kilos fall off instantly. Frowns vanish and the eyes shine again. The only real way to make up after a fight is to confront the fight. Table the issues and deal with them once and for all. The more you run away from the truth, the harder it gets to accept its consequences. Couples who say they always make up before going to bed are probably lying. Or not facing the hurt generated. Some couples find it so hard to maintain eye contact when they are making up, it becomes a counterproductive and artificial construct which collapses very quickly. Sitting across a table and sorting out differences in a 'civilized' fashion is an equally fake move. We lose our civilized selves when angered. Conditioned responses of polite behaviour are thrown out of the window when the gloves are off. Writing long emails is one way of putting your conflicts into some order. But do remember, emails are forever. And can be easily retrieved by an aggrieved party. Text messages are equally incriminatory. Phone calls are trickier still—you can say the most unfortunate things but you can't see the recipient's reaction. What's the fun in fighting long distance? Besides, have you forgotten the recorder?

Considering human beings have been fighting since time immemorial, it's strange that nobody has come up with ways to: a) anticipate a fight and b) resolve it quickly. There are some weirdos who thrive on fights, their own included. In fact, such people instigate fights. They don't admit it, but they exist. It isn't out of a sense of sadism alone (though sadism does figure), often it is out of sheer boredom. An empty mind is a dangerous thing. I've heard men and a few women boasting about their alpha personalities and wearing anger as a badge. They claim they can't help themselves since they fall into the Type A aggressive, assertive personality slot. This is rubbish. I am pretty Type A myself. But I abhor fights and have rarely instigated one. Yes, there is a quick temper (road rage, especially), but I do try to control the urge to let fly—words or hands!

Does age have a lot to do with anger management? Or are some people just more angry than others? Ask me and I will say that age has everything to do with emotional issues—anger management being just one of them. Age affects everything!

Does age have a lot to do with anger management? Or are some people just more angry than others? Ask me and I will say that age has everything to do with emotional issues—anger management being just one of them. Age affects everything! And that's pretty hard to deal with, since you keep remembering your younger, milder self and wondering what happened to that far more likeable person. The answer is obvious—why not leave it there?

~

Marathon, anyone?

I do it. I am sure you've done it too. I have not met a single person who, at some point or other, has not run miles away from something or someone. As a child, I didn't like my maternal grandmother. She didn't like me either. I was told she had slapped her forehead really hard when my birth was announced, lamenting, 'Did we really need another girl in the family? Weren't two enough?' Once this was revealed to me, I admit I found it hard to love her. The feeling was mutual. As a teenager, I would avoid coming straight home from school on the days she was visiting. I would loiter on the basketball court and take a bus which took a longer route to get home.

I generally found her in the kitchen, making some traditional Maharashtrian preparation with my mother as her apprentice. She never smiled or greeted me. In her presence, my mother regressed and behaved differently too. I felt ignored and unwanted. I even wished my grandma dead. This thought would induce far too much guilt within me, and I would promptly distract myself by announcing I was hungry, tired and thirsty—which indeed I was at the end of a really long and demanding school day. Both women would exchange looks of utter exasperation and treat me like an intruder—a nuisance. This was my cue to flee.

There are other ways to flee unpleasant situations too. Mental and emotional fleeing is the hardest to detect. And often the hardest to deal with. What looks like withdrawal and aloofness is often a fear of rejection. Children run away the fastest and the furthest when they sense danger—physical or psychological. Today's youngsters are coping the best they can with a multitude of challenges that didn't exist in the past. They do exist in a parallel universe, and if you can't access it, you will find yourself very alone. As will the child. The most worrying aspect of a young person's virtual existence is the secrecy that surrounds it. Privacy is a relatively new issue, especially with respect to toddlers. I overhear conversations in schools and parks, elevators and movie halls. Mothers seem overwrought and unsure when they swap notes about their kids' privacy. This makes me laugh.

What sort of privacy does a four-year-old require, I asked a young mum recently. She provided an elaborate explanation involving 'time off' and 'not invading personal space' of her cute daughter. My protest that she was still a baby was met with ill-disguised scorn. Said the mother with a smirk, 'You obviously don't know today's kids! They have such packed schedules, it is important for all of us to respect their priorities.' And what were those? She said her daughter was dealing with peer pressure and feeling inadequate. The little girl was not pleased with her 'shape'. I almost yelled, 'What do you mean by that?' But deep down I knew. Body shaming starts in the cradle these days. Mothers express anxieties over their babies looking less than perfect—especially when they themselves post pictures of their babies on multiple social media platforms. These have become 'weighty' issues in more ways than one. Today's dinner-table conversation is more about calorie counts and less about enjoying what's on the thali, forget discussing sociopolitical issues. Intense debates revolve around the intrinsic benefits of quinoa and desi ghee, rather than a cousin's wedding or a sibling's divorce. Perhaps even demonetization and GST.

Families that diet together stay together. Eating together is a different matter. Within this delicate dining-table space, nothing of any consequence takes place, what with every family member engaging with a mobile phone. Menus are customized to accommodate dietary requirements. One person is on a gluten-free course, another eats chicken but not red meat, a third avoids carbs and focuses on proteins. It is a wonder there is any joy left at mealtimes!

I attended a community feast recently and was delighted to rediscover the pleasure of sitting on wooden platforms placed on the tiled floor, being served a *shuddh* vegetarian meal by family cooks and senior ladies of the household. Most of the recipes had been passed down from earlier generations and the mood in the large dining room was lively and relaxed, as along with each dish being served, there were anecdotes and memories galore revolving around other family feasts. Suddenly, the barrenness of contemporary meals struck me forcefully. Why have we stopped talking—really talking—and started 'exchanging' polite noises that pass for conversation? This is where social media also plays the villain. All these links that have to be opened and read, all those videos that have to be watched, and the games that need to be mastered. I confess I have tried and failed to ban mobile phones at the dining table. And since example is supposed to work better than lectures, I never make or take calls during meals. Often, I find myself staring stonily ahead while everybody else is busy punching keys.

Large families mean large problems. They also mean large joys. But it's the problems that act as speed breakers in intimate relationships; they start to choke and gag and stifle, and you want to run away. Mothers and wives are not supposed to admit they want to flee. Most women I know well want to flee from time to time. They are not sure where they are headed, nor why they want to escape. But they do! Some of my more daring girlfriends have done exactly that—run away from home and family. One of them left for Goa and never came back! She is blissed out and content, living the life of an ageing hippy in a beach shack, surrounded by like-minded people from all over the world. After years of 'not forgiving mom', the children are back with her. And she dotes on the grandkids who adore their hip, tattooed grandma. The husband, who had turned into a vengeful demon when she had fled, has reconciled himself to her way of life—albeit most reluctantly. He spends half the year with her and doesn't seem angry any more. But then she is an exceptional woman. She has always made bold decisions. Not every wife–mother–daughter has her guts. Most grit their teeth and stay put.

But what if society 'allowed' women to flee from time to time? I think it would lead to happier marriages in the long run. Fleeing provides perspective. Away from the tyranny of domesticity (I really don't know a single woman who 'loves' housework!), women come into their own in creative and wonderful ways. Most spend time with themselves engaging in activities they may love but don't find the time for, trapped as they are in routine. The basic family fears that the woman will 'run wild', have an affair, drink herself silly and get into trouble are entirely misplaced. The reason families think like this is because families are selfish and insecure. They need the pivot (the woman) to keep their lives going.

When they express their worries about the woman's safety when she is on her own somewhere and they can't reach her, they are, in fact, worried about themselves. 'What happens to us if she doesn't come back? What will we do on our own?' The vagabond/absconder is made to feel terrible about forgetting her primary duty! Most times she backs down, even after her bags are packed—metaphorically and in reality. She shrugs and says sadly to herself, 'Forget it! The family is right. They need me. I should stay. What was I thinking?' And she stays. Everybody claps. They tell her she has done the right thing. They make her feel valued once again. She lulls herself into believing the false praise. She cries a little. Or a lot. Nobody sees her tears. Nobody is interested in her regrets. She tells herself to stop yearning. Stop dreaming. She gets busy in the kitchen. There is a collective sigh of relief. One more escape successfully stalled by those who claim to love her. If only they knew! If only they loved! She'd be free . . .

~

I see you stare, see if I care!

I was checking my Facebook page and came across my youngest daughter's cheeky post. It was one of those 'truthful' personal statements that are peddled by various youth-driver sites. It read: 'Yes, I dance in the car. And I see you stare. I don't care!' And I was instantly ashamed of my many lectures to her in the past.

Anandita was born dancing. She has the music in her. We all admire her unrehearsed moves. Anandita can, and does, dance anywhere and everywhere. That's the way it should be, right? That's what I stated very confidently. But when Anandita was a few years younger, our old faithful who chauffeurs her around told me with some alarm that Anandita was being stared at by other motorists, especially when the car stopped at traffic signals. He said, after carefully lowering his voice, that she had the car stereo on at full blast, and refused to listen to him when he requested her to stop dancing in the back seat.

'People think she's a mad girl!' he blurted out. In my heart of hearts I knew it was they who were mad—obviously, they'd never danced just for the love of it. Obviously, they were not accustomed to seeing a young girl lost in her own world. Obviously, they needed to loosen up. She was not harming anybody, merely embarrassing Choudhary. He, in turn, was being protective towards his charge, and giving her 'good' advice. But I fell for it and did the right (predictable) thing by admonishing her. Anandita looked genuinely puzzled, then hurt. She asked what was wrong with dancing in the car to unwind, relax, enjoy the music. I told her pompously, 'But people stare!' And she replied witheringly, 'So let them stare! I don't care. And you shouldn't either.'

But on one level, I did care. Double standards!

The more sinister side of social media pressure involves the 'coolness' factor. Parents of pre-teens are at a complete loss here. Unable to access this virtual world their children belong to, they feel powerless and excluded. They also feel exceedingly insecure. Most parents I talk to are ignorant about their children's lives outside the home. They have no clue whether their kids are underage drinkers, have experimented with drugs, stolen the family car and taken it on a few spins, had sex, got an abortion or made friends with potentially dangerous people they've met over FB. Nothing is as it looks. The parents are frightened and baffled. 'Should we interfere?' they ask, anxiety written all over their face. I don't understand the word 'interfere' when it comes to children. There is no such thing as 'interference'. Either you are intimately involved in the minutiae of their lives or your children could be dead. It is happening all over the world. Children are getting radicalized, joining cults, playing dangerous games (Blue Whale, anyone?), participating in secret rituals, keeping guns. Parents have the right to know, period. It's a non-negotiable right. Children cannot take away a parent's legitimate concern over their lives and safety.

I had battles galore with my own—and still do—when they felt I had crossed the line and invaded their space. It's 4 a.m. and they aren't back. I am aware of the event they're attending. But know nothing about the 'after-party' and the 'after-after-party'. All I know is my bedside clock is ticking and my heart is pounding. Their mobile phones ring, but of course, I get no answer. I start having morbid thoughts. 'What if . . . ?' I wait for the landline to ring. It could be a call from an emergency ward in

I don't understand the word 'interfere' when it comes to children. There is no such thing as 'interference'. Either you are intimately involved in the minutiae of their lives or your children could be dead.

a hospital. Or from a police station. All sorts of wild stories pop into my head. Finally, my call gets through. I ask in utter despair, 'But . . . but . . . where are you? It's nearly 5 a.m.!' I hear an exasperated sigh. 'Don't worry . . . I am two minutes away . . . we are taking the turn at Mantralaya.' It is always the Mantralaya turn! 'Come on, I am not such a donkey. You are probably at Juhu,' I want to say. But I keep quiet. I feel grateful my call was accepted at all. I remember my neighbour's kid making several distress calls and not getting a response late on a Saturday night, because the poor, exhausted mother had switched off her mobile phone and fallen asleep . . . till that early-morning knock on the door. You know the rest. It has become a common narrative across the country. Why should mothers have to put up with such tyranny?

Today's progressive parents are supposed to 'mind their own business' and stop 'being nosy'. What's nosy about asking basic questions like 'When will you be home?' I really don't get it. We are supposed to respect our children's choices. Mostly, we do. We are also supposed to pretend we are deaf, dumb and blind. I have often felt like chopping my tongue off after saying, 'Oh my God! You are going out dressed like *this*?' Those terrible words tumble out before I can stop myself. It's war after that. I am told I know nothing about how people dress these days. I know nothing about the latest hair and make-up trends. I am not a nail person, so clearly I don't appreciate nail art. As for body-con ensembles—come on, what's the point of going to the gym and working out strenuously if all one can wear is a shapeless tent? Small difference: Mumbai has a posh locality called Malabar Hill. But Beverley Hills it ain't. This is where I sense a lot of clashes between New India and Old India. I am suspended in between. I understand my daughters want to dress like their global peers. But our social environment is far from conducive for flaunting this level of fashion. I worry about reactions to their on-point dressing. I see them through a mother's filter. And all I can observe is risk. Sorry, I am an old-fashioned hypocrite when it comes to safety. In principle I support and encourage every woman's right to dress and behave as she pleases. But I confess I go into panic mode when I see my youngest daughter leaving for a night on the town, dressed à la mode. I fear she will be singled out for verbal or physical attack from people who 'disapprove' of her clothes. 'Showing legs, showing arms, showing so much . . . do these girls have no shame?' That awful word—shame. A shiver runs down my spine. I forget my politically correct stand on the matter of female attire and throw a shawl at her, 'Take this . . .' I call out desperately. Not that she is going to wrap herself up. But, I console myself, at least she has the option.

It takes me back to my own 'shameless' days as a teenager who lived in shorts. I had a legitimate 'excuse'—I lived on the sports field. But shorts remained my most favoured attire, much to the disapproval of my parents. It certainly was a big cultural departure for my family to watch their youngest child running around half-clad, especially since their eldest was compelled to switch to sarees when she 'came of age' at eleven! My father was serving in the hinterlands of Maharashtra back then. By the time our family relocated to Mumbai after ten years in Delhi, I was ready to break the mould and kick-start my life on a fresh note. What must have seemed rebellious, radical and defiant to them was perfectly natural to me. So it must be for my daughters too.

As protective parents, we tend to over-romanticize our own histories. We also concoct myths about our past. Most times we get away with the quasi-lies and half-truths. Children are too self-absorbed, too lazy to probe or dig for the truth. This suits everybody just fine. But what if you decide to table the truth, the whole truth and nothing but? Do you really think your children want to know? Just the other day I was dealing with a daughter's meltdown. One of the siblings told me softly, 'The problem is you confide a bit too much in her . . . she knows all your weak points.' And you know most of hers. That's a problem? I have no real 'secrets'. I prefer my family to know it all—warts and everything. I don't want to hide a thing. Perhaps they are not dying to know about my life before they were born or even what it is today? Why inflict unwanted information on the unwilling or the disinterested?

I started to think about sharing too much with my children after that stand-off. For a couple of days, my new-found insights worked brilliantly. By day three, there I was, dying to perform an emotional striptease once again. Why?

Most mothers and grandmothers crib about the apathy of children. This is universal. There are 'good' children and there are 'bad' children. But all children are indifferent. Mostly. Understandably. Recall your own childhood, if you dare.

No child is born 'bad'. So why do some children turn into brats? Psychologists have their own take on this. Tomes have been written on the subject. History books are replete with examples of 'good' and 'bad' children. After raising a few myself, I think 'bad' children are products of 'bad' parenting most of the time. Poor handling of a difficult kid leads to that kid growing up into a seriously dysfunctional adult. This is, of course, a sweeping generalization. But there is an element of truth in it. I have seen children born of the same set of parents behaving so differently, it's hard to figure out what could have gone wrong. I'd say inconvenient timing is the most obvious cause. Some kids are born too early, some too late. Very few are fortunate enough to be born when both parents are ready for them. It is this out-of-sync accident of birth that dramatically affects a child's personality and psyche.

Most parents are unaware of their own emotional state at the time of conception and after. Young parents are so wrapped up in just managing their time, money, in-laws, health and other priorities, they don't have the energy to invest in a toddler. If both parents work, as is common, the situation gets further complicated. There are pressures galore to cope with—an acute shortage of time being the main bane of parenting at this stage. Supportive in-laws take care of the nitty-gritty of everyday issues—they stand in for day-care centres. Even the most loving grandparents find it hard to manage a tantrum-prone kid. There is confusion and guilt since nobody can figure out why the child is yelling so much or throwing toys around. 'We give our baby everything . . . whatever is asked for,' hapless in-laws from both sides lament. Perhaps that's the problem! Giving a child 'everything' leads to certain disaster. But it's the quickest way to shut the kid up . . . peace is bought with chocolates, video games, unrestricted access to television, some other bribe. Soon the kid realizes their power. And uses it ruthlessly. Not knowing he/she is being ruthless, of course.

I am trying to see the world through the eyes of my grandchildren. It's a daunting task. Not being a typical grandmother, I cannot coo and cuddle for long. I get distracted and bored after a point. I enjoy the gurgling and the drooling, but it doesn't keep me enthralled and engaged as it does most of my contemporaries. In fact, I fail miserably when they attempt to draw me into the grandmom stakes, a silly competition that involves gushing and bragging. No, I don't know how often the babies poop, how much and the quality or colour of their poop. Frankly, I don't care either. So please stop telling me about it when we meet. Then comes the question of how many grandchildren we each have. 'Oh, you have just five? I have seven. Any grandsons? I have three.' Sometimes, I ask why they boast about this, considering they have not physically produced those babies. This doesn't make me terribly popular in the Grandmom Club. I can almost hear them whispering, 'What does she know? She's too busy with her own life and career.'

Indeed I am busy with my life and career. Without that, I'd be an even worse grandmother—crotchety and critical. Demanding and possessive. I want to meet my grandkids as young adults.

Indeed I am busy with my life and career. Without that, I'd be an even worse grandmother—crotchety and critical. Demanding and possessive. I want to meet my grandkids as young adults. I may not be around at the time, but that would interest me far more—I'd be able to converse with them, watch movies together, share books and ideas. Figure out what they're all about. Till such time, I am happy to meet them a few times a month and watch their antics. I confess there is only so much of messing with fake 'slime' and play dough that I can take. I guess that makes me a lousy *naani*.

When the toddler grows into young adulthood, trouble starts. Big, big trouble.

These days, parents don't shy away from seeking professional help either for themselves or their kids. Counselling troubled teens has become big business in India, and I frequently meet teenagers with mega attitude who sulkily boast, 'Aunty, I am in therapy.' Our movie stars have made it trendy to go public with mental health issues. There is an upside and a downside to this. Young, impressionable adults with resources and zero awareness take advantage of their parents' panic-stricken response to crises and seek the services of trained counsellors, who may or may not have the answers the youngsters desperately seek. We are stuck! Today's grandparents lead active, full lives. They don't have the patience to listen to the problems faced by their grandkids. Even if they have the time, they lack the insights needed to conduct an intelligent dialogue.

Kids don't respect what family elders advise, and they don't have faith in their own parents! This is a new development in our social history . . . I overhear children openly mocking parents for being 'so weird', 'so dumb'. I feel terrible! What if my own children say that about me? Then I reassure myself I am not all that dumb or all that weird. Just a little so. That too, not all the time. I try not to be. I want to be able to keep up in a sensible way with a rapidly changing world. Being 'cool' is not the objective. I am embarrassed by 'cool'. It's enough to be curious and interested. I am definitely that—at the risk of being called nosy and intrusive.

Why do we fear the young?

The young! Oh, the young! They really are not at all scary! I wish more of us would accept that. What do we fear about the young? Their ideas? Their energy? Their opportunities? I think the young are frequently feared, not trusted, avoided and occasionally shunned because we see our own inadequacies reflected in their success. We nod our heads sagely and comment on how uncaring, selfish and reckless the young are! Really? Is it that easy to forget our past? It's the birthright of every young person to be flagrantly disobedient and reckless. How else do you discover yourself? Do the unthinkable and see what happens . . . if you don't, you will turn seventy and not have lived at all!

~

The great escape(s)

I did some wild and wonderful things at twenty . . . thirty . . . forty. Fifty too. By sixty, I had become slightly more self-conscious, mainly because my children made me so. Despite their restraining presence ('Mama, it's for your own good . . .'), I sneakily managed a few mad adventures, which I cherish. Those words, 'It's for your own good', had exactly the opposite effect to what was intended. They were the spurs! Who wanted 'good'? Not me. I wanted life! In all its rawness and glory. It's a wonder I didn't run away by myself to some exotic destination, without a backward glance. I felt tempted many times. I still do! I hear a tango being played, and I want to jump into the nearest aircraft and head to Buenos Aires. This has been a consistent fantasy. I am sure that irresistible word 'escape' obsesses millions of women. I have yet to meet a woman who has not thought at least once, if not a hundred times, of abandoning her family, children, parents, pets, lovers and escaping into another reality.

This obsession with escaping goes beyond class and circumstances. From the poorest to the richest, women dream of escaping. Not necessarily because their lives are wretched or deprived. It is something beyond that. It is a reaching-out to possibilities and fantasies of the kind nobody sanctions. It is a yearning for more. More of everything. It has nothing to do with having or not having money. Insecurity is the leitmotif of every woman's secret life. Insecurity fuels and feeds on itself. Half the time, we don't know what we are feeling insecure about! Even a confident woman, if prodded a bit, will admit to a near constant state of suspended insecurity. Very often, it is driven by her dissatisfaction with her body. If a woman does not like what she sees reflected in the mirror, she feels less about herself on other levels. This feeling is not connected to perfect proportions. Top models worldwide talk about their low-self-esteem issues.

Of course, the pressure on them to conform to an absurd ideal is far different from the self-image 'problems' the rest of us face. Beyond physical beauty, what we recall are childhood slights. Even the prettiest little girl is not spared a highly personal and absurdly pointed remark by an insensitive relative during those early years. 'Your head is too big!' 'Pity you didn't inherit your mother's complexion!' 'Oh dear! Your sisters are so much taller! What happened to you?' 'I hope your parents are getting those teeth fixed!' 'Your eyes are not like your father's—don't worry, the rest of you is nice!' Do adults not realize how terrible they sound? And how permanent these early scars are? Taunting a kid with crass comments about his/her appearance seems to be a particularly nasty Indian trait.

So much for early scars. Our fear of the young reminds us a bit too acutely about our lapses and omissions. We cannot forgive ourselves. We lament and rewind our memory spools. 'Had I got better grades in class ten, I would have . . .' 'If only my father had respected my decision to pursue art and not forced me to opt for science . . .' 'My mother was such an emotional drain on me during college—she was going through a lot of stuff.' Excuses. At sixty, there is no time left to redeem those old promises made to oneself. It's a done deal. Accept the foolish decisions and move on bravely. So long as you have had a good time falling flat on your face at twenty!

Envying the young adds lines to your face! I keep saying that to my close friends—men and women. Who, after all, easily lets go of vanity? At any age, we want to look our best . . . as good as is possible. Some of us use a superior quality of hair dye and happily believe we are fooling the world if we cover the grey. Are we? I am tempted to stop 'touching up the roots', as it is politely referred to by hairdressers. It is my husband and children who dissuade me. 'Going grey is not for you,' they insist. Often, I am not aware that more grey is now showing at the temples in a shorter span of time than earlier. If I went for a 'touch-up' once a month in the past, I need to make the trip twice a month these days. I find the process time-consuming, tedious and expensive. But I go through with it dutifully, so as to not let the family down.

Every aspect of my physical self is scrutinized on a daily basis by family members. If I gain a kilo or two, I am advised: 'Cut back on the vino—it's sugar, you know.' If my saree blouse doesn't fit well, someone says, 'Change the bra . . .' If my walk slows down, I am reminded, 'It's those heels! Why not switch to some other footwear?' I wear spectacles to read and write, and I am fine with being seen on public platforms wearing specs. But a child will helpfully suggest, 'Get lenses, na?' In a way, this level of personal and highly critical examination is really touching and sweet and displays an intense level of involvement. But . . . I do feel like screaming sometimes. 'Leave me be! I am nearly seventy years old! It's okay to wear specs, have grey hair, weigh extra kilos, deal with a slower gait, be seen in a baggier blouse. So what?' Then, I hastily retract my rebellious thoughts! I tell myself they are right. They love me. They want me to look good. And I suppress a loud laugh! They. They. They. It's all about the 'they'. My entire life has been about the 'theys'. When will my time come? Will it ever?

My time is mine only when I write. And that time is sacred. Precious. Priceless. I am jealous of this time and space. I guard it. Protect it. Am proprietorial about it. It is this time that keeps me going. Keeps me sane. It is this time I value the most. Above all else. Which is also why I have no fear of the young.

My time is mine only when I write. And that time is sacred. Precious. Priceless. I am jealous of this time and space. I guard it. Protect it. Am proprietorial about it. It is this time that keeps me going.

~

Superwoman one day, Minnie Mouse the next

This was the thought bothering me as I drove down to Mumbai from Pune. It was a familiar route—I knew practically every overbridge and tunnel. I was feeling uncharacteristically 'out of control'—feeling small and diminished. I was searching for a parent to tell me what was wrong. Even as I neared seventy then, the child within was yearning for advice and guidance from someone wiser, if not older. I wanted to be soothed and comforted, not taunted and mocked. The incident in Pune may have been the trigger, but in itself, it was pretty insignificant.

Many women of my age group have told me they feel fatigued 'acting their age'. They often want to just be. I don't call that feeling irrational or childish. To the outside world, we are fossils—way past our sell-by date. But within, we are still girls! We remain vain and petulant, flirtatious and capricious, demanding and silly. Why not? Most of us suppress this sudden and crazy urge to let go because we are overly concerned about the consequences. 'What will the children/grandchildren, husband, in-laws, neighbours, relatives say?' Think about it—what *will* they say? *Log kuch aur hi kahenge. Logon ka kaam hain kehna.* That you are immature, irresponsible, selfish? What if you are? Do you care? Let them say whatever the hell they want to. You are what and who you are. It's okay. Selfish *toh* selfish. *Bas?*

Age and wisdom are not interlinked. Wisdom is fluid. Flashes of it come and go. Nobody is consistently wise. Women are entitled to their foolishness. An overload of wisdom can seriously impact our health! The pressure to be wise, caring, giving, nurturing to all the people in our lives is such a huge and oppressive burden! There are times you just want to take that damn weight off your shoulders and flee. Is that so wrong? Who hasn't felt this urge? The ones who act on it are the blessed ones. They pay a price, but at least they don't have to pay that to themselves. They are gloriously free.

The only 'wise' decisions worth making concern the health of loved ones. You can't fool around with someone else's life. Your own? Well, women can be foolishly negligent. Men and wisdom is an entirely different story. Most men never really grow up—they just get more practical as they go along. A rare few have the gift of wisdom. These are the ones who don't talk—they provide the required support during crises, silently and efficiently. They don't remind people around them about their contribution. They guide without lecturing. They find solutions during an impasse. You can count on them and trust their advice. Generally, the advice is offered without any strings attached. Sometimes, no words are exchanged. The reassurance comes from being in the presence of these wise men.

I miss such a powerful presence in my life sometimes. More so because I am supposed to *be* that presence in other people's lives. I get tired of other people's confidence in my 'efficiency', my 'capability', my 'strength'. I want to be weak, dependent, foolhardy sometimes. I don't want non-stop responsibility. I want the option to be badly behaved if I want to. I want to indulge my fantasies. Be reckless and self-centred. At such times, I need my own personal rock. No judgements. No criticism. Only unconditional understanding and acceptance. Of course, my husband is that rock for the most part. But my reckless self worries him. Perhaps my expectations are unrealistic—I want a granite mountain.

So many supposedly 'strong' women are forced to live up to some unrealistic and fake image of what the world thinks they are or ought to be. Of late, I find myself getting irritated when strangers walk up to me and say, 'You are such a fearless woman. We admire your guts!' I want to yell, *'Gupp bass!'* That's Marathi for 'Shut up!' When said rapidly, it sounds like 'GUBBBBASSS'. I feel like using that word a lot these days. If they only knew. I am no more fearless than they. Confronting my own fears and saying, 'Yes, I feel scared. Yes, I am intimidated,' has not been easy. In our family, we have coined a quaint word for it—*shepti*. This refers to a dog's tail-between-the-legs posture when he is unsure, insecure, afraid. We have devised secret ways to warn one another when we sense fear/diffidence creeping up in innocuous social situations. We mouth the word 'shepti' discreetly . . . and smile. Most times, the 'warned' person gets it and snaps out of that zone instantly. Projecting 'strong' versus being strong—huge difference. Strength comes and goes—just like wisdom. But women who are expected to stay strong 24/7 often break down and crumble when no one's looking. Who is there during those fraught and vulnerable moments to hold us and say, 'It's fine . . . it will pass . . . I am right here . . .' Then again, I wonder whether we ourselves push people away with our fictional 'strength'. I feel like screaming, 'Hold me! Take care of me! I'm afraid.' But I keep my mouth shut. That cry never escapes my throat even by mistake. People often tell me they feel intimidated to start a conversation with me or take the initiative. But why? I don't bite. I don't breathe fire. I haven't grown talons. I want to plead, 'Please . . . I'm really very nice and sweet and kind and gentle. Really! Don't go by what I write in my columns and express on television.' Very few would believe me. It's their 'shepti'. But when someone does make the effort, I feel thrilled. It is so energizing to talk to a confident stranger rather than a familiar coward.

Like me, there are others who feel like Superwoman one day and Minnie Mouse the next. It's a schizophrenic existence and exhausting to boot. I do not possess answers. I am just as 'weak' as the next person. I want to shout this out but at this point in my life, nobody wants to hear it. A mould has been cast, a box created, and it seems I have to obediently sit in it.

Or else what? That's the tough question.

Received wisdom instructs women to steady the boat when it rocks. 'It is your job to keep the family together, it is your duty to make sure peace is maintained. You cannot place yourself first, no matter what. *Ghar banana aurat ka kaam hai.*' Discussing this with my younger friends, I found I was not the only one who was sick of these platitudes—the rules and regulations define our 'domestic responsibilities' that insist we, as women, are born to ensure stability and peace in the home. That we are the ones who are called 'shaadi fail' if our home life is chaotic. That we must possess the skill to roll out perfectly round chapattis if we want a perfectly sound marriage. Above all, we must obey. Obey the 'rules' if not an individual or a set of individuals. But what if we are never consulted? What if we are left out of decisions that lead to anarchy and chaos—whether domestically or in global politics? What if we have no real say in how we lead our lives? That's pretty much what it is at present. Has always been.

It is only after systems break down irreversibly that we, the damage-control experts, are summoned to restore order, bring about peace and maintain the status quo. Most of us oblige. It's the ones who refuse to play ball who get 'punished' and end up feeling guilty and terrible about situations they may have had nothing to do with in the first place. Women are frequently forced to take sides: A belligerent husband may demand, 'Are you with me or against me?' glowering menacingly, while a petrified child looks on. It can happen in the presence of domestic staff, employees and, worst of all, mutual friends. One half falls out, the other half has to follow. Even if the fight has nothing to do with you, and you quite like the friend who will soon become an ex-friend. Unless the issue is major, nobody should have to choose sides.

To avoid embarrassing social situations, one can negotiate skilfully and still maintain a civil relationship. It's much harder if the choice involves a close relative. Mothers who pick a child over an aggressive husband find out soon enough that unless the child is as strong as the spouse, life can become pretty uncomfortable. As adults, the freedom to choose is in our hands. Difficult choices demand hard decisions. A nifty plan B helps. More and more women are discovering the power of a plan B. Financial independence is the first, most crucial step. Getting a home of your own is integral to maintaining your self-respect. Most women of a certain age get stuck in awful marriages because they have nowhere to go. They have assumed their marriage is permanent. They have assumed they are secure on all fronts. They have assumed their husbands are not ruthless. They have assumed their children will look after them if something goes wrong. Please, ladies, make no such assumptions. I have friends who could have bought their own flats with their own resources or with a bank loan (as I did), but they didn't want to. They preferred living a lie. They chose a life of compromise when they could have opted for dignity. When such women find themselves in a dreadful domestic situation, facing daily abuse and insults, they discover they have zero options. Where does a fifty-year-old woman go if she is thrown out by her husband of twenty-five years?

No man or woman should stay in a nasty relationship only because there is no roof over their head. Preparing young daughters for this is the toughest challenge for mothers. If you place too much stress on independence, the subliminal message that gets out is this: 'Your dream life may not work out as planned. Your dream partner may let you down. Make sure you are not in a trap. Keep the exit door open.' I still believe this piece of advice is worth passing on. A young woman who has been raised on highly romanticized notions of marriage and its 'happily ever after' ending may find herself entirely unprepared if

A young woman who has been raised on highly romanticized notions of marriage and its 'happily ever after' ending may find herself entirely unprepared if faced with an unexpected twist in her marital paradise and the possibility of a separation/divorce comes up.

faced with an unexpected twist in her marital paradise and the possibility of a separation/divorce comes up. She is generally so ill-equipped to deal with the emotional shock, the last thing on her mind is the practical fallout of the development. She panics. She suffers a complete breakdown. All sorts of 'advisers' step into the picture. Her family distances itself. She takes a disastrous route (alcohol, drugs, adultery) out of sheer desperation.

I have seen this happen over and over again. And yet, how does one tell a daughter madly in love with an unsuitable boy that she needs to take off her blinkers and take a good look at the guy before taking the plunge? She might hate you for stating the obvious. Ditto for a son who has lost his heart to the wrong woman—does one 'warn' him? Or keep mum? Having been in so many such situations, I can tell you, there is no right way to deal with it. Whatever you say, suggest or do will be held against you. If you are blunt, you will be called a cynic with no empathy. If you keep quiet and things don't work out, you will be accused of not being a responsible parent. Either way, you are the loser. So my method is to just be myself. Be upfront and straightforward. Take it or leave it. I say what I need to and hit the ball back over the net. After all, I was not involved in the decision. Nobody sought my permission before falling in love. And deciding to get married *phata-phat*. As a parent, my job is to guide, period. Not threaten. Not impose. Taking or rejecting my advice is up to the person. Yes, it's tough. It leads to months of bickering and arguments. But your children must know you have a spine. And that you are willing to stand up and speak up when required. No question of 'shepti' here.

Which is also why I refuse to 'pick' partners for my children. I may select someone with the best of intentions. It's possible my choice is totally off from the sort of person the son/daughter is looking for. If things don't work out eventually, I will be blamed for choosing the wrong partner. For imposing my will in a personal matter. No thanks. We live in a modern world. The children have all the access required to locate, meet and court their own mates. I am happy to bless the couple once they decide to tie the knot. That's it. Better still, I frequently half-joke, elope and tell me all about it!

Arranging the weddings of children has been my least favourite part of raising them. For most parents, it's an absolute nightmare, even if they don't admit it. Since I have not taken the assistance of wedding planners so far, and foolishly attempted to do it on my own (albeit with some help) I can tell you one thing: There are still three weddings left. I won't survive them if I have to handle all the arrangements. I am hoping the three unmarried children will spare me and my husband the *chhota sa* trauma, by discreetly and considerately opting for a *swayamvar* in a distant forest.

~

Throw away that hair shirt!

On one particular drive from Pune, I was in review mode. I was figuring out the major and minor mistakes I had made in seven decades. I knew I was cheating a bit and using filters. Giving myself more credit than I deserved. Or was it the opposite? Was I being 'shepti' and underplaying my own contribution? Had I done enough? Too little? Too much? Women and guilt. Guilt and women. We put on hair shirts when we needn't. So much emotional energy spent on self-inflicted wounds.

During the longish drive, I also managed an intense conversation with Anandita, my youngest daughter. It was about a very successful television commercial for a top global brand of sneakers aimed at today's sporty woman. To her, it spoke about the true empowerment of women in India—urban and rural. It was a positive and she connected instinctively with what appeared paradoxical to me. Was I being cynical? Or was she being naive? Was it just an age thing? Would I have seen this commercial differently twenty, thirty years ago? I genuinely don't think so. When I told her the slick ad had nothing to do with female empowerment and was just about selling more sneakers, she was upset. When I wondered aloud what the price of a pair of those sneakers was and how many families of the same rural women featured in it those pricy shoes would feed, she said that's not the point. I withdrew. My withdrawal at this stage was a 'wise' decision. Or let's just say it was practical. Did I really want to spend the next three hours squabbling over ridiculously overpriced sneakers?

It is when 'practical' wins over 'emotional' that problems start. Very often, we step away from confrontational situations because we don't want to handle the consequences. It's easier to drop the issue and look away rather than see it to its logical conclusion. Men frequently accuse women of being quarrelsome and 'naggy'. I find it an annoying stereotype. What they actually mean is that women don't like to leave things alone. If there is an unresolved conflict, we don't run in the opposite direction, even when good sense tells us to do just that. Does playing ostrich resolve issues?

In my own life, this game has never worked. I guess I am not an ostrich. I vastly prefer a no-holds-barred one-to-one to clear the air and sort out areas of hostility, getting to the bottom of that particular conflict for starters. Where does it stem from? Why is it there? How can it be diffused? Not too many people agree. Most think if you leave conflict alone, it disappears. If it does, it is temporary. It festers—a dormant monster that can awaken any time and strike when you are least prepared for the attack. There are times when a flimsy Band-Aid is expected to do the job of a surgical procedure to stop a wound from haemorrhaging. Is that possible? But we foolishly attempt just that—a quick fix, when what is required is amputation.

The counterargument is, why not leave a superficial scratch alone? Why dig deeper and infect it? Forced to make a morbid choice, I'd prefer amputation to gangrene. One limb less is better than a weakened heart that threatens to give up every few days. Sometimes, when I spot a gorgeous three-legged dog in the neighbourhood chasing a garbage truck, jauntily and happily guarding its turf, playing with companions, looking after puppies, my heart soars. The dog seems to be doing just fine. So can we!

~

Still looking for Aie

Is it okay to miss my mother, even though I am a grandmother myself?

Last night, I dreamt of Aie. Again. It was a scene straight out of an Almodóvar movie. I dream of her frequently. I continue to miss her. She died at seventy-eight. Soon, I shall reach that age myself, if I live that long. I have five grandchildren. There will be more in the future, I am sure. God said, 'Go forth and multiply.' I took his word for it. I happily went forth and multiplied. I hope my children do the same. Despite all the wonderful people in my life, I still miss my mother. And there are times when I experience feelings of such despair, I want to rush to her, just to place my head in her lap and have her stroke my hair. Her lap. I have never found a good enough substitute for her lap. I miss the tactile joy of her saree against my cheek. Those *naram naram* sarees which absorbed my tears, allowed them to soak in and create small wet patches on her thigh. What comfort!

She didn't have to say much or even ask why I was upset. She just had to be there, seated on her bed or on the living room sofa, ready to comfort me in her own way. I still long for the touch of her fingers as she pushed a strand of stray hair away from my face and tucked it behind my ear. It is the quietness of the moment that I miss most. A moment filled with tender reassurance. A moment stripped of drama. A moment so complete in itself it didn't demand a thing. I would rest there for a short while and leave. Sometimes, we would sit silently in the kitchen while she prepared tea. I would stare at her tiny frame, looking for clues. But I still don't know what those clues were for. What was I seeking? What did I really want to know about her? Why didn't I just ask?

So many years later, I keep wondering: Did I ever know her as intimately as she knew me? I held nothing back. I trusted her with a ferocious totality. Was that ever a burden for her? She knew more about me than anybody else. My confidences remained safe with her. I felt safer with my mother than I do with anybody else. I 'sensed' her. But beyond that? Why did we never speak of love? Or disappointment? Why did I not probe gently to discover the woman behind the mother? Isn't that what we all need to do? We create convenient boxes and stick our nearest and dearest into them. I certainly did that with my mother. While I told her everything about my life, I never asked about hers. She knew my secrets, she kept them. I didn't know hers. I thought she had the perfect marriage with my father. Did she think so too? Towards the end of her life, she seemed just too exhausted to even attempt a proper conversation when we met. I would watch the faraway look in her eyes, as she restlessly tapped her fingers, and I would wonder what was going on inside her head. Her aloofness stumped and frustrated me. After a point, I would get restless and bored, make an excuse and leave. Her pain—physical and emotional—stayed with her. She chose not to share it. I chose not to probe. Was it out of consideration or something else?

Do we ever invest enough time in figuring out our parents? Or is it easier to think of them in generic terms?—'Oh . . . these are my parents. They brought me into the world. They will look after me. They are good people. Once I find my feet and move out, I will reconnect with them later.' Later rarely happens. This is one of my life's greatest regrets. Late one night, she was gone. Just like that. I wasn't there. I will never know. There are far too many unanswered questions. But at least the memory of placing my head in her lap remains vivid and strong. It comforts me when I am lost and feel like I am drowning. I miss Aie, my mother.

Childhood is what you choose to remember . . . and forget . . .

My mother's comfortable lap. That sums up 'childhood' for me. We didn't have to converse. In fact, I preferred the peace and silence of those all too brief minutes, as I surrendered to her love and the love I felt for her. My siblings insist they have no such precious memory to cherish. To one of them, our mother was a taciturn, undemonstrative person. My late brother, Ashok, remembered her with intense emotion and a sentimentality that was otherwise absent in him. I am surprised at these dramatically varying versions of our mother. Could she have been all that different with her other three children? Could she also have been all these contradictory people simultaneously? Was our bond extra special? If so, was it because I was the youngest child? And she, in a far happier place in her own life at that point? Why question? She's gone. I am here. My memories of her soothe and nurture me. That's all that matters.

I am sure I had a few rows even with my non-confrontational mother. I had several with my father. But honestly speaking, I cannot recall a single row with Aie—not one! Have I blotted out the memory? Am I in denial? Perhaps. I prefer it this way. Why hang on to negative images you can do nothing about? This is what I say to my siblings when

My mother's comfortable lap. That sums up 'childhood' for me. We didn't have to converse. In fact, I preferred the peace and silence of those all too brief minutes.

they start recounting their own less-than-pleasant memories of the same woman—our mother. 'Don't tell me . . . I really don't want to know,' I entreat. I want to stay with my own nostalgia. It's mine! I'm entitled to it. Nothing needs to be proved. We are not in a court of law. My 'proof' is in my attitude towards my own children. I think I owe Aie a big one. Recently, my sister Mandakini gave me Aie's stainless steel masala dabba. I just have to look at it to smell her *aamti*.

I miss my father too. Perhaps I could have managed that relationship better than I did. But on many levels we were a bit too alike. That was the strength as well as the weakness of our relationship. He was blunt and outspoken. Sharp and cutting. He was also madly charming when he wanted. Upright and uncompromising. Our conversations were candid and cerebral. Philosophical and also surprisingly wicked! We could swap dirty jokes and laugh at life's peccadilloes. But we remained wary of each other. I am presuming he didn't want to deal with a repeat of my many acts of defiance and rebelliousness when I was a young adult. We became 'equals' much later in life. I needed to earn that privilege. He liked the 'famous' me. The daughter everybody recognized. I am not sure he liked *me*! Where do we err when it comes to these two fundamental relationships in our lives? People say these remain our biggest challenges, no matter what the nature of the bond. Even the most nurturing, loving relationship comes with fault lines.

After my father passed away, I suddenly realized I had been 'orphaned'. I was a married woman with children of my own. But I felt strangely alone and insecure all of a sudden. With all our differences and arguments, he was one person I respected and admired—and that had nothing to do with his being my father. By that time we had become friends—sort of. It was an uneasy friendship, but it was on a reasonably balanced, fair footing. I enjoyed the liveliness of his mind. His sense of humour. His ceaseless curiosity. He was, I suppose, 'impressed' by my life and fascinated by the dramatically different professional direction I had taken as compared to the career choices of my more conventional siblings.

Our conversations were anything but pedestrian. From world politics to Madonna's latest song, my father was interested in it all. His vast knowledge of and love for literary classics combined with a staggeringly high IQ provided the fodder I needed at a time when Google Devta didn't exist! He was my reference file—one quick phone call and he'd fill in the gaps instantly. Our emotional equation is a different story. Even though I shared important aspects of my life with him pretty openly, it was almost like a man-to-man chat—brisk, practical, to the point. His advice was matter-of-fact and spot on. I admired his detachment . . . and it still makes me wonder how he managed to maintain that level of distance, even formality, with all his four children. Did he realize how deeply this attitude affected each one of us, individually and collectively? Since I have never asked my siblings. I can only guess.

How do we connect with our parents without going nuts?

These thoughts make me ask myself the same question about the sort of mother I am to my children: How different am I with them? Do I show my preference for one over another?

If so, which one? Do I make it obvious? Do the others know? Do they discuss it? How do I appear to them? Fair-minded or prejudiced? Sometimes, when my anxiety levels are high, I look into the eyes of whichever child is around and search for signs . . . answers. Have I spoken too harshly? Should I have waited to reprimand? Do I show my love sufficiently? Articulate it clearly? Does the person recognize the intensity of my feelings? Are comparisons drawn constantly? On the whole, do I get pass or fail marks as a mother? This is the single most important aspect of my existence. It supersedes everything else. Everything! I torment myself endlessly thinking about where I have fallen short. My friends tell me I am crazy! One of them advised me, 'This is your time, baby! Be selfish. Think of yourself and yourself alone. Your children are all adults. They should be worrying about you!' I looked at her face and was confused. She seemed so happy! She confirmed it! 'I am very happy! The day I decided I was the most important person in my life, I freed myself. I love myself the most in the world! Now, I first make sure I am happy, before I think of anybody else—including my children and grandchildren.' I mentioned the conversation to my husband. He laughed! He doesn't really care for this friend all that much. Considers her a 'bad' influence (as if I can be 'influenced' at this age!). He told me bluntly, 'Look at her life dispassionately. Is that what you want for yourself? Could you live like her?' The answer was obvious. Even so, I couldn't stop thinking about how easily she had made crucial choices . . . and lived with the consequences. Despite her rash and selfish ways, she was admired and adored by her friends and kids and grandkids. Even her husband worshipped her. What was so terrible about that?

Our deepest feelings towards our mothers define and colour nearly every aspect of our lives till the very end. I feel fortunate to have nothing but warm and wonderful memories of a childhood that was 'normal'. My children mock, 'What is "normal"?' I can't answer that! 'Normal', as in undramatic, untraumatic. In today's times, that is already saying a lot. Especially for a girl who was not at all 'obedient'. My mother understood my 'disobedience'. And never punished me. She absorbed. She accepted. She understood. That takes a lot.

I tell young mothers today to let things go. I say that to young couples too. What does it matter if your child is not 'performing' as per your demands, the school's demands, the peer group's demands? Are you going to treat that as a personal failure and make your child feel responsible? Before you blink, your childhood is over, your child's childhood is also over. You watch your grandkids with some level of detachment . . . soon, their childhood will vanish too! What will all of you remember of this precious time years and years later? A report card with poor grades . . . or hugs that comforted you when you were feeling awful about letting everybody down?

I was not the teacher's pet, either in school, or later, when I dutifully attended my children's PTA meetings and looked visibly bored. At these dreadful PTA mornings, I would spot just a handful of fathers. The rest were overwrought mothers fighting for five more marks with the Hindi/maths teacher. My children wanted me to be that mother—competitive and on edge 'for the sake of the child's future'. Ha! Not worth fighting for. I would submit meekly and pretend I was most upset that my daughter had received poor grades in maps in geography.

Sometimes I think today's parents have it much tougher. Everything seems to be spinning at a dizzying speed. Connecting both ways—children to parents, parents to children—is a daily balancing act that involves enormous reserves of patience and tact. Keeping families sane and together is the single biggest challenge of our times. I keep learning my lessons from unexpected sources and I marvel at how wise and evolved our rural communities were—and still are. They are pretty unaffected by change and stick to tried-and-tested ways to keep the family show on the road. These ways have worked for centuries.

Sometimes I think today's parents have it much tougher. Everything seems to be spinning at a dizzying speed.

One such friend of mine is a master craftsman from Barmer, Rajasthan. Khemraj is proud of what he does and has a strong sense of legacy. Once when he was visiting Mumbai to participate in an arts-and-crafts fair, he stopped by for tea. One by one, he unrolled his Pichwais, all of them unique and painstakingly embroidered. He pointed to one particular beauty and told me it had been embroidered by his daughters-in-law. 'My wife makes sure the young girls are kept busy and they acquire our skills. To generate healthy competition, she rewards the bahu who finishes her portion of the embroidery on time and excels. That girl gets a silver or gold ring. The gift is recognition of her hard work. But it also keeps her motivated. The other bahus try harder so that they too can earn a ring or a bracelet. This is a simple way to keep the family together. It has worked for our forefathers. It is working for us as well.'

Khemraj is a relaxed, happy man. Being one of nine children himself, he has known deprivation and starvation. It is craft that kept them all alive when they had nothing else. His respect for each and every Pichwai in his collection is something he has passed down to his young son. Each wall hanging has its own story. And Khemraj knows that story. He wants his large family to know it too. We modern-day parents have stopped sharing stories. That is the problem. Who has the time? I try engaging my own children in stories that have a special meaning for me—it could be a simple story about a favourite saree. I would love to talk about where I bought it, when I had worn it for the first time, how long I have had it. Small things. But of importance to me. I can see their eyes glazing over. They wait for a tiny pause in my narration and immediately change the subject. My past has little relevance or interest to them. It makes me sad. But I keep quiet. Parents of today have taught themselves to keep quiet. It's better this way, they sigh. At least there is more peace in the home. Is there, really? Should one call it peace . . . or a strategic ceasefire?

~

Who pays attention to mood boards?

To start with, you have your own mood swings to take care of. And believe me, those are the hardest. As I get older, I am astonished and, frankly, rather disappointed by the way my emotional pendulum goes from one end to the other smoothly, effortlessly, but leaving a totally wrecked me in its path.

Earlier, I could anticipate, sense a potential typhoon heading purposefully towards me. Today, even if I do recognize the signs, I feel powerless. 'Your fuse is getting shorter, Ma,' commented a concerned daughter, when I exploded with rage over what she considered a minor transgression, but which appeared monumental to me. I saw the panic in her eyes and immediately stopped. I retreated to a quiet part of the house and asked myself, 'Are you going mad? You have never behaved like this. Never!' I didn't find a convincing answer.

My daughter was not exaggerating. She loves me. My outburst was not aimed at her, but at a young house help who had done the exact opposite of what I had requested five hours earlier. She's a girl I am fond of—eager, soft-spoken and polite. It had been a genuine mistake—we all make them. But seeing a large, red suitcase balanced precariously on top of an antique cupboard infuriated me. Why was it there? The girl replied, 'You had asked me to place it there.' No, I hadn't. So she had not understood my instructions. All I needed to do was request her to take it down. That's it. Instead, I threw a hissy fit and alarmed my daughter.

That night, I spent many restless hours trying to figure out why I had been so harsh. 'It's age. Age does that to people, you can't help yourself,' said a well-meaning friend. She is wrong. Age makes one grouchy, that much I do concede. But age is no excuse for being unreasonable and rude—which I had undoubtedly been towards the young girl. I woke up determined to make it up to her. I looked for signs of resentment when she brought me tea. I thought she would sulk. Worse, I thought she'd quit. Nothing of the sort happened. She was her usual smiling, cheerful self and that made me feel terrible.

I have been monitoring my mood swings closely. I know the triggers. I have been monitoring other people's mood swings too. But I don't know their triggers. Hunger definitely affects my mood. I have seen it affect the moods of my family members. At my age, people tell me it is related to low blood sugar and manifests itself around teatime, when energy levels dip and a certain light-headedness takes over. That is the time to have a quick snack before someone's head gets bitten off. I have found this pretty effective and generally carry some dark chocolate in my handbag when I am travelling. I shun all drugs. I do not pop pills. No uppers, downers, sedatives or sleeping pills by my bedside. Counting sheep, or cows, is a far less damaging way to induce sleep. If all else fails, watch an old film—the one that bored you the most. I guarantee it will put you to sleep within ten minutes. Of course, moodiness and age are connected. But when moods affect very young people in a way that cripples them from carrying on 'normal' activities, then it's time to seek professional help.

Mental health problems have still to receive widespread attention in our society. There is far too much stigma attached to being thought 'mad'. It's 'mad' or nothing! Given our ignorance about the myriad mental issues we deal so clumsily with, it's important to educate ourselves, starting with those we share our lives with. Try telling a spouse or a child that counselling may just solve a recurrent emotional problem, and chances are the suggestion will be met with hostility and outrage. 'Are you trying to tell me I am nuts? That I require electric shocks? Neurosurgery? Do you want to drug me? Kill me? Why should I be on medication? There's nothing wrong with me. I refuse to take those tablets. The side effects are worse than what I am going through. All I need is love and sympathy. Not drugs.' Partly right. But mostly wrong.

Women are not 'allowed' mood swings. I have noticed we create categories for those who are entitled to mood swings and those who aren't. One poor lady I know figured out instinctively that her mood swings (even when she was menopausal) would be misunderstood and crushed. I know I am a borderline case in my own family—I can't push it beyond a point. It simply won't be tolerated. 'Snap out of it!' I'll be told. And in all probability, I'd do just that . . . though inwardly, I'd be seething. Mothers have to be mothers 24/7. Their moods must be controlled at all times. They must not show 'excessive' emotion (who defines 'excessive'?). They must smile a lot and distribute hugs and cuddles on demand. Mothers must not frown. Or cry. If they do, the family feels guilty and upset. And as we know, mothers can't upset the family. Mothers can't fall sick either. That also upsets the family and interrupts everybody's busy schedules.

At the moment, I am definitely having 'excessive emotion' issues. So are a lot of other women I know—some younger, some older. They are feeling the same way I do—isn't it about time we let our emotions show? I want to be shameless about mine! If I feel like crying for some odd reason—I am going to cry, period! Who can question my

At the moment, I am definitely having 'excessive emotion' issues. So are a lot of other women I know—some younger, some older. They are feeling the same way I do—isn't it about time we let our emotions show?

tears? Why should I 'justify' them? To whom? I realized with a bit of a start that I hadn't wept in years, perhaps decades. Properly wept, that is. Howled. With tears streaming down my cheeks, nose running, loud sobs escaping my unconstricted throat. Just the way one is supposed to cry. Not the decorous sniffles . . . tiny, little gasps that indicate 'I am upset', but the full-throated cry that sounds animal. I want that desperately! Just to find out if I am still capable of feeling the same intensity. If my tears are still there in a deep, dark well within. Or have I let them evaporate . . . just like that? Like the thousand laughs I have lost in a similar fashion? Laughing or crying, urban women feel self-conscious about openly indulging in both. Even in grief, an unreasonable, unwritten code says, 'Please control yourself. People are watching. Stay dignified.' What rubbish! So when do women 'like me' actually cry, if not during a tragedy? Why are we made to feel weak if we break down? I remember everybody praising Sonia Gandhi at her husband's funeral. She was a picture of stoicism—dry-eyed, upright, taciturn. We all found it remarkable and discussed it later. 'It's because she is Italian. Foreigners are trained from a young age not to show their emotions. Look at the Queen of England. Can you ever guess what she's feeling?' We reluctantly admitted our own lack of sophistication and control when it came to such calamitous occasions. Or even less dramatic tragedies—the death of a favourite chacha, for example. We asked each other, 'Did you cry at your own wedding?' I confessed I was pretty dry-eyed. I did try to squeeze out a few tears. I dabbed my eyes, pretending I was overcome, but I actually wasn't. I was quite relieved, as a matter of fact.

The other women said they had indeed cried—but weren't sure why. Were they crying *because* they were getting married? Did they not like the man they were marrying? Most women sheepishly admitted that was indeed the case. Some were abandoning old loves, some were panic-stricken at the prospect of 'adjusting' to a brand-new family, some were terrified of walking away from the security of their maternal homes. Most hated the idea of obligatory sex with a person they may or may not feel attracted to. It was a new phase they actively suspected but dared not challenge.

Young brides of today don't have the same misgivings. Their anxieties are differently couched. Their emotional landscapes differ, and they appear much tougher, as they toss back their *ghunghat*s inside the wedding mandap itself and ask for a drink halfway through the ceremony. Everybody 'understands'. There's no choice!

I am waiting for my full-blown bawling session. If I tell my daughters I want to howl, they always ask for my reasons. I don't really have any. Or perhaps I have too many to list. Why should I have to provide 'reasons'? Is it still okay to turn on those taps? Where should I cry? The location is important. I don't want to lock myself in a room and wet my nice pillow covers. I don't possess pretty lace handkerchiefs to cry into. I could cry by the window as the sun goes down . . . but then again, I like to enjoy my sunsets. Should I cry in a darkened movie hall? Maybe. If the movie is tragic. But what if it isn't and I still feel like crying? Would I make a fool of myself sniffling through a comedy? No, no, no. I want to make a production out of it. I need a great setting, a gorgeous locale . . . somewhere abroad. I know—I want to cry in Paris! Sitting by myself on the banks of the Seine. It has to be autumn, great October skies stretching over the world's most beautiful city. An accordion needs to play in the distance. And around me, young lovers about to kiss or make love right there and then. Paris is good for tears. And regrets. And longing.

And where do I go to laugh?

In New York. Definitely New York. Because New York accepts mad laughter. New York gets madness. Likes it, even. So does Paris, but differently. New York encourages laughter. Paris prefers tears. But I live in Mumbai. I am not sure Mumbai understands and accepts either. Or at least not in the way that suits me. I can't picture myself sitting alone on Marine Drive and weeping my heart out. Or laughing in the rain at Chowpatty Beach without risking arrest, for that matter (*'Yeh pagal aurat hass kyon rahi hai?'*). I rarely laugh these days. I rarely see women my age laughing any more. They smile a lot—but it looks like a reflex action. 'We are polite and we know when to smile', that sort of thing. If they laugh at all, it's by mistake. And they don't show their teeth. They cover their mouths and lower their heads, as if they are ashamed to be caught laughing. That worries me. Especially because I used to laugh a lot, even at silly stuff, mainly because I enjoyed laughing. We have to unlearn our habit of frowning, and relearn laughter.

New York encourages laughter. Paris prefers tears. But I live in Mumbai. I am not sure Mumbai understands and accepts either.

~

Lights, camera, Diwali

I have mixed feelings about celebrating Diwali. Somehow, I always feel a little let down. When I was a child growing up in Delhi, I enjoyed the festival of lights much more than I do now. I suppose the expectations were modest, and I used to take delight in small signs that indicated bigger thrills to come as the days became shorter and nightfall arrived around 5 p.m. Colony life in Delhi ensured a sense of community, as I watched neighbours feverishly scrubbing their homes in time to welcome Lakshmi, Goddess of Wealth, when she slipped regally into their homes, took a good look around for cobwebs and uncleared dust, before deciding she wanted to linger a little longer to bless the family with increased prosperity in the new year. I would be told by my mother to make sure my little corner in the bedroom I shared with my sisters was kept spick and span, in case Lakshmi looked hard under the desk and found crumpled paper. I believed my parents when they said Lakshmi would arrive in the still of the night and inspect each nook and cranny of our government home. My tired eyes would strain to stay open as long as possible to catch the glory of the goddess, clad in light and magnificent jewels, as I imagined her bending over my head to bless me. Next morning, I would ask anxiously, 'Did she come last night?' And my mother would assure me she did. 'But why didn't I meet her . . . ?' I would wail. 'Because she came just after you fell fast asleep.' That would mark disappointment number one.

I still wait for Lakshmi to come a-calling. I have visualized the moment countless times. I know what I will say to her. Accurately and vividly. I can see her clearly, dressed in a sky-blue Chanderi saree. She has diamond *kudi*s glittering on her earlobes. And her chest is covered in gold. Her crown is studded with rubies and emeralds. Maybe I am waiting for my mother? I don't know. But it is a lovely wait.

I have tried hard to keep all the old traditions alive in my own family. I was delighted to read a mini interview of my daughter Arundhati in a special Diwali issue of a popular glossy, in which she has recounted my efforts at sharing the Diwali magic with my loved ones. I was most touched that she had acknowledged the rituals and understood their significance. For all these years I used to think I was wasting my time plodding on, while the family stayed pretty distant and disconnected from the process. Almost like none of it really mattered, and even if I were to abruptly stop, nobody would notice or care. Apparently they would! This was such a tremendously reassuring feeling! I felt motivated and energized all over again! And told myself I must carry on while I still can.

Why do rituals matter so much in our lives? Is it the sense of continuity they provide to us in these frenetic times? I ask myself why I bother. I do it selfishly for myself . . . to feel I am fulfilling some family duties that need to be marked, passed down and hopefully perpetuated by the next generation. What does it matter? No answer. It matters. I care. That's it.

I have a friend who is incredibly enthusiastic about celebrating all Hindu festivals in right royal style. She has been at it for decades. I asked her once, 'Doesn't it bore you? Aren't you tired after all these many years?' Her shining eyes provided the answer I was seeking. She lives alone. So . . . she is not looking at posterity. She does it for her own pleasure. And the rituals give her enormous joy. Her religious routine requires time, resources and passion. She possesses all three. Recently, I watched her performing an impromptu garba raas at a function she had organized in memory of her parents. I had seen her dance at my daughters' weddings in the past. So many years later, she had not tired of dressing up every single day, carefully picking jewellery to match her sarees, stringing fresh jasmines in her hair . . . all this entirely for herself. How wonderful to saturate your life with so much beauty, fragrance and meaning. As I watched her whirl and twirl during the garba, I felt a tiny twinge of regret. I asked myself whether the responsibility of keeping a large and growing family in tune with my own sentiments was worth the effort and occasional disappointment. Well, on some days it seems entirely satisfying . . . on others, I silently exclaim, 'Fuck it.'

These days I have been saying 'fuck it' to a whole bunch of stuff. Am I 'evolving'? Or just getting old? Girlfriends say we are all 'evolving'. And I say, 'Bullshit!' We are just tired! And don't want to go that extra mile for anything or anyone. We think about sleep a lot—we never seem to get enough. Then we remember what our gynaes used to tell us during pregnancy, 'Make the most of this short period before the baby arrives. Once you become a mother, you will remain sleepless for the rest of your life.' Too true! Now that most of us are grandmothers and still severely sleep-deprived, we figure the reason for this has to be something else. I mean, if thinking about Diwali can unleash so many long-buried memories . . . !

These days I have been saying 'fuck it' to a whole bunch of stuff. Am I 'evolving'? Or just getting old? Girlfriends say we are all 'evolving'. And I say, 'Bullshit!' We are just tired!

~

Where is the old, familiar 'me'?

Women keep asking themselves this pointless question. They miss their organized selves. They either miss the person they imagine themselves to have been, or they long to be another person altogether. Even though that annoying phrase, 'Who is the real "me"?' has been reduced to a cliché, even the most accomplished, talented, successful woman spends sleepless nights looking for herself. These disruptive thoughts generally emerge when women meet other women they have shared histories with. They look at the other women and lament, 'Where did I go wrong? How is it possible that my friend looks happier, younger, sexier? I was like her to start with. In fact, I used to beat her at everything in school/college. I won more medals and prizes. I came first. I married before she did. I had my son before she conceived hers. I earned more. My husband is better educated. We live in a larger house. I travel abroad twice a year. Even my pet dog is a better breed. But she looks happier. And I miss my older self—the happy self. Now I wonder if it is too late. That other self may be lost or dead.'

I suffer from this sinking feeling pretty often, but a little differently. I ache for my other self. I meet her accidentally—when a familiar song plays, and every fibre of my being wakes up. Like it happened when driving back from Pushkar to Ajmer with friends. The entire experience overwhelmed my senses. I fell in love with Pushkar and wondered why I had never bothered to visit this jewel of a destination earlier. I didn't go during the touristy camel fair on Kartik Poornima. This was in December and Pushkar was not crowded. Staring at the architectural beauty of the ghats, while listening to the strains of itinerant sarangi players, I fell into a trance of sorts. Strolling down the narrow strip, lined with shops selling gaudy souvenirs, I met myself in a small antique store. As I started rummaging around, I kept meeting me—was I that angel in the old Tanjore painting? Or the plaster-of-Paris baby Krishna with chipped paint? I must have been the woman made out of seasoned teak—her painted, kohl-lined eyes staring unblinkingly with wonder and amusement. Yes, I was her. She wasn't expensive as compared to the other objets in the cramped space. But she was special. I loved her. And I found me.

Later, I was idly listening to the car stereo playing a Bollywood song ('*Mera jee karta . . .*'), and I started to cry. I didn't want to startle my hosts—we didn't know each other beyond a polite exchange of social niceties. So I stared out of the window at the rapidly fading light, and pretended there was something in my right eye that was making the tears flow. One of them must have sensed the mood, for the volume was gently pumped up. We were driving past sand dunes. I wanted to get out of the car and start running. I wanted to get to the other side of the hill and escape into the Aravalli Range, never to come back. I felt like joining a gypsy tribe, smoking ganja, dancing on the sand, singing to the half-moon, taking off my clothes and freeing myself. From whom? From what? Maybe from me—this me.

All of us have another me. Or many other 'me's. We generally hide them or hide from them. We start suspecting that other me. Like it's dangerous and disloyal to allow such thoughts. How idiotic! Why should all our 'me's be incompatible? We could coexist. And not be hostile. I don't feel threatened by the other me. I like her. I enjoy running into her, as I did in that bazaar in Pushkar. She was me in my early thirties—the best period of my life when I had grown new wings. I was flying. I was happy—truly happy. Happy about my choices. Happy about life's possibilities and promises. That's the me I don't want to let go of. I stood still in Pushkar inside the Brahma temple. The marble under my bare feet was cold. I looked at the image of the creator, the one who saw everything. I searched for answers in his eyes. Someone rang the temple bell behind me. A child was crying in his mother's arms. I started to pray. The prayers were a thanksgiving. Brahma already had too much on his plate. Walking down the steps, I wondered—what next? Should I take a drastic decision? At the bottom of the steps, I saw a local vendor chucking guavas at a group of monkeys sitting on the roof of a low haveli. We started chatting. He said he fed them five kilos of the fruit every day, three times a day. At that moment, I wanted to switch places with him and spend the next few months—maybe years—feeding guavas to monkeys in Pushkar.

> Why should all our 'me's be incompatible? We could coexist. And not be hostile. I don't feel threatened by the other me. I like her.

My old me smiled. The scene was so intimate and familiar. She knew. I knew. All was not lost. I had offered a chaddar earlier that day at Ajmer Sharif. The heady fragrance of the world-famous Pushkar roses was still making me dizzy. I had asked for *dua*. I was sure the Sufi saint had heard my prayers and blessed me.

Sometimes, we need to stop for these 'guava moments' in our mad lives. These guava moments make far more sense than all the other stuff we do. They are untarnished by external expectations. In this story, both the parties are in sync and happy. The monkeys and the man who feeds them. As for me, the spell wore off as the evening transformed into a more recognizable reality. I was seated in the back seat of a luxury car, driving to Jaipur to meet a group of wealthy, young entrepreneurs at a palace hotel. The talk would be about money and where to spend New Year's Eve. I would 'perform' my role with finesse and expertise—the same role I have been playing for decades. I did. Everybody appeared pleased ('She's exactly as we thought she'd be'). I smiled sardonically to myself—who is 'she'? Do I know her?

Later the same evening, the night lamp in my gigantic suite kept flickering. Was it trying to tell me something? Or had I just had too much wine?

I am sure there are many, many women who have mixed feelings about Diwali and other celebrations . . . Xmas, New Year's, Holi, Id. Let's call it performance anxiety. Since it is the woman of the house who is expected to get it all together *and* look terrific *and* impress the in-laws . . . it's a bit of a double-edged sword. Especially given the shrinking space and time for organizing traditional festivities. Most young working wives leave everything to professionals—party people with great ideas and expensive suggestions. My daughters tell me cheerfully Diwali preps are a click away . . . there's nothing that can't be sourced, purchased, installed if you know which website to hit. I feel terribly under-equipped when I hear all this. I still think it's important to do it the old-fashioned way . . . go to the vendor, place the order after physically examining every diya, haggle with the family flower seller (a flower seller who buys marigolds in the wholesale market as opposed to a florist who wants to sell imported peonies).

I feel pretty smug about my own Diwali enthusiasm. Much as I try, it hasn't quite rubbed off on the children, who expect me to remotely control their homes, and we send each other hourly reminders like, 'Have you organized the *toran*s for the front door! Please don't recycle last year's faded *kandeel*s. Remember to wash and clean your altar before performing the Lakshmi Puja. Get fresh chandan agarbattis, and extra oil for the diyas, and wicks! Please don't use those cheap, battery-operated Chinese diyas. I know they are convenient. But let's stick to inconvenient, at least during Diwali. Last year your terrace lights looked more like disco lights, so avoid UV blue. Your terrace party shouldn't compete with the nightclub next door. And make sure the children wear pure cotton only, and keep them away from firecrackers, flames, rockets and those disgusting "snake" crackers.'

Just as I keyed this bit in, I received a call from one of the daughters with fresh instructions. She needed mini kandeels of a particular colour and specification. Check. A son was looking for *kadak boondi* laddoos. Check. Another daughter required *chakli*s and cornflake *chivda*. Check.

Aaaah . . . Diwali!

~

Bye-bye, this year . . . hello, new year!

My children love December. They find it a 'party month'. They start planning for December in November itself. I guess, many moons ago, I used to love December too. These days, I am a little ambivalent. If November has been reasonably well spent, December appears like relief! A relief!! I mean . . . this is age! I have survived one more year without breaking a hip or getting a cataract! Help! It boils down to basics eventually, doesn't it? And I think of my friends—most, much younger, some, much older, just a few who are of the same age. We have very, very different attitudes to December. I long for those old excitements—the anticipation of meeting new people at a party. Dancing! Flirting (that too!). Planning a glamorous getaway. Acquiring a new something—anything. But I keep mum. Older people are not supposed to nurture such childish dreams. Sometimes, my children reprimand me for acting juvenile. As if that's a huge crime. Sometimes, I reprimand myself! But don't we all have that frisky child in us? Why do we not indulge this precious aspect of ourselves a little more? I feel best when I regress. And with a small start, I immediately pull myself out of the zone.

Recently, at a pretty dull dinner party, I ran into someone I had known many years ago. He reminded me of a Xmas party we had attended (separately). And then he said, 'That was the last time I saw you smile with your heart, and eyes.' I was taken aback for a minute. It made me wonder: Was that also the last time I was happy? Happy, in an unalloyed way? Happy just being who I was—who I am? What happened to that person? He smiled and assured me gently that it was fine. We all have that one phase in our lives when we are in perfect sync with ourselves—and not faking anything. Looking back on that Xmas, so many decades later, I still don't know what I was so happy about. Was it my appearance (I was in my prime)? My 'success'? Or was I in love?

I look at my children as they prepare for the end-of-the-year celebrations, how meticulously they plan everything. Some of my friends also enjoy the jolly season tremendously. Their feelings aren't synthetic or manufactured. I long to be the woman with a huge orchid tied on a satin ribbon around her neck. Wearing an off-the-shoulder dress. Sitting in a mint-green convertible. A slight chill in the air. Long hair streaming in the night breeze. A cha-cha-cha playing inside her head. Silver lamé and French chiffon. Sparkling conversation and promises! Women love promises. That doesn't make us fools. It makes us romantic. We can dream and yearn. And imagine all those promises coming true. Take away promises, and what do we have?

Despite it all, I enjoy creating a 'jolly' ambience throughout the month of December. Just as I love creating it for Diwali. Lights! How quickly and economically a room can get transformed with the right lighting. All it takes is a candle or two to make my spirits soar. And fairy lights, of course. This Xmas, I feel as if I am not myself (whatever and whoever 'myself' is). And I dare not ask myself why. On the surface, everything appears to be 'normal'. Nothing much has changed. Or has it? Am I just sick of 'normal'? Questioning 'normal'? Are women 'allowed' to question normal? Most men would scoff, 'What rubbish! Is this some new thing you've started? What's the matter with you? Don't give such vague answers. If something is wrong, if something has happened, just come to the point and say what it is.' But what if nothing specific has happened? What if the change is deeper than a superficial cut? What if old wounds start festering without a warning? Should one just act normal and say nothing? Why are women terrified to admit everything isn't okay sometimes? Why do we feel we are being cussed if we voice it? Why should there be justifications and explanations?

It's really okay not to feel or behave as if everything is okay. I have decided to do just that in the coming year. And have said as much to the family. If they find my attitude unacceptable, they are keeping quiet about it. And I feel like a naughty schoolgirl about to play hooky and jump into a passing train headed for an unidentified destination. Just the thought of it is liberating. What did I tell you about crazy dreams?

I am busy making a bucket list of all the places I want to go to in the next few months. I am just being practical. Right now, I am able to walk, run, jump, dance, shout, sing, read and drink as I choose to. Who knows about next year? Or even next month? Should I do it? Just take off on my own? A strong inner voice is urging me to do just that. 'Go!' it keeps saying. 'You won't regret it! Go!' And my heart lurches—Argentina and tangos! Sakura season in Japan. The big migration in Africa.

I have to get there. Have to!

End-of-the-year blues were unknown to me till 2016. By any standards, the year had been 'good'. I became a grandmother for the third time in December, and even though it was a familiar feeling, the excitement I felt waiting outside the delivery room was something else. In fact, as I held my grandson for the first time, just about an hour after he was born, I felt an old urge tugging at me—so complete was my identification with my daughter, Arundhati, who looked exhausted but radiant, like only a new mom can. Her husband,

It's really okay not to feel or behave as if everything is okay. I have decided to do just that in the coming year.

Sahil, known as 'secure' to all his friends, for being the most dependable man in the group, was smiling sweetly . . . with all his heart! I wanted to carry my own baby, just to experience that unbeatable exuberance of giving birth. I confessed that to a friend. I said, 'I feel like having a baby too!' He replied, 'You just did!' Empathy this intense can be scary sometimes.

Despite the high of that moment, I came home feeling low. I forced myself to fake excitement as the Xmas tree was getting spruced up and decorated. Earlier, I would go out in hideous traffic to shop for new baubles, and end up buying far more than was needed for the small tree. This year, I merely took the carefully stowed carton down from a high loft, and got on with the job. When evening fell, and the lights came on, I felt zero joy. For the first time in years I didn't bother to keep the fairy bulbs blinking all night. I boredly, indifferently, switched them off at 11 p.m. and went to bed feeling let down, I still don't know by whom.

A few nights earlier, I had attended a charming seventy-fifth birthday party of a dignified lady who had been very kind to me at a point in my life when I had felt totally abandoned. To dress for the party, my friend had hired professional make-up and hair artists, and was looking lovely. A person who obviously knew her taste in music very well was playing her favourite love songs on a keyboard. There were affectionate speeches and tributes from old and true family friends. I looked at the faces of the assembled guests and nearly wept! When it was my turn to speak about her, I broke down and found it difficult to finish my sentence. Was I weeping for her? Or myself?

At Dilip's seventy-fifth, the entire family had gone flat out to make it extraordinary for him at every level, starting with a simple puja at our favourite temple in Colaba and ending with a party at home, with surprise guests—his close friends. He seemed overcome and overwhelmed as he thanked one and all. And he looked smashing that night in his perfectly fitted Jodhpurs combined with a velvet *bandhgala*, a silver-topped cane in his hand for that extra swag.

Something was going on inside my head and heart. It was disquieting and I have still to come to terms with this unfamiliar emotion.

The birth of Adhiraj Pramod Raju was as tranquil, calm and gentle as the mother who had carried him—Avantikka. This is her third child, and she, along with her husband Pramod, had meticulously prepared the two older girls for the new arrival, involving them at every stage of the pregnancy. When they saw the newborn, just fifteen minutes after his birth, the little girls were awestruck, and also a little confused. Pramod, a former doctor, had been inside the delivery room, and appeared entirely in control (That's very characteristic of him! I definitely want to see him plastered some day!), as he beamed, his eyes visible and smiling from behind the surgical mask. It was a quiet, golden moment, as we all gazed at the infant and came up with the usual comments: Whom did he look like? The common consensus was: Indumati Kilachand (Ba), his maternal great-grandmother.

With Adhiraj, there are five grandchildren in the family at this point. In the past year, we have welcomed the birth of Arundhati and Sahil's adorable Aryaman. His birth too was marked by such an overwhelming sense of peacefulness, more so because there were four generations from Sahil's side to welcome the little fellow. Radhika and Bobby had their son in Chandigarh. Radhika was certain she was carrying a boy. When I asked her how she knew, she answered simply, 'Because Guruji told us.' Such is the power of faith. Both she and Bobby are on a deeply spiritual path, and little Sudhir is an intrinsic part of that journey. That leaves two sons, Ranadip and Aditya, and one daughter, Anandita, who have still to make the big decision. I get the feeling 2018 is going to be a really, really crowded year. It may see a hat-trick taking place!

~

Women need caves too . . .

What do women of my age do when they reach these crossroads? Men retire quietly into their caves and solve crossword puzzles. The more adventurous ones start looking around, cranking up the rusty old mating machine. If they have money, style and a good car, there is any number of women willing to provide company. So many women are in the exact same situation these days—they have money, style and a fancy car, even two. I meet so many women in similar situations these days. They have money, time, fancy cars, style, looks and the inclination to play with the right partner. Some are single. Some aren't. Even so, they generally hesitate before moving forward. But I also have girlfriends—with or without money—who have never hesitated or looked back with regret. They have gone right ahead and grabbed the moment. One particular friend, who has fascinated me for decades, laughs at my attitude. 'Look at me,' she chuckles. 'I do whatever the hell I want to and my family still loves me, because all the members know this is the only way I can live, contribute and grow. Place me in a cage and try to control me—oh God! Everybody loses, most of all the family.'

This works for her. Always has. Her energy levels are extraordinary. I adore and admire her tenaciousness and boundless creativity. There is nothing she won't attempt at least once. Today, a ravishing woman in her sixties, she divides her time between three cities, maintaining lovely, welcoming homes in all of them. She can go from being a beach bum in Goa and dancing every single night at her favourite club to transforming into a hands-on country girl in the Himalayas. That is, when she isn't stopping off in Mumbai to attend an important corporate event or two with her far more subdued husband. She isn't harming a soul by being her own woman. And yet, this is not how society judges her. Does she care a hoot? No, which is why she can afford to be who she is.

I was reminded of her when a much younger friend phoned out of the blue and found me in a pensive mood. 'Free yourself!' he urged. Free myself from what? He laughed, 'Your own hang-ups!' But how? He wasn't being helpful when he signed off with a jaunty, 'Find a way—if you dare.' I spoke about this conversation with one of my daughters. She agreed with my friend and added, 'About time, Mom!' Ten minutes later, I was on the phone trying to book myself a trip to Iceland to see the Northern Lights. This has been my dream since I was a little girl. If not now, then when?

Women who feel the same way hesitate to take even baby steps to 'free' themselves. What are we afraid of? Our own potential and power? Freedom scares us. That is the worst kind of conditioning. The inbuilt censor is forever inhibiting our every secret dream and saying, 'No, you can't!' What a waste that gigantic heap of 'can'ts' becomes over time. A futile and expensive waste of a woman's best years—her best energies, talents, her most passionate feelings of love. If only women could discard all the 'can'ts' and embrace the 'cans'.

What a waste that gigantic heap of 'can'ts' becomes over time. A futile and expensive waste of a woman's best years—her best energies, talents, her most passionate feelings of love. If only women could discard all the 'can'ts' and embrace the 'cans'.

I plan to do just that. And this time I am not looking for endorsements from the family. I am doing this for me. I am pretty confident I will find it within myself to give this 'project' a wholehearted go, if nothing else. I am a realist. I will start small. Travel continues to be my biggest passion. And I intend to make up for lost time by identifying destinations on my long-buried bucket list. Where should I start? How about Marrakesh?

~

Remember what you want to, discard the rest!

How we deal with painful memories is revelatory. No two people remember any incident in exactly the same way. The details vary. But, crucially, so does the meaning, even the context. I have unconsciously trained myself to leave the negatives of the past behind. I am genuinely not tormented by thoughts about what someone did to me or said to me years earlier. Under hypnosis, most of these suppressed memories will undoubtedly surface. They come up in dreams, of course . . . but I don't allow them to blur my todays. What's the point? Easier said, right? When I talk to my daughters about this aspect of life, I am not sure they are convinced. They tell me I am in denial and they aren't. They may be right. But if denial helps me, why not? Suddenly, I become defensive and start wondering if they are trying to tell me something about my behaviour towards them.

Women remember things differently. Men think we are making up stories because their recollection of the very same incident is something else altogether. So whose memory is to be trusted? I would say the woman's, most of the time. Men are far more selective in how to maximize storage space inside the brain. They discard what they term 'garbage', and retain what they believe is essential. We hoard it all, every gruesome detail. All kinds of rubbish are carefully stored, consciously or otherwise. I ask myself, 'How the hell do you remember that silly remark?'

I forget a great deal of really important stuff, and retain rubbish. My daughters and girlfriends confirm the same affliction. When we meet, we recall in excruciating detail the most mundane occurrence that had taken place years ago. We recreate with obvious and annoying relish several small things—what someone wore, who said this, who said that, the precise sequence, the colour of a saree, the joke nobody understood, the cruel nicknames given, the gifts everybody received and hated, the slights and taunts, the reluctant compliments and praise, the hurts and barbs. Women hang on to hurts the most. They easily or conveniently overlook what men describe as the 'good stuff', and dredge up memories of emotional wounds inflicted through a careless observation or, worse, a deliberate insult. Men lightly dismiss this response and dub it an 'overreaction'.

Men invest in emotional dumping grounds where unpleasant memories get trashed permanently. We store ours like we store our precious jewellery—in vaults. An intelligent academic friend of mine narrated how her husband always tried to put her down in public by trivializing her work and personality. Being an accomplished and articulate person, she began to get annoyed by his dismissive conversations about her multiple achievements. She recalled how he had told an artist friend of theirs that his wife preferred destinations that boasted of glamorous nightclubs, not world-class museums! She was taken aback since she wasn't the 'nightclub type', as she put it. It was a painful memory she couldn't free herself from, because she felt it was such a gross misrepresentation of all that she stood for. He would also say, 'She goes to Florence to shop. Her temples of learning and culture are designer boutiques. I prefer taking the Michelangelo trail . . .' I told her to forget it. It was just her husband's insecurity talking. But the hurt was too deep. He promptly forgot or at least pretended to. 'It was just a light-hearted remark,' he explained lamely. Was it, or was it a well-aimed barb? There were countless 'light-hearted' remarks she had endured over the years. She'd let them go. 'Why start a fight?' she'd argue. But had she protested the first time, perhaps these barbs would have stopped.

Men invest in emotional dumping grounds where unpleasant memories get trashed permanently. We store ours like we store our precious jewellery—in vaults.

Women often hesitate to confront their partners, adopting the same reasoning: 'Why pick a fight over a trivial issue?' They are unable to see it for what it is—an attempt to devalue the partner in public. When women friends ask me if such 'jokes' are worth the fights that follow, I answer with an emphatic 'yes'. Most men cannot handle a mild, critical remark passed in the presence of outsiders. But women are expected to laugh indulgently when they are insulted. Those that refuse to laugh are made to feel petty and small. If the rare woman chooses to speak up or argue her point, she is called shrewish, ill-mannered, bad-tempered, aggressive, arrogant and lacking a sense of humour. I have watched, aghast, as husbands bellow, 'Shut up!' at a party, and their wives freeze mid sentence. Or men who discount what a partner has said, with a small laugh and an apologetic comment, 'Don't mind her. She thinks she understands politics! If you get her started, she'll tell Narendra Modi how to run the country, and instruct you how to run your company too!' I am not making this up. Too many wives keep mum. Not just in India, but across the world. They are conditioned to believe it's 'unwomanly' to contradict men in public, and they are too scared to do so in private. The original sin gets compounded many times over, a pattern develops, and that is how it remains forever.

In such a scenario, women often develop their own secret codes. Sometimes, just eye contact is enough. We teach ourselves to provide the much-needed 'calmsutra' to other women when things look rough. Women train themselves to become reluctant warriors, even if they are born meek and submissive. They become sly chameleons. Quickly change colours. Adapt. Merge. Survive.

Friendships, close ones, with other women have always been my bedrock and comfort zones. I think of them as my duvets. When low, I snuggle into my favourite 'duvet' and feel instantly comforted. When there is even the slightest dent in one of those trusted relationships, my world gets shaken. Slanging matches in the presence of people are ugly and embarrassing. If the conversation is heading in that direction, and the mood is torrid, one of you must have the good sense to leave the room. Make any excuse. Go to the loo, breathe. Close your eyes. Steady yourself. Regain composure. Then rejoin the party. I have witnessed too many ugly scenes, most of them alcohol-fuelled, and always wondered why the couple had ventured out together if they were mid-battle to start with. Hosts who are accustomed to outbursts handle the situation expertly. But most people are taken aback and don't really know what to do—step in and risk being told to butt out, or leave the two to slug it out. Then comes the ugly aftermath—the taking of sides. Everybody present feels obliged to comment, dissect, judge and advise. In my judgement, it is best to pour a fresh round of drinks and change the subject. Post-mortems can wait.

The younger generation of women sees this differently. Confrontations don't scare them. When they fight with their partners, they refuse to stew in silence. They see strife as a part of the relationship and don't want to run away from it. Dealing with issues in an upfront way is best, they claim. And they are right. Women of my generation were told to 'ignore' matters that didn't directly threaten the marriage. We were urged to 'adjust' (that awful word!) and wait for things to blow over. But what if 'things' didn't blow over? Well then, that was your funeral. Discussing this with a couple of friends late one evening, I said out of the blue, 'Men mate. Women marry.' The two men present exchanged looks and one of them gave an expert response on why this is so. Then he turned to the other man and asked, 'Do you ever discuss intimate aspects of your married life with other men? Do you talk about your wife with your best friend when you've had a fight?' The younger chap shook his head and said emphatically, 'No, never!' Both men turned to me triumphantly and gloated, 'See! We don't discuss personal matters with others. It is you women who do that.' I agreed enthusiastically and wholeheartedly. That took the guys off guard. They had expected vehement denials and protestations. Instead, a new channel was opened up and my gal pal said, 'If we didn't talk about how miserable we were, we'd go mad! It helps women to share and to know they aren't alone. We crib, we bitch, we betray confidences and break pacts when we are distressed and panicky. We can only turn to each other. It's cathartic. It's therapeutic. Without this valve, we would have to deal with all your nonsense without expressing our hurt and rage. That's bad for our emotional systems. Why suppress our anger? Why get ulcers? It's so much better to call up a friend and tear you apart!' There was stunned silence, followed by uneasy laughter. Some sort of a taboo had been broken. A dam had been breached. It felt good!

Twenty years ago, I wouldn't have dared articulate any of this. Here I was, talking boldly about what I really feel from time to time, and taking the chance that my frank words might lead to a fresh confrontation. Maybe I had taken a cue from my daughters. They refuse to sweep their conflict under the carpet. When they argue and fight, the

Portrait of a wife/lover/companion, through the eyes of the newly minted artist Dilip Dé

The Pandit sisters: Shakuntala (Aie) with Vimal and Nirmala

Those championship years! Right on track!

Beloved Aie, my most trusted ally

Writers I love and admire

With Nayantara Sahgal and Kiran Nagarkar at the Dhaka Lit Fest

With V.S. Naipaul at the Jaipur Lit Fest

With Amitav Ghosh at the Singapore Lit Fest

With Vikram Seth at the Kasauli Lit Fest

With Ben Okri at our home

With Nobel laureate Amartya Sen in New Delhi

With former Reserve Bank governor Raghuram Rajan, after his book launch in Mumbai

With Prime Minister Narendra Modi in Mumbai

With Kangana Ranaut in Mumbai

With our SPG—wonderful men and women in uniform, during an ugly crisis in Mumbai

With Sunita Saxena during our Ranikhet adventure

With Aryama Sundaram and friends at his sixtieth birthday party in New Delhi

How old is 'ageless' . . . ?

Tea for two with Gong Li

Jhoomo-ing with close friends at Arundhati's mehendi evening

With my constant travel date, Anandita, in Sydney

Radhika with her son, Sudhir, in Chandigarh

With Ranadip and Aditya at our Alibag farm

With Avantikka at her wedding

Adhiraj comes home with Avantikka, Pramod, Anasuya and Ahiliya

Baby Aryaman's day out in Seychelles with Arundhati and Sahil

The official family portrait with all the bachchas, at Mr Dé's seventy-fifth birthday celebrations

Traditional Diwali aarti for my husband—an annual ritual we both look forward to

Our Tricolour . . . and a charming honour at Reims, France

gloves are off and problems are tabled, no matter how tough they appear. It's done, they exclaim. And they are right.

Ask a man about this new development, and he will say, 'Oh . . . these kids are irresponsible and *moophat* (loudmouths)—they say the first thing that comes into their heads. It is not correct. Let them stay married for twenty–thirty years like we are, then talk!' Not realizing what a ghastly prospect it would be to stay married for 'twenty–thirty' years to men like them!

~

Do you not 'see' old people?

As I get older, I notice a callous attitude towards the elderly more and more. We think nothing of pushing past senior citizens, making them apologetic and self-conscious about their own slowed-down speed of walking. This happens wherever queues are involved—airports, in particular. Younger, more impatient co-passengers glare instead of helping a senior citizen struggling with a strolley or a heavy package. They snigger and laugh if the old person across the aisle doesn't know how to order from the snack card available on budget airlines. Yes, the queue does slow down, and yes, everybody is tired, but surely a little consideration for the old is not such an unreasonable demand?

Agreed, older people tend to talk too much. Or talk too loudly. It's probably most annoying to pretend to take an interest when someone close to your grandfather's age starts on an ancient, unending tale beginning with the line that renders the young instantly deaf, 'When I was your age . . .' As soon as I hear those lethal words, I gently kick my husband under the table and hiss, 'Stop! Can't you see how bored those kids already are? And you haven't even begun!' I get it—nobody is in the least bit interested in how things were thirty, forty, fifty years ago. Just look around you—the attention span has shrunk so alarmingly, and conversation as my generation understood the word has all but disappeared. Even though I have managed to figure out most of the abbreviations commonly used to convey just about everything from life-and-death issues to existential concerns, there are still times when I find myself out of the loop. That's when eyes start to roll, and one of my children pats my hand kindly and says in a soothing voice, 'Oh . . . you won't really get it.' I want to yell, 'Try me! Why shouldn't I be able to get it? What is there to "get"?' But I force myself to smile, shrug and say indulgently, 'Okay! I guess it's not for me to get . . .' Nobody contradicts me! Of course, I feel hurt. In my mind, I am still thirty and totally with it. I believe it's my natural state! I don't feel close to seventy inside my head. It's difficult to accept—but clearly my children see me differently. Others may compliment my attitude, and say how refreshing it is to be with someone who gets such a kick out of life. But my children find it hard. I understand. One of them actually wants me to feel tired! I remember coming back from a short trip to Delhi, getting home and participating in a demanding television debate the same night. My daughter sounded positively annoyed! She asked me, 'But why aren't you exhausted? In your place I would have been pretty finished by now. Why do you have to do this show? Take it easy. Put up your feet . . . get a massage . . . relax!' It was my turn to get annoyed. 'I am far from tired,' I snapped. Which was 100 per cent true. I wondered why she would want me to be tired. Later, while I was still searching for an answer, I figured: a) it was out of concern, b) people my age are supposed to feel tired after a hectic trip or c) she feels tired after a trip. There is another reason too. The other mothers in my children's friend circle lead different lives. Most are much younger. The few that are close to my age are happily retired and enjoying their leisure. Perhaps my manic travel and work schedules are hard to compartmentalize. Slower is more 'normal'.

A few days later, I came across an interview with one of my heroes—the indomitable Germaine Greer. I was distraught to see her ravaged face and read her harsh words. For some reason she had picked on Jane Fonda, who is about the same age as Ms Greer. Jane Fonda's obsession with staying young was mocked by Germaine Greer, who sneered it was a pity that Fonda couldn't replace her brain the way she had replaced her hip, knees and other body parts. I was very disturbed by Greer's remarks. And I asked myself, 'Will a time come in the not-so-distant future when I too will become as embittered, as judgemental, as cruel? What was Jane Fonda's big crime, anyway? She had said, perhaps truthfully, that men liked younger women. And she wanted to look young—for men. That was a pretty naked confession. I respected Fonda for saying it upfront. Greer said what she had to. But the big difference here is that Fonda was not hurting anyone—besides herself—through that politically incorrect admission, whereas Greer had launched a pretty formidable assault on a contemporary. Where does tact end and spite begin?

There's absolutely nothing wrong with being self-delusional from time to time. In fact, I think it's essential and positively wonderful, especially when your morale is low, and there are enough people bitchily reminding you about all that's terrible in your life. Like during one of my recent birthdays. There I was feeling pretty loved and cherished by my family and friends, when a lady I really like and consider close called late at night to wish me. She made the standard excuses about the late call, saying she assumed I'd be madly busy dealing with hundreds of calls and messages. She asked me what I had done the whole day, and I started to narrate everything in detail, with the enthusiasm of a child. Abruptly, she cut the call short and said, 'Okay, Shobhaa. I have to go. There's someone at the door. Let's catch up soon.'

Why did she call, then? Why did she ask what I did? Was she being hostile? Was there some level of jealousy? I hated to think of her as a jealous friend. It is demeaning to friendship. Jealousy is for the insecure—those who perceive the other as a threat. But this girlfriend was like family. I felt snubbed and hurt.

There's absolutely nothing wrong with being self-delusional from time to time. In fact, I think it's essential and positively wonderful, especially when your morale is low, and there are enough people bitchily reminding you about all that's terrible in your life.

I found it difficult to get over that cryptic birthday chat. I recalled other recent conversations with her. Hadn't they all been pretty negative? I suddenly remembered her words when a close friend had passed away. She had offered zero solace.

Instead, she had reminded me we were the same age, and suggested it was but natural that I would feel disturbed and lapse into a panic attack or get extra depressed because of how 'vulnerable' I had allowed myself to become. Almost like she was saying, 'It could be your turn next!'

'Shobhaa, it is not her you are thinking about—it is yourself. You must be worried about your own health and future,' she had said. Even though I was puzzled by her attitude, I let it pass. Perhaps I shouldn't have! She was deliberately pushing the wrong buttons and I was falling for the trick. Why didn't I tell her to bugger off? Was I giving her the benefit of the doubt because of an old association, or because I didn't want to lose her friendship? I still think about her conversations during that low period and wonder why she spoke to me the way she did. I think she was transferring her own emptiness on to me, which made me feel worse. Maybe I needed to get out of my little world and access hers. I needed to extend myself, and not the other way round. How well did I know her, or she me? Was it time to disconnect and move on? Is it that easy? Something was wrong. We needed to talk about that 'something'. I still haven't found the required emotional boldness to confront her. Till I do, I will keep feeling lousy, or worse, looking for an alibi.

When we give another person the power to affect our feelings this strongly, we need to ask ourselves why. And why did we choose that person or persons. I seek out friends who make me feel good about myself and whom I feel good about. I make every attempt to let them know how much they mean to me. Sometimes, wires cross, and I feel terrible. I am sure they feel terrible too. What does one do? As I discovered through multiple negative experiences over the years, one shuts up and puts up. Or one walks away a sadder, disillusioned person. Assuming everyone around you is on the same wavelength and tuned in is one of the world's most foolish assumptions. I am at once trusting and sceptical, optimistic and cynical. Perhaps I read friends wrong, depending on which emotion dominates on that particular day when we connect.

I want to tell you, we can fail when we try too hard to keep relationships ticking along as per our memories of old ties. 'We used to be so close' is a sentence we repeat and hear being repeated. And yet, if we try to deconstruct that phrase to understand the remembered closeness, more often than not, it is one that is far removed from reality. We cling to a version of idealized 'love' or 'fondness'. But did it ever exist, at least in the form we recall? I look back on interactions that are fifty-plus years old and smile indulgently. As I did when a school friend called on my birthday, as she unfailingly has every single year for five decades. After we exchanged enthusiastic greetings, inquired after grandchildren, there was absolutely nothing to say. Nothing! We promised to 'catch up'. We both know that's not going to happen. It's a part of the annual ritual and it hurts no one. Not even us. But if the calls stopped, now that would hurt! There are a few regular birthday callers. We talk just once a year. The calls last a few precious seconds. But they mean a lot to me. One year, I didn't receive a call from a talented photographer I had hired during my editor days. He was silent and watchful, dependable and respectful, a perfect teammate. Along with an equally lovable art director, we chatted in Marathi and inquired after one another's families.

When I didn't get his call, I figured he had forgotten. After all, he wasn't a young man any longer, just as I wasn't a young woman. Around 4 p.m. the next day, as I was driving back from Pune, the art director called. After wishing me a long life and good health, he informed me that our photographer friend had passed away on my birthday. His wife, who had called the art director to convey the tragic news, had added, 'Please call and wish Shobhaa Bhabhi. He would have wanted to.' I choked back my tears and said a small prayer. It was that kind of relationship which didn't need words or an exchange of gifts, promises or pledges. Just pure, unconditional affection and a deeper understanding that doesn't demand validation. Now that he was gone, it would be one phone call less every year. I will always miss Vivek's call.

That's how we start coming to terms with our own mortality. Too scared to deal with dying, we run away from imagining what it must be like to be sick, alone, living with the knowledge that death is a few days, maybe even a few minutes, away. And then contemporaries start dying. You scan newspaper obits, your eyes go to the birthdate of the person who has gone to his/her 'heavenly abode'. You realize it is someone younger than you. And involuntarily, you thank God for keeping you alive. But alive for what?

Lucky are those who have specific goals and ambitions for each stage of their lives. I am not one of them, alas. I roll along, and improvise as I go. Some things work, some don't. I shrug and keep walking, as the whisky ad goes. But for the past couple of years, deaths of people I have known and grown up with have started to affect me a lot more than I could have imagined. 'You sound so uncharacteristically sentimental these days,' a girlfriend commented. It was like an accusation. As if to display vulnerability was somehow shameful. I instantly grew defensive. 'Really? I wonder if that's an accurate observation,' was my weak comeback. She persisted, 'We need to talk. You brood too much. So-and-so's death has really affected you!' She was right, and wrong. The person she was referring to was hardly a close friend. But yes, her death did shake me up. I said a bit testily, 'It's not as if I am morbidly preoccupied with death or something. But yes, I do think about it more than I used to.' The word 'morbid' made me stop. What's morbid? Is age morbid?

People ask me where I want to be ten years from now. In my head, I say, 'Having fun in heaven/hell. But definitely dead.' I mean that. But it's not the expected response. Most people want a seventy-year-old to turn pious overnight and talk of going on a pilgrimage. They want philosophy, words of wisdom, distilled knowledge. I feel like laughing out loud and yelling, 'Screw your conventional/boring expectations. I am not about to alter my essential being because it makes you uncomfortable to think of a seventy-year-old woman whose world is not draped in a shroud. This attitude is exclusively reserved for seventy-year-old women. Men, please excuse!

People ask me where I want to be ten years from now. In my head, I say, 'Having fun in heaven/hell. But definitely dead.' I mean that. But it's not the expected response.

I was recently called a 'bombshell' in print. 'Sizzling at Seventy,' read a caption. Somewhere else, I was described as 'the sexiest sexagenarian'. Was I supposed to feel flattered? Initially, yes! It felt good, till I thought about the subtext. Why do we have to deal with a universal assumption that women of my vintage are nothing more than sexless, old bags? Why does our sexuality pose such a threat and repulse younger people? Is it the aesthetics that create a problem ('Oh my Gawdddd! Who wants to bed her? Is she cuckoo? Can you imagine her without her clothes on?')? Some of my women friends have not stopped looking at themselves, or at men, for that matter. When they spot attractive men, they look! Check them out. It does not mean they want to instantly bed them, though, why ever not? Mostly, they are paying a genuine compliment. It's soothing to the eyes to observe a man at ease with himself and the world. He needn't be a 'stud', or even good-looking. Perhaps he has wonderful hair that moves? Or shoulders that speak? A manner that pleases? A lovely voice that caresses words? Age is really pretty irrelevant. Women are not known to lech openly. But my daughters laugh when I say that. They tell me they have no problem leching. My daughters? Leching?

I stare a lot more at attractive women too. And go up to some to say, 'You are beautiful!' I do that sometimes with ladies manning security booths at airports and malls. So many of them display their marital status with sindoor in the parting of the hair, bangles and rings, mangalsutras and bindis. I like those touches. I like the vanity. The rest of their appearance is masculine—they wear standard-issue shirt-pant uniforms like their male counterparts. Most people regard these mandatory checks with hostility, even resentment, and refuse to greet the uniformed ladies, forget about smiling or paying them a compliment. I like brief interactions, especially if I notice a telltale detail like mehendi patterns on the palm. I ask cheerfully, 'Just married?' Most times, the young bride is taken by surprise and blushes, covers her face and giggles before briskly patting me down. It's a respite for both of us.

And it's a sweet moment. Her job is tiring and monotonous. My journey is equally tiring. That brief exchange always energizes me. I am sure it energizes the other person too.

~

Sugar-free at seventy

I was never a sugary person. Not at seventeen, and certainly not at seventy. I don't like sugar. Even as a child, I preferred savouries to sweets. Birthday cakes and pastries? Give me spice over sweet any time, any day. I can bite into, enjoy and digest chillies, but not mithai. I find myself gagging when force-fed *pedha*s and laddoos, chocolates and macaroons. But these days, when I refuse dessert, other guests look at me sympathetically and ask, 'Diabetes?' At seventy, your systems start slowing down. I have always listened to my body. When I get an urgent message from a body part that says, 'Whoa! Cut the speed!' I generally listen. I also talk to my body parts and make them listen, except perhaps when I am having too much fun.

Fun does have its limits, though. Airports! I hate them. I used to love entering one in the past. I would saunter in, my eyes gleaming, my step light. Just the thought of a new destination would make my heart race in anticipation. These days, I groan at the prospect of those interminable walks from one terminal to the next. The shuttle trains and endless immigration queues. The strained shoulder weighed down by a heavy bag. The change in attitude is inevitable. If, after a long flight, I used to be in a rush to disembark and start my trip as quickly as possible, I now take my time to get out of the aircraft and into the bus or air bridge. I let other passengers rush past me. I don't really care if I am the last one to leave the aircraft. I wear flats most of the time. And watch my step on escalators and stairs. I used to do that earlier as well. But these days it's a lot more obvious. In fact, observant younger companions instinctively offer their arms when I travel. Some say, 'Hold my hand.' Others take my packages and bags and considerately walk behind me. I am always touched and filled with gratitude. Was I this thoughtful at thirty or younger? Perhaps not. I was too self-absorbed to bother about a much older acquaintance.

Dependencies induce anger. Even when you know the person whose extended hand you have grabbed is being courteous, you are reminded of your own inadequacies at that moment. And you feel awful. I do! 'Are you scared of stairs?' a young man asked me at a function. I admitted I was. 'I was looking at you when you went up on stage—your body language had changed totally.' That was pretty sharp of him! I grinned and confessed I was terrified of climbing steps, ever since a nasty fall in London years ago. Once that was out of the way, it was fine. I felt freed.

I notice my children are being extra solicitous towards their mama these days. It's a recent development. It amuses and saddens me. For years I used to nag them for not looking out for me during our frequent travels. They used to be genuinely puzzled by my scolding. 'But, Mama, you leave us panting at the back! You walk faster and you have far more energy. You need looking after?' It was at once a challenge and a compliment. It was also true. We would hit our destination, wherever it was, and within minutes of checking into the hotel, throwing my bags down, I'd be hustling them to join me in the lobby and start exploring. They would groan, protest, not take my calls, plead fatigue and fall asleep, while I would briskly take off on my own. I still do that. But if they are around, they don't let me wander off now without someone accompanying me. I am touched. But I also feel cross. I say those awful words that I never thought I would utter: 'Come on, I am not *that* old yet!' They smile indulgently and lie, 'No, no, we felt like grabbing a coffee.'

Slowing down is not fun. Not when your mind is racing.

My husband has framed a picture of me as a sixteen-year-old track and field star. I am wearing alarmingly short shorts and carrying running spikes in my left hand. It's a black-and-white picture, grainy and somewhat out of focus. But he loves it! And often says with enormous longing in his voice that he wishes he had met me then. It's all about youth, isn't it? And why not? The cycle of life doesn't stop spinning for anybody. Today, I look at similar pictures (taken on their mother's nifty phone), of my granddaughters winning track events during their sports days. I am shy and afraid to participate in the charming 'grandparents' race'. What if I don't win? Some of the grandmoms are ten or fifteen years younger, fitter, hotter. What if I suffer a cardiac arrest trying to beat them to impress my grandkids? I can't do it!

What my body can no longer accomplish, I hope my mind still can, and must. I say that to all my contemporaries as they struggle with the same issues. I run into them at airports and note their 'comfy' (read: dumpy) attire, flat shoes or bulky sneakers, mouse-coloured shawls and handcrafted pullovers, coiffed bob, light foundation, discreet make-up and standard pearls. I can never become that kind of woman. I stare guiltily at my own attire. I must resemble a leftover relic from the hippy era, in my hoop earrings, gypsy skirt, silver bangles and large handbags. My hair (so much thinner) is still left loose and untamed. My make-up has not varied (a touch of kohl, lip gloss), and my attitude remains the same. It's the gait that gives the game away—cautious and watchful.

My hyperactive mind is in overdrive, noticing everything minutely. As always, I am devouring sights and sounds. An unfamiliar accent makes me spin around to see who it belongs to. I stare at the bright green nail polish on my neighbour's overgrown toenails. I shamelessly eavesdrop on conversations and smile to myself. I start writing my next column mentally, or imagining a new character for my next novel. There are dozens of parallel conversations going on inside my head. I am never bored. I like my own company. I talk to myself a lot. Not aloud, of course. But even before falling asleep, I indulge in some 'me talk', review the day, think about my life, figure out what I have done wrong, congratulate myself for doing something right. So, when I finally shut off my mind, there is nothing incomplete left to carry forward to the next day.

Here's a confession: When it's difficult to fall asleep, I design clothes. Yes. I love doing that. In my mind. I start by reviewing the contents of my cupboard and figuring out what to keep and what to discard (I end up keeping everything!). Then comes the all-important mix-and-match session—I get excited when a new way of wearing an old favourite pops into my head. I make mental notes and tell myself to try it soon. That never happens! But I enjoy the game. Some may find this superficial, I find it most creative.

We all have to find our own 'games'. They are harmless and they can be most entertaining. Our games allow us to keep the mind active, alert and energized. A lazy mind sans stimulation becomes dull, leading to the onset of depression, loneliness and possibly other more serious medical conditions. The more you exercise the brain, the sharper your perceptions are. It works on the same principle as physically exerting yourself to keep those muscles more toned and efficient. I hardly exercise my body. I have never worked out in a gym nor engaged a trainer. As and when I can grab a few minutes, I stretch and attempt a few basic yoga asanas. My latest is the 'chair suryanamaskar'. Not sure what good it does, but it makes me feel virtuous. I confess it's not terribly smart of me to ignore a regimen recommended by far wiser folks. I just feel restless and bored jumping around by myself. But this is short-sighted as some form of exercise is essential for the system. I could climb stairs, walk, swim, do a few real suryanamaskars. Each new year, I make the same resolution: start exercising! Each year it's broken by 10 January. Doing housework is perhaps the best exercise of all. Unfortunately, I am no domestic goddess either.

~

Okay, I can be an ostrich sometimes . . .

Aah! Now comes that magic word—denial. Most of us fall back on it when the alternative is hard to change or absorb. When I am faced with a no-hope situation, I take my time to react. Generally, I walk away and retreat into myself, scrambling to find a solution. There is no problem on earth that does not have a solution. It may not be the ideal one—but it's comforting to know it exists at all. These dark phases are the hardest. Especially if one has to present a 'social face' at a high-profile event and smile at strangers, when all that time, there are demons within, and enormous, tempestuous emotions to deal with. Anger, rage, hurt, disappointment, disillusionment, contempt—it's a cauldron boiling over, but the surface has to stay calm and controlled. Or else—what will everybody think?

Of course, I am often trapped in these highly conflicting situations. And I have sort of trained myself to deal with them with a level of equanimity but only I know what price that extracts. The public persona stays in character (can't let the side down), but I am so emotionally churned up within, my heartbeat accelerates dangerously, my head pounds, my gut rebels. Yet I give nothing away. I realize this is detrimental to my physical and mental health. I try to control my mind as best as I can, and then I wonder—is this the solution? I know the answer. I am evading truths. I am being a coward. I am running away from dealing with a crisis upfront.

Unspoken arguments are running through my mind as I go about my day, dutifully filing columns, attending to domestic chores, handling children, all the while making sure my voice and expression remain 'neutral'. But why? I want to yell, cry, hit back, argue, but I don't. My mother was not like that, I remind myself. When she was angry or upset, she expressed it. My father would say, 'She wears her temper on her nose' (an untranslatable Marathi phrase that says it all). Her subterranean rage would surface, her eyes flash, and her voice would go up a few decibels. The outburst would subside fairly quickly, and then she would sulk. Her brow would stay deeply furrowed for a few days but she would carry on with her 'duties' regardless. She would retreat in silence to the kitchen to prepare the family's meals, just like I rush towards my laptop and start keying in stuff blindly. We would walk around her without daring to intrude into her space. I have no such protection, alas! So I do the next best thing. She cooked. I write. Both adopting a life-preserving tactic, for the same reasons. She must have found cooking as therapeutic as I find writing. It's a pity I never asked her that question. Her answer might have surprised me. Nobody asks me either. Just as I took it for granted that my mother cooked for us, every day, twice a day. I guess my family takes it equally for granted that I write every day, most of the day. It is assumed my mother and I had the same choices—and we chose! Did we really? Maybe she wanted to write. Maybe I want to cook. Too late to ask her, but not too late to ask myself!

It is assumed my mother and I had the same choices—and we chose! Did we really? Maybe she wanted to write. Maybe I want to cook. Too late to ask her, but not too late to ask myself!

Denial is a dangerous place to be in. It resolves nothing. It delays everything. Eventually, whatever it is you don't wish to face will not evaporate into nothingness. It will wait. Sometimes for decades. And it will bite. Then what?

I have no original answers to offer. For decades, I have struggled to make sense of life's tricks—the big ones and the small ones. The one thing I have observed is that those who deal with inner grace rarely crack as badly as those who wilfully hurt innocents. Sensitivity is about other people, not yourself. I remember pointing this out to a good friend when she was harping on about her own high levels of sensitivity and passing judgements on those in her life who didn't possess it in the quantum arbitrarily decided by her.

After hearing her out for half an hour, I stopped her mid sentence and asked what the definition of sensitivity was. As expected, she spoke about herself, her emotional response to family situations, friendships, colleagues, and how intensely even tiny rebuffs impacted her. At this point, I sensibly backed out of the conversation. But years later, she reminded me about that afternoon and said she thought about our exchange and realized how selfishly she was living, only thinking of her own reactions, without pausing to think of anybody else. It happens to all of us when we are smarting from fresh hurts. We can't think beyond the hurt. Unable to cope with the intensity of the emotion, we run in the opposite direction. Denial strikes again! Accumulated denials start piling up, till one reaches a breaking point and something gives—generally the body, which protests vehemently against years of suppression. Even at that critical stage, most of us treat the physical symptoms, without bothering to find out what caused them.

Younger people are suffering from stress-related conditions. Some of them are acutely aware of the triggers that generate stress, but plead helplessness. 'It is our hectic lifestyle these days,' they rationalize. And if anybody says the obvious ('Change it, in that case'), they shrug and change the subject instead. I am terrified when I look around me and see twenty-somethings trying in vain to cope with multiple issues and failing to resolve most. The levels of competition they are compelled to deal with are frightening. The pressure to conform to near impossible ideals of what constitutes a 'good life' makes them chase ridiculously unrealistic dreams. The reassurance that larger families provided troubled household members is absent in today's nuclear units. With little or no guidance, kids are adrift, left to their own devices to seek bigger answers to deeper questions than the ones they respond to robotically in their exam papers.

I grew up with kids who came from far wealthier backgrounds, whether in school or in the building my family lived in. As a government officer's daughter, there was a tacit acceptance about what we could and couldn't afford. Of course, I did feel frustrated at times, but I also understood in practical terms the extent to which my father could stretch the budget to accommodate my needs. As a competitive athlete, I needed spiked running shoes, for instance. These were expensive. I ran barefoot or wearing regular 'tennis shoes' (not today's exorbitantly priced branded sneakers) till my wonderful coach (who didn't charge fees), the late Ullal Rao, managed to get a pair for me. It was a huge, unforgettable moment. I actually kissed the new shoes! And slept with them under my bed, waiting for dawn, when I'd make my way to Azad Maidan for my daily training with 'Sir'. I am not sure I ran any faster with the spikes, but they remained my most prized possession for years. I guess I felt I had earned them . . . and that 'Sir' saw enough potential in me to gift a pair. I was being taken seriously as an athlete—and I didn't want to let 'Sir' down.

Today, when I read inspiring stories about a ten-year-old milkman's son (Shubham Jaglan) winning junior golf trophies in distant Las Vegas, my mind goes back to my own childhood. Shubham's story is unique and extraordinary when compared to mine. But I like narrating it to my children—how privileged their lives are! What do they not have? They could achieve any target if they set to work with that incredible level of dedication. They have access to the best clubs, the best facilities, the best trainers. And then I check myself. Their dreams and hungers are different. They have skills I don't possess and I am always marvelling at the 'smartness' of their generation. They appear so confident as they travel the world on their own, meeting friends across the globe—for wedding celebrations, significant birthdays, anniversaries, bachelorette parties. It still appears terribly posh and exotic to me, as I shamelessly eavesdrop on conversations laced with amazing details about magical soirées on the edge of the Asian side of Istanbul (only wannabes stick to the more touristy European shore, they sneer). Is it just the new wealth pouring into India that is responsible for this directionless generation aimlessly chasing hedonistic goals? That may be part of the explanation. But beyond the urban, super-rich party scene lies the other Indian reality of educated professionals seeking the good times in cities like Bengaluru, moving at a very young age to an alien environment from the one they have grown up in, discovering an alternative lifestyle of sprawling malls, coffee shops (remember the tag line—'A lot can happen over coffee'?), pubs, nightclubs, gated communities, romance, break-ups, drugs, booze . . . sometimes murder and suicide too. Never before have I read as many accounts of young people either taking their own lives or killing someone else. There is so much subliminal violence in daily interactions with family, friends and colleagues. There is also no great fear of the law . . . no shame, if caught. When I ask them the reason for this apparent lack of any contrite feeling, they say they take their cues from the older generation! 'Look at our politicians . . . look at some of our industrialists . . . or even sportsmen. They get away with cheating, bribing, killing . . .' Without a moral compass, either in the public space or within their own homes, there is a gigantic chasm which is growing at an alarming pace. Too many young lives are being thrown away . . . destroyed. I fear we have let them down.

~

Let's play role reversal

Most times, I am the person who likes to take charge in family situations. My family indulges me. They let me believe I am indeed in charge, even when I am not. That's pretty sweet of them. It has become such an old habit that they allow me to set the pace during family gatherings or when we travel. These days, I notice a subtle and touching shift. The children have taken over. And I like it, especially when we go out together and there is a huge crowd. In the past, I would be holding their hands and leading the way. It's the other way round now. Packages are gently taken from my hands, car doors held open, the roomier seat vacated for me. The children are not submerged in themselves and their priorities, as they once used to be.

My youngest told me bluntly, 'Of course, I think of myself first, but these days, I also look out for you. Haven't you noticed?' I had noticed and wondered about the newly minted concern. Was she working on me because she wanted something? My cynicism had resurfaced. I asked equally bluntly, 'So what do you want this time?' She looked stricken! And I felt instantly guilty. She had actually waited for me, helped with the luggage, shared her snacks, looked for chairs and toned down the music blaring on the car stereo. It was a big change. Did she recall the times I used to carry her across busy roads as a child, afraid her tiny hand would slip out of mine if I merely held on? Do the other children also remember small but intensely loving gestures from their past? Are they 'paying back'? Is it duty? Or, dare I even say it, love?

I miss being the 'totally in charge' person sometimes. It's nice to be 'looked after' by one's children. It's even better to do the looking after. 'I feel so useless these days,' an older girlfriend cribbed, adding, 'nobody needs me any more!' I consoled her—or tried to—by saying needs change constantly. True, she doesn't have to slave for her family now that the children have their own lives and homes, but what about emotional needs? Why not focus on sharing experience and wisdom? 'I don't think they have the time to pay attention to what I am saying . . .' she responded softly. Our generation behaved as insensitively with parents and family elders. Have we forgotten and forgiven ourselves? Who had the time to listen to aunts and grand-aunts talking about the Mahabharata or even a juicy family feud? I can recall my eyes glazing over as I'd stare stonily and rudely at an imaginary spot on the wall and escape at the first opportunity.

Rule number one these days: Stop being petulant. Rule number two: Don't demand attention. Rule number three: Forget self-indulgence. These are luxuries one gives up at fifty. Self-sufficiency is the only survival tool available now. Self-sufficiency can be fun. I find it freeing not to wait for someone to accompany me if I feel like going to the movies or even to a new bar in town. I pick up my bag and go. Travel remains my biggest turn-on. Why wait for a friend or family member to fit into your plans? Go ahead and book. Let the others know. If they are interested, they can book too. If not, you don't miss out.

Feeling unwanted can be such a depression-inducing feeling, especially for people who have felt wanted most of their lives. I watch retired men and women closely these days. And tell myself fiercely, 'Never retire! You don't have to, you don't need to.' I have observed the sudden and visible deterioration in the personalities of people who have held positions of power for decades—chairs of large corporates, for example, or politicians, even movie stars and sportsmen. Once their position is gone, their charisma fades overnight. The body language changes, so does the voice. Some start stooping. Others begin to droop. Those who pretend to be 'relieved' not to have to deal with responsibility are the worst hit. They are forcing themselves to act tough when they are crumbling within. This little pantomime is kept up for a year or two after retirement. Then, one fine day, realization seems to dawn that nobody gives a damn. That's the day they straighten their shoulders, stick their chin out and carry on.

'It's all about the position, occupying that damn *kursi*, isn't it?' a friend asked despairingly. She had just lost her job in a media empire and was smarting from the 'nasty sacking'. Well, all firings are essentially nasty. She'd enjoyed a great run for thirty years, heading features and bringing out a weekly supplement for the publishing group. Staleness had set in years ago. But then, the management didn't want to upset this particular apple cart. She knew too many people—advertisers at that. Too many people knew her. The brand was associated with her a bit too closely. That was also the main problem. Only, she didn't know it. Feted and toasted, she loved playing the opinionated diva, sweeping late into events, followed by cowering minions. Her travels took her from one glamorous global destination to the other. Luxury brands wooed her with fancy gifts. She herself kept repeating the old cliché, 'Who needs marriage? My job is my lover.'

When the marching orders came, she was instantly felled. Loyal staffers recalled how she froze for a couple of minutes, and then collapsed, crying, howling like a child. 'We had never seen her vulnerable. It was too much! We didn't know how to handle her tears. We only knew how to handle her tantrums.' Like several before her—and there will be several after—she foolishly believed her faithful flock would stand by her and quit en masse. Nobody did. She thought her influential 'contacts' would display loyalty and pull out of the media group. How wrong and delusional she was!

In less than a week after news of her exit became public, all the invitations dried up. A much younger editor replaced her. The old staffers stayed put and quickly shifted allegiance to the new boss. She was left gnashing her teeth in utter frustration. Her calls were rarely returned. All those glamorous junkets to the world's top fashion/lifestyle destinations dried up overnight. Nobody courted her to attend and cover the weddings of billionaire brats. And worst of all, the lady who would airily state, 'If it's champagne, it had better be Dom,' to quaking hosts, discovered that she could barely pay for her beers.

The story doesn't end well. She tried to launch several independent ventures. She relied on old associations. She should have worked on her goodwill instead—the goodwill she ought to have accumulated over thirty years but clearly hadn't. This is how the cookie crumbles. It is always about the position, rarely about the person. Younger is better. Younger is smarter. Younger is hungrier. Accept it.

The media world is full of similar stories. There are television anchors who assumed networks would collapse with their exits. But even high-wattage star power is as good as the vehicle that allows it to shine on the right platform. Take away that platform, and what you are left with is a vague memory of a person who did a decent job of yelling at everybody, night after night.

Ditto for corporate fat cats who delude themselves into believing the company runs solely because they run it. Not so. Ask the shareholders. Even the most successful top dog comes with a sell-by date. Nobody remembers, nobody cares. While attending the prayer meeting of a legendary (and genuinely loved) head honcho of one of India's pioneering engineering giants, I looked around at the motley crowd with some amount of distress. Where were the fawning executives who used to trail this man, hanging on to his every word, treating him like a demigod? Most of them expressed surprise that he'd been alive all these years. Once he retired, he was metaphorically dead. They were unaware of his many years confined to a wheelchair after suffering a massive stroke. I have seen this indifference over and over again. Power comes with the designation, not the individual. Is that so hard to fathom? Look at what happened to some of our most-watched television anchors once they left the mother ship and floated their own. Where are those amazing men and women today? Where is Oprah Winfrey, for that matter?

Spending a few days in Kolkata, I was enjoying a cuppa on the lawns of a popular club, when a familiar figure shuffled past me. His head was bowed, and he had aged dramatically in less than a year. Was he suffering from some ailment? I asked a common friend anxiously. She laughed and said, 'Yes. The ailment has a name—joblessness.' He had once been the *burra saab* of all burra saabs, the head of a tea company, occupying a sprawling bungalow and not deigning to talk to the 'natives'. He would state loftily, 'I only talk to God.' Here was the same man, shabbily dressed and completely withdrawn. 'He took his retirement very badly,' my friend explained. And I wondered, 'How does one take retirement well?' People will lie and say, 'Oh! It is such a boon! The best period of my life has just begun. I have the money to do what I want with my time. I can do nothing if I so choose. These days I spend time with my grandkids, play golf, meet friends for an early drink at the club, read books I have been collecting over years, travel to places like Peru. Never felt better! Don't I look it?' You smile and lie glibly, 'Retirement suits you, you're looking great!'

No, darlings, nobody wants to retire. Not at sixty. Not at eighty. There is something inexorably tragic about that word. It's the closest sentiment to death and perhaps prepares you for it. Retirement demoralizes most people, which is why I get bugged when smug, fit, clever and hugely successful youngsters claim nonchalantly at parties that they plan to retire at forty. These are the very people who remain players till they drop dead. By saying they'll retire at forty, what they actually want to convey is how affluent and chilled out they are. They want you to know they can *afford* to retire and still maintain the same lavish lifestyle. A tall claim, but also one that could be true, depending on how much they have stashed

No, darlings, nobody wants to retire. Not at sixty. Not at eighty. There is something inexorably tragic about that word. It's the closest sentiment to death and perhaps prepares you for it.

away. When asked their post-retirement plans, they trot out well-rehearsed lines about working for the 'less fortunate', 'giving back to society', starting an NGO, mentoring younger colleagues, taking up a teaching assignment in Brazil, lazing around in a Phuket villa they've invested in, and other such meticulously constructed fantasies.

Then why the stoop and shuffling gait when they actually do retire? Why the hollow eyes and strained smile? What poor actors we all are. Most of us run away from acknowledging that when it's over, it's over. Everybody of a certain vintage has a replacement. And the replacement is younger than your own children. Hard to digest? Sure. Does that stop the ageing egoists from clinging on, chewing on memories and talking about the glory days even when nobody is listening?

What poor actors we all are. Most of us run away from acknowledging that when it's over, it's over. Everybody of a certain vintage has a replacement. And the replacement is younger than your own children.

~

FOMO

The first time I came across the term 'FOMO' was on a family chat. Arundhati was pregnant at the time and unable to travel with us or attend the many fun events, weddings, birthday parties. I saw a 'sad face' emoji with the word FOMO, and asked what it stood for. Fear of missing out, she explained. I had learnt a new *young* expression! Speaking the language of today and tomorrow is key. If you want to keep up with the times, and not feel left out in conversations, make sure you listen keenly and pick up new phrases.

I remember liking the sound of 'ewwwww' when it was introduced. I liked 'yuckkk!' But I never liked 'whatever'. 'It's a bummer' is great and covers a lot of ground. 'Let's bounce . . . !' is jaunty and I do use it, much to the embarrassment of my kids. I haven't taken to 'yaaaasss!' so far. And even less to 'daayyuum'. That's the thing about slang and new idioms. Every generation has its own lingo. And every generation is possessive about its usage. If parents try to appropriate 'their' words, they often resent the intrusion. But I can't help myself. My love for language and new words supersedes sensitivity in this regard. I happily speak to them in their idiom, and recall the same thing happening with my own mother—but for entirely different reasons. My mother taught herself conversational English by speaking to us. That's how she learnt Hindi as well—by listening and not feeling shy to boldly go ahead and chat with anyone, throwing in Marathi words when stuck. She sounded charming and naive. Perhaps I merely sound like a wannabe. Like a mom trying hard to sound cool, hip, with it. But that isn't so. I just adore the way languages shift, get twisted, and become richer into the bargain. As the anointed godmother of 'Hinglish', I can't get enough of the new additions to this unbeatable form of easy communication. *Jhakaas* does not translate to 'awesome'. Jhakaas is jhakaas.

As far as FOMO goes, yes, it's true parents feel left out when they watch their children having a grand time. Oldies start lamenting, moaning and groaning, talking irritatingly about their own rollicking years that nobody wants to know about. Does there come a tipping point when parents turn into insufferable bores? I am terrified of reaching that point. When I repeat myself, my stories, I can see my children exchanging looks ('There she goes again . . .'). And I am baffled. Whatever happened to the old scintillating conversationalist? She grew old! That moment comes for all of us. Subjects we find fascinating are old hat, irrelevant to the young. We assume they will benefit from our wisdom. We fool ourselves that they want to learn life's lessons from us. They want to learn from their own life or their peers' lives.

I think of my father, desperately trying to take control of family conversations and contribute to the overall noise. His voice was loud and his personality commanding. His life had been pretty eventful and inspiring. Yet. It's the 'yet' that separates generations. Nobody wanted his views on Pandit Nehru or pre-Independence India. If he quoted Keats or Kalidasa, there were blank looks from clueless grandchildren more interested in Beyoncé and Brad Pitt. '*Zamana badal gaya hai,*' I would remind him. Now, I have to remind myself!

This awful truth was driven home at a destination wedding when I joined my children and their friends, as they sat at a poolside bar, chatting and gossiping about those not present. Initially, they welcomed me with whoops of joy ('Shobes is here . . . yay!'). Soon, they wanted to light up. In our family, we all pretend the children don't smoke. They use a so-called code word (tabac) when they feel like smoking a ciggy. I go instantly deaf and pretend I haven't noticed the swift movement to an open space. Well, in this case, we were in an open space. And I was in the way, an inhibitor. Plus, I was narrating what I thought was an amusing titbit that they were clearly not interested in. After two minutes of fake politeness, one of them pleaded, 'Mama, now enough! Just go!' So I went. Did I feel hurt? Initially, yes. But I immediately reminded myself of my own reaction to my father's presence when I wanted to enjoy my after-dinner smoke (for years I smoked precisely one cigarette a day and thoroughly enjoyed it, before giving it up totally).

So long as you maintain that distance from your sensitive ego and someone else's sentiments, you are fine. To the best of my ability, I try to never talk about the distant past when I am with young people. They really don't give a damn. Why subject yourself and them to nostalgia? Why thrust yourself into their space when you are not entirely welcome or accepted? We all guard our spaces. The young are entitled to put up a sign that reads, 'Oldies, stay out!' No offence meant. So, none should be taken.

At the same wedding, I found myself sitting at a table tapping my feet to the DJ's amazing Bollywood tracks. I knew every song and practically every move. But I also knew my children would feel embarrassed if I hit the dance floor and started grooving to '*Kala Chasma*' and other catchy hits. So I sat tight and was enjoying myself watching others on the dance floor, when my daughter reached over, placed her hand over mine and said quietly, 'Mama, go dance,' I was so thankful. Permission had been granted by at least one member of the resident censor board. It was just the green signal I had been looking for. Once on the floor, I let myself go. It was fantastic and so liberating. I was dancing on my own, for myself. My eyes were shut. I had entered another zone. Dancing is meditation. I love it! I can dance anywhere to any music. I dance for myself. It is not a performance. I don't need a partner. I dance for me, with me. Maybe that is what my children fear. They watch me closely in public spaces—at airports, for example, or inside a mall. Wherever piped music plays, if I as much as snap my fingers to the beat, I feel a restraining arm clamp around my shoulders, a voice hissing, 'Please, Mama. Not here!'

Those words, 'Not here!' or 'Not now!', are familiar to me. In my younger days, I ignored them disdainfully. Who decided where or when I could dance or sing? I did! Nobody else had that right. Today, I meekly give in. Obedience is not my strong point. My husband chides me constantly—sometimes he is genuinely angry, other times he does it indulgently. He reminds me, 'You are behaving like your ten-year-old self—rebellious and childish.' He is right. Then again, I ask petulantly, 'Why should I grow up? Why should anybody grow up? There are characteristics and traits we possess that define us but don't have to confine us. I like some of my childish habits. Dancing is one of them.'

Knowing this, the children organize family gatherings at their homes, where they ensure there is a steady supply of Sauvignon Blanc and great music. 'Mama—you can dance tonight as much as you like.' And I do. I think it is very considerate of them to recognize my weakness and indulge me. I want to thank them. I want to keep dancing as long as my knees and feet allow me to, before my toes fall off!

Dance is life.
And then your aching knees disobey.
Age is also life!

Dance is life.
And then your aching knees disobey.
Age is also life!

~

Do *buddha*s and *buddhi*s really have sex?

Don't go 'ewwwww' at the thought of senior citizens at it. After a certain age, 'at it' has many interpretations. Of course, it isn't the 'at it' of the twenties, thirties and forties. But in our scrambled and confused society, it is considered 'indecent' for anybody over fifty to have a sex life or even think about sex, especially women. Hitting fifty renders a woman instantly sexless. Her thoughts are meant to turn to God and matters spiritual. She is seen as a 'person', not a woman. Past her childbearing years, her womb loses its value. She herself gets demoted. Worse, she demotes herself. She is by now used to being called 'auntyji' even by men ten years her junior. Her husband prefers snores over sex. If she shows mild interest in a man, she is called a 'frustrated nympho'. To some, she is a soft target. She can no longer get instantly impregnated. So it's safe to screw her and scoot. If she is in a stable marriage, she is spared the nuisance of dealing with beer-bellied seventy-year-old lecherous strangers eyeing her and even propositioning her. Men at that age figure a woman of fifty has nothing to lose and they have nothing to fear.

There are far too many assumptions in this narrative. Let's get one thing straight: Senior citizens have sex, okay? Senior citizens like sex. Senior citizens think sex. A lot. Deal with it! Surprisingly, women at fifty and above these days seem to be far more sexually active than their thirty- or forty-year-old counterparts. They look after themselves better than my generation ever did. They are fit, well groomed and confident enough to wear swimwear on a beach without shrouding their bodies in voluminous kaftans. Despite that, when it comes to getting between the sheets with someone, the same glamorous ladies baulk at the thought. 'I can't possibly undress before a man, or make love with the lights on.' But why? 'It's so awkward! I also don't like the idea of looking at a naked man. Besides, I am far more fastidious now about tiny but important details—like smells, BO, personal hygiene, bathroom habits. Sex at my age involves far too much work!' But at least, there is a certain lively interest in and a naughty discussion on the subject. And if the 'work' part is made less of a chore, I know quite a few of my girlfriends who'd be actively interested in resuming this familiar and pleasurable activity.

By contrast, the young wives I meet seem to lead pretty bloodless, sexless lives especially after they have children. They stop having sex with their husbands as soon as the pregnancy is confirmed. Most say it's because they feel scared of 'harming' the baby. But that's a lie. Many sheepishly admit they experience a welcome sense of relief to not have to provide 'duty sex' or sex on demand. They all complain of constant tiredness. Their souls seem more fatigued than their bodies. Their eyes are lost and listless. It's hard to think they have lost interest in sex. Sex that keeps the world spinning. It almost makes life worth living. It's a whole lot more interesting than planning for the next destination wedding. And yet, urban couples seem disconnected from the sensuous world altogether. Do they smell mogras? Like the feel of Chantilly cream on their bodies? The taste of each other's skin? How can an erotic thumri not arouse them? Why are they dead to beauty? Is their body obsession nothing more than vanity? Do they ever see their body in the context of 'the other'? Does it at all interest them to see their bodies with their partner's as one form, intertwining, disentangling, making patterns? No? Why not? Ed Sheeran's 'Shape of You' was displaced by Luis Fonsi's 'Despacito' as the most watched video of all time. Both songs are sexual, erotic and impossibly catchy. The young love to dance to these hits. But they don't love sex? Or not as compulsively as my generation? A contradiction!

It alarms me when young girls confess they are 'bored of sex'. Have they had too much of it at twenty? What is 'too much' in any case? Or is it partner fatigue? Too much bad sex with the wrong partner? How can they be 'bored' of their own sexuality? Knocking off the veil of discovery and mystery from the act of love is to insult what is the ultimate act of giving. When you share your body wholeheartedly with another, you share more than pleasure. You share complete trust. There can be no greater intimacy than when you become one.

This tender feeling should stay and sustain you at whatever age. Yes, even at seventy. You are not going to be a throbbing, panting, sweating mass of unbridled desire in your seventh decade. But you have a body that still responds to stimuli. You aren't dead—emotionally or physically. There is no shame to feel what you feel. There's nothing more comforting than a caress from a loving partner when your self-esteem is low. A caress—not a friendly hug. A lingering, gentle caress. A caress that makes you feel like a desirable woman. A caress that makes you forget those extra kilos, the wiggly bits, the wrinkles and lines, the cellulite and grey down there. There is a more devastating honesty in an expression of physical love at my age than there ever was when I was younger. There are no games to play. No facades. No filters. And you have the leisure of time on your side. No hurried couplings. No tricks to prove how adept and 'hot' you are. Just a mellow coming together of all the years shared and the many mistakes made. You can laugh in bed finally. And that's so damn liberating!

Self-consciousness kills sex. Women want to look perfect when they are naked. They are never happy with their bodies and that intense preoccupation destroys any enjoyment of sex. I doubt they even look at their partners, so entirely absorbed and self-critical they are. As we all know, if two perfect bodies try to make love, it ends in disaster because acute vanity gets in the way. Young mothers look for easy solutions. Sometimes they suppress their sexual urges and sublimate those energies into some other activity by jumping energetically into a demanding sport. Their husbands do the same. So we have two fit people who share a bed but do not have sex regularly because they are dead beat at the end of the day. This provides a convincing alibi as well. They declare how much they love each other and they mean it. 'It's just that we have loads of stuff to deal with to have sex in addition to all that.' The occasional sexual romp is reserved for a semi-drunken Friday or Saturday night. Fuelled by alcohol, inhibitions sufficiently lowered, they get home and make feeble attempts to get it going. Most times it doesn't work. Or as they put it bluntly, 'It's too much effort for a few minutes of fun.'

Funny how those two words—'too much'—colour so many aspects of young lives. I hear the phrase 'Too much fun, yaar' and smile to myself. Better that than 'too much boredom'. Short attention spans have shrunk everything. Try having a conversation that satiates all the senses at once like a gourmet meal. It has become rarer and rarer with any person of any age group. At some point your eyes glaze over and, abruptly, the interaction is declared finished. There is an immense sense of relief as the bored person looks around frantically for someone more interesting to talk to. I remember feeling really awful at a family wedding when the elders were abandoned and left to amuse themselves while the younger generation chatted animatedly. I told myself, 'You will soon join the ranks of those family elders left on the sidelines to fend for themselves.' No way, I say defiantly, looking nervously at myself in the small mirror I discreetly fish out of my large handbag.

I don't want to be the little old lady who once had an interesting life. I don't want to be the woman waiting to be served her meals at a function because she is unable to walk to the buffet table and help herself. I don't want to be the woman people walk up to uncertainly to ask, 'Aren't you so-and-so? I wasn't sure. So what are you doing these days?' An ego is a terrible curse. I tell myself mine is a healthy one. It isn't exaggerated one bit. I ask my family if I am doing fine all the time. They are tired of reassuring me. When I questioned Avantikka for the hundredth time, she told me gently, 'You are used to people looking at you. That's how it has been for most of your life. It takes time to get accustomed to a different response, when that happens, if that happens. Don't think about it right now. Knowing you, there will always be something else you will find that is enjoyable and fulfilling. Maybe some other passion that will fascinate you. That's the person you are.' It's difficult to view yourself turning into a non-entity, a non-person, an old person. Old in spirit. Old in thought. Old-old. Will it happen to me?

I console myself with memories of M.F. Husain at ninety-five. Productive, active, agile, attractive, alive—physically and mentally. What broke him was not old age but rejection. He aged quickly after he was banished from his beloved India. He had no will to carry on. Even though he had everything else—enough fame, money, admirers—what he didn't have was home. Rootless and despairing in the end, the person I met on his hospital bed in London a few hours before he died was a broken man. For the first time in his life, Husainsaab looked like a sick, old person, which indeed he was. But till that moment when all was taken from him—his izzat—he had been the legendary, iconic Husainsaab. Ageless and gorgeous, exuding vitality in every jaunty step, as he traipsed all over the world, restlessly forever seeking beauty.

Where will my 'rejection' come from? In what form? Will I recognize it in time? Should I even care? One part of me says, 'To hell with such boring thoughts. You will deal with whatever it is, if and when you have to. For now, drink up the moonlight. Stay thirsty. Stay hungry. Dance!'

Some people take rejection in their stride, as if it's the most natural thing. But it isn't. Nothing and no one should feel rejected. There is room for all. The space in this life, in this world, is vast. And yet, most of us experience rejection several times in our lives. Most of us deal with rejection very badly. People say foolishly, 'Don't take it personally,

Where will my 'rejection' come from? In what form? Will I recognize it in time? Should I even care? One part of me says, 'To hell with such boring thoughts. You will deal with whatever it is, if and when you have to. For now, drink up the moonlight. Stay thirsty. Stay hungry. Dance!'

it's not about you!' Then who is it about? You just fired me. You turned down my proposal. You ditched me for someone else. You hated my project. And you are telling me not to take it personally? Even an infant understands rejection. Watch an unloved, uncuddled child. Even if that baby is well fed, cleaned and taken care of, the absence of love will register. Love has no substitute. A baby that isn't held and rocked and soothed and kissed responds very differently to the world, not just when he/she is a baby but for the rest of his/her life. The importance of touch cannot be underestimated. That applies to old people too. Nobody thinks of holding them. In some cultures, it is considered 'improper' and perhaps disrespectful to hug elders. How absurd!

Overfamiliarity is actively discouraged in certain communities. Daughters are not hugged by fathers or brothers or uncles or grandfathers after they attain puberty. Who is not trusted? The young girl? Or do the men not trust themselves? I have never understood nor accepted this attitude. We are so stiff and aware around one another. A little boy learns very quickly that he must not cling on to his mother—at least not in public, unless he wants to be teased for being a sissy. Little girls stop dead in their tracks before rushing into a male relative's arms, with just a ferocious frown of disapproval from a senior family member.

By the time we are ten or twelve, we have been well-trained to restrain ourselves from touching anybody. Like touching is dirty. Touching is a sin. Soon, we forget what touching feels like. The only touch we condition ourselves to recognize is a sexual touch. We hear about mothers teaching their kids the difference between 'good' touch and 'bad' touch. I feel wretched watching little children staring warily at friendly adults greeting them in a park, for instance. Not every adult is a pervert. Then again, how does a parent take such a chance? So we have overzealous parents constantly reminding their children not to talk to 'strange uncles', not to accept sweets from an 'unknown aunty', not to, not to, not to. And soon the kids grow into suspicious teens, constantly looking over their shoulder to check whether there is a dangerous stranger waiting to molest them. And soon they forget the comfort of an innocent embrace. Sad!

~

The 'age thing'

So here I am, contemplating what to wear to a chic cocktail and supper party being hosted by two grande dames. One is older by a few years, the other one younger, also by a few years. I checked with my son, Aditya, and confessed I was thinking of ditching. A certain ennui has definitely set in of late. By 7.30 p.m. I start asking myself whether the effort required to don party clothes and a party face is worth it. Most times, the answer is no. This time, I surprise myself by saying, 'Maybe I should go. New people!' It's funny. I thought I was done with 'new people'. I could barely handle 'old people'. Then again, I don't enjoy meeting people my own age. Most are tired, cynical and jaded. They want to discuss visits to the orthopaedic surgeon who has recommended knee surgery, hip replacement, God knows what else. I always feel like joking morbidly and saying, 'Why not a heart transplant? A new brain?' But I shut up. I really don't enjoy discussing ailments—my own or other people's. To each our own hernias, if you know what I mean. Why should seventy-year-olds feel compelled to discuss 'seventy-appropriate' topics? Who decides what those are? I am not dying to know more about the swankiest senior citizen facility in the Himalayas. Nor am I keen to track a grandchild's every burp and loose motion.

I want to talk about fun stuff. I can do that with much younger people, or much older. But not seventy-year-olds. It's like seventy is a strange number. An in-between number. You are not entirely decrepit, nor are you technically middle-aged. You are old. But not that old. Most of my gal pals are in their forties. Some in their fifties. They have lived life. They've seen the world. They have stories to share. I like their attitude, the way they dress, talk, hold their drinks, hold a conversation. We enjoy the same things—movies, food, dancing and books. We love to travel. We are vain, but not self-obsessed. We are pretty cool, or so we like to think!

Summer holidays these days have nothing to do with summer. Or even holidays. The only reason people take a vacation now is for the pictures and selfies they can post on social media. Does anyone have as good a time as they project in those carefully curated, perfectly art-directed shots? While planning our family breaks, I am no longer surprised when someone asks, 'But is the destination photogenic? Can we wear cool looks?' Narcissism has taken over our lives! I laugh and go back to more research. I have been made the designated holiday planner. I have earned the post, I can tell you! For years, I would wait and wait and wait for someone to take the initiative and let the others know: 'Okay. Here's the plan. We are booked to go to a tiger/hippo/elephant/rhinoceros reserve. These are the dates.

Here are the tickets. Start packing.' That never happened. One fine day, I decided to announce my own travel plan. I made it clear I was happy to go on a solo trip, because I was plain sick of waiting for everybody to make up their minds. The family stared in horror and disbelief. 'What's wrong with you? How can you go by yourself? You will hate it! You'll have the worst time. You'll miss us. Forget it. Please cancel immediately.' I stood my ground and said, 'Try me. I am going. That's that. Next?'

Within a few hours, I had five people signing up for the trip. That grew to ten. We had a plan! We cheered. We went. And we had a brilliant time. Of course, not all of it was smooth sailing. There were several goof-ups and hiccups. But overall, a good time was had by all. Now that it is official, I take my role very seriously. The minute one trip concludes, I start dreaming about the next. We all have individual dream destinations, but mine get preference! Why? I play the 'I'm getting on . . . my knees protest, my bones creek. All of you are young enough to climb Kilimanjaro a few years from now. But this is my time to do fun things while I still can . . . who knows about this time next year?' I further dramatize the situation by clutching my left knee and saying, 'I have been neglecting it. Must see the orthopaedic guy next week.' Blackmail! It always works. It's one of the advantages of growing older. I exploit it to the hilt.

When I think of my own childhood years, apart from a few road trips around Delhi with my parents, I cannot recall any major holidays. Our 'native place', as we so charmingly call it, was Bombay itself. Once we moved here (I was ten at the time), we stayed put. Holidays meant additional expense. My father simply did not possess the resources to give himself, our mother or us a much-needed break. But it hardly mattered. I don't remember feeling left out when my school or college friends enthusiastically discussed their summer holiday plans to go to hill stations around Mumbai, or farther to visit grandparents in Shimla and beyond. For me, that break from studies meant cycling on hired bicycles down busy streets near our home, and going for a walk on Marine Drive in the evenings to watch a brilliant sunset, and if in possession of some loose change, eat an ice cream sandwich at K. Rustom's (it still exists, and the ice cream sandwich remains amazing) near Churchgate station. Of course, that walk also offered a chance to chat with boys from the neighbourhood who 'accidentally' timed their walks with ours.

These days, our plans are far more elaborate . . . and I suspect they are going to get further pumped up. I travelled abroad for the first time when I was in my twenties. It was the single most important individual decision for me back then. Abroad! Alone! The whole world was waiting! The love affair was on—a crazy, adventure-filled one. Every minute, every pound and dollar counted. And now? My children are seasoned travellers. My grandchildren with their own passports at three months have taken enough international flights. Everyone is so blasé and relaxed. While my heart still thuds when I get into the car taking me to the airport. I count the hours to take-off. I never tire of rechecking my handbag for passport, travel documents, soft shawl, phone charger (key!). Arriving at a foreign destination fills me with anticipation as I take a deep breath and look around me, hoping to identify a brand-new experience at the arrivals lounge itself! I hope travel continues to enchant me. I hope I never become blasé and say, even to myself, 'Ooooof! Been there. Done that!' Thanks to my travels, I have gotten over my old fears—fear of sleeping alone, fear of darkness, fear of ghosts. It took me a while to sort out my fears, but I told myself it's that or staying put. The answer was obvious.

When I wrote a book to mark turning sixty, my publisher Ashok Chopra and I discussed the cover and agreed we needed to break the stereotype of a little old lady of sixty imparting distilled knowledge to her sistaahs. At around the same time I had shot for *Vogue* (India) for its annual Age(less) Issue. The images were uber stylish. We both picked the same one—of me in an electric-blue one-shoulder gown, my hair carefully windblown by the studio fan, and a mischievous smile playing on my lips. 'This is the one!' Ashok Chopra declared gleefully, and we had a glam cover. Almost all the reactions were positive, except for a few which we sensibly ignored.

Ten years later, I am pleasantly surprised the book sold at all. I was debunking age and talking merrily about how to make the most of the sixth decade. Had I posed in a demure saree and said the same things, would the reactions have been different? I'd say yes. Stereotypes are just so annoying. We should all be free to be whatever age suits our temperament. I can go from feeling sixteen to looking and feeling eighty. Give me that flexibility, please. Don't put anybody into a box with a number on it. And if anybody tries to do that with you—fight with all your might. On days when I want to pull out my 'I am seventy' card, I do just that. But that's my call. It works to my advantage in certain situations, and I can manipulate it beautifully to generate an array of reactions. But most times, I have to remind myself I can no longer hop, skip and jump through life like a twenty-year-old. As the French would exclaim, '*Quelle horreur! Quel dommage.*'

There is a phrase I hate hearing myself utter—'as one grows older'. What happens when you get older? Do horns appear? Do your toenails fall off? Well, they can. Your hair certainly does, from *all* over. Teeth too. Your equipment dries up but doesn't rust. You may get cataracts, and knees might require replacement, as could hips. It's all rather pitiable, dreadful and messy, so why talk about it? Nobody but other fuddy-duddies wants to know what really happens 'as one grows older'. Your bowel movements should remain a deep dark secret. Along with flatulence and fibroids. As some star said, 'A good doctor can give you what God didn't.' So please spare the world. Your medical history is for you and you alone.

The other equally irritating line is, 'When you get to my age!' I say that less. But when people around me use it, I feel tempted to pipe in with a cheeky and rude, 'Yes, honey, when I get to your age, I will still be wearing high heels and red lipstick. And deep-purple outfits.' Or I feel like mocking the person with an offensive comeback, 'Oh dear, are you referring to adult diapers?' These responses are not intended to offend my age group. I know we all have to endure some terrible affliction or another and suffer. I prefer to suffer privately and not inflict suffering on others.

Age has its uses too. I use mine when it suits me, like asking for an airport buggy after flashing my senior citizen status. Or promptly accepting help from youngsters to carry heavy shopping bags. If you can't leverage age, don't mention it. When I am on a flight, I often meet interesting people. It starts off with a studiedly casual, 'My wife is a big fan of yours' (Lies! The man needs an excuse to strike up a conversation!), then comes the selfie request ('for my daughter . . .'), and once this connection has been established, a free-flowing conversation begins. I wonder what sort of a thrill these men get by chatting with a strange woman they are never likely to meet again. At some point, we end up discussing children. And I mention grandchildren. Something goes 'boinggggg!' inside the fellow's simple, little head. The expression in his eyes alters in an instant. His voice drops. Sometimes he folds his hands and says, 'Namasteyji,' reverentially. A few men actually dive for my feet. A perfectly normal conversation abruptly changes course, and we start talking about pilgrimages. The age thing again. This is just so silly! I am not the one who has initiated the conversation. Is the man terrified I might bite him? A little later, I get it. The man is nervous. To start a conversation with a strange lady is not part of our great Indian culture. To start a conversation with a lady who is a senior citizen? A grandmother? A naani—hey, bhagwan! A dialogue needs a filter, a justification ('My wife is your fan . . .'). Or else, guilt happens.

At the time of writing, I am a good few months away from hitting that silly number. But my sweet family is busy planning many surprises, which may include a cruise. We are serial cruisers. I believe families that cruise together, stay together, and drink a lot together! I don't want to cramp their enthusiasm by interfering. But I have a few plans of my own, should someone ask me. A few things I am certain about—there has to be lots of singing and dancing. A few things remain fluid and open. Being an improvisational artist, I like the idea of deciding in December what to do in the first week of January. Everything is possible, if you dream it. Who knows what December may inspire? It's important to keep options, and the mind, open but I notice most people at seventy are creatures of habit. They don't want to change a thing. They like their routines. They are comfortable with the familiar. Anything else throws them, and leads to confusion and disorientation.

I want to urge them to break out of that cage of fixed notions. Give life a try—raw, real life. It's not all that scary, you know. In fact, doing something totally unexpected, even potentially dangerous, may turn out to be the most exciting risk you have ever taken! At the very least you will go to the great beyond having experienced an adrenaline fix, an unbelievable high. That should be tempting enough. I hope my children are skipping this part—or they may tie me up!

Watching the sequel to *The Best Exotic Marigold Hotel* (rather unimaginatively titled *The Second Best Exotic Marigold Hotel*), I was most amused by a scene in which Richard Gere, playing a tired hotel inspector, first appears on screen. I for one gasped audibly and loudly cheered when one of the senior citizen actresses in the movie commented, 'The Lord have mercy on my ovaries!' Yes, it was an age thing. Most of the women in the cinema hall were 'over the hill' like me. So were the actresses in the movie (except for the hero's fiancée). We were responding to a memory—and not the man in that scene. Our memory had frozen, and we were swooning over Richard Gere's character in *Pretty Woman*, which had just celebrated its twenty-fifth anniversary. Just as we were twenty-five years older, so was

Richard Gere. That's a quarter century of nostalgia. We were no longer 'fan girls' of Gere—we were fan *buddhis*!

That cruel word—buddhi! It has such a deeply wounding effect when hurled at a woman well past her prime. And this is where a small story comes in. At a family gathering being celebrated in a trendy, new midtown cafe, the earliest reservation given to our party of twelve was for 10 p.m. By the time family members started to roll up, the scene outside the cafe was pretty lively—lots of young, affluent people were gearing up for a long and hard night of partying (it was Friday night, after all). Three ladies from our group arrived together and struggled to push their way past the crowded door, where clumps of youngsters were enjoying a smoke.

Spotting the ladies, a cheeky girl, cigarette in hand, turned to them and said loudly, 'Wow! What an inspiration you guys are to our generation. Keep it up, aunties!' One of the 'aunties' bristled at this 'insult' and ticked off the person sharply. The others were equally miffed. It made me wonder—are we getting extra touchy when it comes to accepting age? Is that why the lady in our group reacted so strongly to what could have been an innocent compliment? Perhaps the young woman had spoken out of turn, perhaps she was a little high, perhaps she was acting smart, perhaps she was being spontaneous. By not giving her the benefit of the doubt, we had betrayed our insecurities. We were talking about the 'incident' two days later, thereby giving it far more importance than it warranted. Of course, young people are cheeky and merciless. They appear to lack sensitivity sometimes, but have we forgotten our own youth and how we used to be? In the eyes of the outside world, we are indeed 'buddhis'—our hair is grey or greying, our gait is slower than it used to be, we look like we may require the use of a walker soon, and our posture is not exactly upright—in fact, we slouch and stoop. So what? Aunty or buddhi—there is no escaping age.

Women who embrace their years with grace and charm exude a unique glow they may not have possessed in their youth. Acceptance of advanced years is different from resignation—it shows. Most times, I am perfectly in sync with my biological age and happy to be a seventy-year-old woman. Of course, I am vain enough to revel in compliments as and when I receive them. But I don't get upset if I am called 'aunty'. This is our 'Indian' way of showing respect to our elders. If it sounds odd to foreigners, that's fine. It is culturally acceptable to us. We address anyone older as 'uncle' or 'aunty'—no offence meant or taken, generally. Young colleagues often ask how I like to be addressed—ma'am? Shobhaaji? Mrs Dé? My answers vary. It really depends on the person and my personal level of comfort. I am perfectly happy with just 'Shobhaa'—that's my name, after all. I don't like Shobhaaji—I find it a bit too Bollywood. Mrs Dé is an option with strangers. Or else, call me 'aunty'. I am fine with *maasi*, but draw the line at *buaji*.

Age-related issues are extremely sensitive, and it's important to respect another person's feelings. Certain women friends are relaxed about being their age and never bother to hide it. Others are positively paranoid and go to great lengths to disguise the year of their birth. 'I don't feel old,' an eighty-year-old exclaimed agitatedly, 'Why do people want me to state my age? It's none of their business.' Still others, younger by a couple of years, love announcing to people within earshot, 'I have always looked up to Shobhaa ever since I was this high in school.' I laugh off the lie, adding, 'Yes, I remember she used to come up to my knees way back then, and look at her now!' We all have our little tricks to hit back at someone who is not quite in line, don't we?

Some of these 'tricks' land us in trouble occasionally, as it happened to a friend of mine who is a couple of years older. How do I know she's older? We used to model together when I was still a student in college, and she was already working. Growing up in the same city has its advantages. The disadvantages are as many—there are very few secrets left to guard. Everybody knows everything. Well, the lovely lady, who had been recently widowed when I ran into her, was hard to recognize initially. Not because the tragic death of her dynamic husband had aged her overnight. On the contrary, she looked twenty years younger and was positively glowing. I complimented her enthusiastically and she seemed suddenly bashful—like she had been caught with the wrong expression on her face when she was meant to look grief-stricken and low. She went into a lengthy explanation as to why she was dressed so elaborately and wearing so much make-up. I had not asked her a single question. Why did she feel like she owed me some bogus-sounding rationale about how her late husband would have wanted her to dress in a particular way and enjoy her life to the hilt, since he loved her so much?

I recognized her dominant emotion at that particular time—guilt! There was no mistaking it—the lady was feeling sheepish. Our cultural conditioning being what it is had made her suddenly self-conscious about her ultra-glamorous appearance so soon after the tragedy. It was also pretty apparent she had had 'work done' (as make-up artists politely refer to cosmetic surgery). I didn't really care but I had noticed. She had also noticed me noticing the obvious changes—the plumped-up lips, stretched skin and eyes that were now looking distinctly oriental. She started to fidget, and said hastily, 'Such a bad allergy. You noticed how puffy my mouth is looking? I don't know what to do!' I could have said, 'Oh please, come off it, that's no allergy. That's silicone.' I kept mum. It wasn't any of my business but I thought it was pretty silly of her to lie blatantly to someone who had watched her closely for over forty years. Here we were, two middle-aged women playing 'pretend' and being awkward with one another. Did I really care a damn whether or not this person had gone under the knife? No. But she clearly did.

Here we were, two middle-aged women playing 'pretend' and being awkward with one another. Did I really care a damn whether or not this person had gone under the knife? No. But she clearly did.

You may think this is a superficial, inconsequential, urban 'problem' about vanity and etiquette. It's much deeper. It's about games all of us play. And the energy we invest in such trivial matters. The facades we protect so fiercely—just in case the truth spills out and we stand exposed. I am still trying to figure out what the lady was embarrassed most by—her upbeat, cheerful attitude so soon after her husband's death? Or her botched-up surgery? Or perhaps both? What about my attitude? Did my critical gaze give the game away? Did she sense hostility on some level?

Did my body language suggest I was critical? What right did I have to be critical in the first place? Or to judge her? But most of us do that without even realizing it. The encounter I cited is not a significant one if seen in isolation. But put several connected stories together and it points to the same thing—dealing with the ravages of age.

Age affects women in ways that are terrifying. To dye or not to dye? I asked my children this question when the first strands of grey started showing at the temples. I was unsure what to do about the very visible grey. Children are the only individuals who are allowed to be ruthlessly candid. They put it bluntly, 'Mama, please do something about it. The grey makes you look really old.' They were right. And I wasn't one of those fortunate ladies whose grey strands make them look distinguished and elegant. Mine added twenty years instantly. I wasn't prepared to be treated 'like an old woman'. I started touching up the roots, fully aware there was no going back. Once you begin dyeing, you dye forever. It's frightening to come across women at hair salons when they are between colouring appointments. I was now one of them. Stuck! More than anything else, I found the whole thing tedious and time-consuming, especially since what starts off as a once-a-month ritual soon progresses to once-in-ten-days torture, spread over a minimum of two hours. It started to get me down. I felt depressed at the dependency. Hair colour became an emotional trap. It still is. As it must be for countless women who cannot step off that wretched drill. I admire women who don't give a damn and go silver with grace and courage. I am not one of them. Should that make me feel like a coward? As if I have succumbed to something that makes me feel less diminished? I don't know.

What I do know is my vulnerability. And I have to train myself to deal with this one, like I deal with far bigger ones. Anxiety is a condition that is hard to find easy solutions for. I have never taken anti-anxiety medication, no matter how intense the stress. Perhaps it is not what I imagine it to be—it can't be all that different from popping a tablet to get rid of a throbbing headache. But I was raised in a family that resisted any artificial interventions—the most dreaded word was 'dependency'. It still is in my vocabulary. Stoic acceptance of suffering, big or small, was ingrained in us as children. There was a healthy disregard for the sort of aches and pains that saw neighbours in a tizzy, calling up specialists 'to rule out anything serious'. We pretty much saw a doctor only when there was an emergency—a cut that was bleeding profusely or an acute attack of appendicitis. Anything that wasn't considered life-threatening was meant to be borne with fortitude and patience . . . till the bloody thing went away on its own. Issues that were 'emotional' by definition (anxiety attacks, depression, stress, low self-esteem) were dismissed as 'imaginary problems' and not worth taking seriously.

My own teenage conflicts had to be resolved privately. Any show of 'extra emotion' (as if there is a predetermined quota for emotions) was aggressively discouraged and labelled an attention-seeking stunt. At times, my anxiety levels did escalate radically (before competitive sporting events, before exams), but it was pointed out to me that my older siblings had coped on their own and excelled at whatever they undertook. True. Today, more than fifty years later, I wonder just how well they had coped in real terms. Were they given a choice? Was an attempt made to provide emotional support when they required it? Or were they meant to keep their chin up and soldier on? What was the price paid for this? There is always a price. Parents who refuse to acknowledge the varying emotional needs of children and dismiss them as 'tantrums' designed to 'trouble parents' play havoc with their adult lives, often without realizing the far-reaching consequences. I plead guilty too. My children's lives baffle me occasionally. I just don't get it. Are they being a bit too self-indulgent? Is that child a real 'softie'? Why can't that one be more assertive? Less assertive? Calmer? Expectations! Which parent is free of them? Which child?

The more we mutually expect, the higher the disappointment/disillusionment. There are times when I am chatting informally with friends and family and the conversation gets over-nostalgic. Everything goes back to 'In our time, girls had to be home by 7 p.m.—latest!' And I laugh inwardly. Occasionally, I stick my neck out, risk being misunderstood, and ask, 'But girls can do at 2 p.m. what society fears they will be up to at midnight. It's not about deadlines and timing always.' Then there are those touchy moments within family when someone decides to blurt out old truths—buried or forgotten. Flashbacks reveal unpleasant incidents revolving around childhood traumas and ugly memories of being belted, threatened, excluded, insulted, demeaned . . . the standard horror tales of difficult years, shared by millions across the world. It's no use saying, 'But that was decades ago . . .' Yes, it was. But the wounds never healed. Or else why would we still be discussing these awful memories?

How do we communicate with those closest to us? How truthful is 'truthful'? My wiser self (it exists!) warns, 'Truthful is hurtful.' Yup. That's true. Is it even necessary to be candid with people you truly love? Do they want to hear what your interpretation of a situation is, especially if that is likely to hurt them—you? Both of you? Discretion within families is a delicate matter. In our society, we believe we should be totally transparent within the family, and say it like it is. Children are supposed to listen without interrupting elders. Elders are entitled to tell everybody off. Distant relatives are encouraged to express their views on personal matters—this is what we have been conditioned to accept as 'normal'. No secrets. No filters. You feel something—you must articulate it. On one level this is healthy and cathartic. The pressure-cooker valve in our families works overtime 24/7. But I notice today's generation has discovered Western-style 'privacy'. I hear ten-year-olds demanding their own 'space' and talking about feeling hemmed in by parents and siblings. Mothers think twice before opening their mouths and correcting kids, in case they are accused of causing 'emotional scars' later! Fathers talk with caution and exaggerated respect to young sons, afraid the boys will answer back, rebel or leave home. Drugs and alcohol issues are never addressed in an upfront way—because parents don't want to deal with the truth. Sex as a topic of family discussion is strictly taboo—unless it is about other people. Forget acceptable, non-threatening topics for dinner-table conversation—these days, conversation itself is next to impossible. Children have better things to do (video games, Internet chat, outings), and they behave like investing even twenty minutes of their precious time on eye contact and chit-chat with the family is a waste of time. Which of these two scenarios is better: Too much communication, which can be intrusive and lead to volatile situations? Or minimal communication restricted to exchanging information ('I am leaving for a meeting at 7.30 p.m. . . . early dinner? Please collect the laundry tomorrow. What sort of grades is junior getting in class ten? Better organize extra coaching. And remember—there's a boring Sunday lunch with that auntyji . . .').

People hurt people. That's a given. The closer you are to someone, the deeper the wound. What can one do to minimize these painful incidents? I read self-help articles and books constantly. I practise deep breathing. I have tried counting to ten before reacting to provocation. Nothing works. It is only family that can affect you this intensely. But a few ground rules that I try to adhere to have prevented small arguments from escalating into major battles. It's easy to tell others not to hold grudges. Can you do it? I have a peculiar memory. I remember what I need to and focus on pleasant happenings . . . but all of a sudden, when I least expect it to happen, there comes a vivid flash reminding me of a really disturbing exchange which may have taken place a long time ago. All my self-regulation goes straight out of the window and I end up saying some pretty awful things. Later, I feel terrible . . . it's too late to take back those ugly words. I apologize. But the apology has little meaning, the person's justifiable anger has not subsided . . . and I am hitting a stone wall with my sincere words. Sincere from my side—but hollow from the other person's. It becomes a stalemate. And there it often stays. What should one do? I

People hurt people. That's a given. The closer you are to someone, the deeper the wound.

recommend a cooling-off period. Leave troubling situations alone. Give yourself time and watch the developments calmly. You have done the right thing by offering a genuine apology. The other person is not receptive at that point. Perhaps a change of heart will follow. Perhaps not! But at least you have attempted to make amends.

Ditto for tact and diplomacy when you sense the other person is experiencing an emotional low and saying things that are not expected, or behaving uncharacteristically. Switch on your empathy button. Switch places. Put yourself in the other person's situation . . . and suddenly the picture will change. Some people say defensively (and obstinately), 'Oh, but I can't be diplomatic. I am very upfront and blunt. I say things the way I see them . . . too bad if that attitude is mistaken for rudeness.' I feel like pointing out the obvious—it is rude! A little kindness doesn't hurt. It may not help either. But at least the recipient is spared more pain. Like when a young person is about to step out for an important meeting or a crucial romantic date. And he or she asks, 'Am I looking bad?' There's no need to be 100 per cent candid and say, 'Yes—since you asked. Hate the colour on you.' The impact of those spontaneous words can be lethal! The confidence levels instantly plummet—there goes the job! There tanks the romantic date. Because all that you have achieved via your bluntness is to generate low self-esteem. Instead, if you say gently, 'Well . . . you always look good. This isn't your best look. But your smile is fantastic! So wear your smile!' You haven't lied. But you haven't emotionally injured another either.

This is something to keep in mind when dealing with young adults. They are so sensitive and touchy about their appearance that a crucial meeting can get totally ruined by an unguarded comment from you. One of my siblings is a great one for 'telling it like it is'. I keep reminding the person, it is a pretty counterproductive approach and should be corrected. But no! So I have stopped giving unheeded advice. I have decided to change my own responses to such exchanges. The other person rarely changes. But you can—that's entirely in your own hands. It's worth doing, especially at the workplace, where bluntness is a real handicap and may cost you a promotion or two.

People confuse diplomacy with hypocrisy. There is a huge difference. Hypocrisy involves manipulation and falsehoods. Diplomacy is about sensitivity towards the other person's state of mind. You can always go back at a more conducive time to say what you didn't earlier. There will be more receptivity and respect when that happens.

People confuse diplomacy with hypocrisy. There is a huge difference. Hypocrisy involves manipulation and falsehoods. Diplomacy is about sensitivity towards the other person's state of mind.

I used to be pretty brash and bratty years ago. I was also living up to an artificially constructed 'persona'. Strangers expected me to be aggressive, outspoken and frank to the point of being ill-mannered. This was a natural consequence given my sharp columns filled with opinions on pretty much everything around me. Some would draw conclusions without meeting me. Others would take their time to greet me and start a conversation. And somewhere along the way, I started to prefer this shield that acted like a filter and helped me to retain my privacy. Later, I realized how much I was missing out on! There were wonderful people out there who were staying away from me—without giving me a chance! My children assured me it was okay and asked whether I really wanted to interact with so many nameless strangers I wasn't likely to meet again. My answer surprised me as much as it surprised them—I did! I had figured the loss was mine . . . and I had to do something about it. Gradually, I let the mask slip little by little. I smiled a lot more—and that got my children all worked up! They pointed out that I smiled at strangers who looked vaguely familiar, and those people didn't know how to respond! I said it was fine. A smile doesn't cost a thing. It was their decision whether to smile back or not! Gradually, things started to change. The energy field around me had obviously altered. My body language shifted as well—from stiff aloofness to a more open, welcoming posture—relaxed, not cross-armed. I hugged much more and received many hugs in return. It felt lovely! There was a new openness when I met people and this deliberate switch liberated me on many levels. I wondered why I had allowed myself to move so far away from my essential self. What was I 'protecting'? What if a few didn't 'approve'? Had I ever given a damn? Not really. So why now?

Age has a lot to do with that too. It is really most annoying! That's our social conditioning. I couldn't greet people with a warm hug in my much younger 'avatar'. It would have been misunderstood. As a woman, I was raised to be very frugal with my hugs and kisses. One only kissed babies in public—that's it. Kissing adults, even people much older than yourself, was deemed 'inappropriate'. I never saw my mother kissing anybody other than her own children when they were kids. I don't remember receiving a kiss from my father, except on his ninetieth birthday, when he kissed my forehead awkwardly and permitted me to kiss his! Hugs were equally rare. When one grows up with so much self-consciousness about any physical demonstrations of affection, those inhibitions are difficult to shed later. One of my daughters does complain that I don't hug her enough! I wonder what 'enough' means? She retorts that if I have to ask such a dumb question in the first place, I don't understand the value of hugs in life! She is right. But I still can't hug 'enough'. I'm trying hard to break this obstinate bastion. And learn from Anasuya Devi, my granddaughter, who has come up with a new word and a fresh definition—she asks for 'huggles' and likes 'huggling' her parents before falling asleep. I asked her, 'What's a huggle?' and she answered quickly, 'Oh . . . it's a hug and a cuddle—see—like this!' Gosh! I've missed out on a lot in life, I suddenly realized. I need huggles now!

My childhood did not feature too many 'huggles'. I was raised in a family that did not demonstrate emotion easily. Anger, yes! Impatience, yes! Irritation, yes! But not affection. Not appreciation. Not spontaneity. Restraint was a highly prized 'virtue'. Exuberant greetings or full-frontal hugs were deemed unbecoming, even vulgar. My parents would look witheringly at our north Indian neighbours in Delhi, and remark on their loud conduct, excitable conversations and frequent backslapping. If they '*galey dabao*-ed' during Diwali, Holi, Id, even that gesture was frowned upon. Almost as if physical contact was somehow abhorrent and 'unnecessary'.

My own children don't remember being hugged and kissed by my parents. When we did exchange 'forehead kisses' on his ninetieth birthday, it was a little awkward, and my siblings stared at me in that strange way which indicated they were surprised and embarrassed. With my mother, I was a little more relaxed and would place my head in her lap while she stroked my hair, and we chatted companionably. I don't remember hugging or kissing her too many times and vice versa. My grandmother was a taciturn, spry lady I barely knew. I always got the impression she disliked me intensely, so the question of hugging her did not arise. Both my grandfathers and the other grandmother were dead by the time I was born. I used to wonder whether this minimal physical contact within the family had anything to do with just our family—were we cold and peculiar? Unfeeling? Uncaring? Uptight? That too! But I think it also had a lot to do with our austere Maharashtrian upbringing, which glorified sacrifice and suffering above all else. There was an absence of joyfulness . . . Laughter had to be rationalized and rationed. Mirth had to be calibrated. You couldn't laugh for 'no reason'. Elders would remind us, 'Only idiots laugh at nothing . . . for nothing.'

And I used to think laughter was therapeutic!

To my absolute horror, I find myself using similar words when Anandita, my youngest daughter, laughs at a private joke she doesn't wish to share. I glare at her accusingly and demand, 'What's so funny?' She shakes her head and says, 'Nothing, Mama . . . it's just something I remembered.' I get bugged. I do. It's hard to shake off childhood memories and instructions.

~

My 'beef' with *khana–peena*

My son Aditya conducted a family puja at his beautiful home soon after our return from Iceland. It was a puja to mark the start of an auspicious period. But we all knew the puja was his way of expressing gratitude to God and saying 'thank you' for the positive developments that had taken place in his life after a long period of frustration and struggle to get an ambitious project off the ground. As the panditji chanted the Gayatri Mantra 108 times, and all of us participated in the *havan*, I looked around at the faces surrounding the holy fire. The panditji from Jaipur was a seasoned Arya Samaj priest who knew his shastras. He also knew urban attention spans and had reduced what can be a ritual spread over hours and hours of sitting uncomfortably on the floor in mid-April heat, to a forty-five-minute *jhat phat* affair, gently adding ghee to a fire with flames rising higher as blocks of dried wood kept getting added to the cast-iron urn.

A lavish feast was planned for later, once the prasad had been distributed to all. I stared in disbelief at the overladen dining table, with platters of rich vegetarian specialities piled on it. Knowing my children's dietary hang-ups, I wondered who would eat all those calorie bombs. I brought up the word 'waste' and my son glared at me. He came up to say, 'Nothing will be wasted. Don't worry. I want to share the food with all the people who work for us and are responsible for our daily comforts which we take so much for granted.'

Suddenly, that word 'waste' acquired a new dimension. Nothing is a waste if we know what to do with our resources—

limited or otherwise. Waste not, want not, my father would often say. Well, I still want! But I needn't ever waste.

I sometimes wish I had discussed beef-eating with my father during his lifetime. He was a progressive person on many levels, but as a Saraswat Brahmin, he had his beliefs. We ate simple, nourishing, healthy vegetarian meals at home. Except on weekends, when mutton was cooked. Mutton, never chicken. I wonder why. Fish and prawns were enjoyed occasionally, and we waited to devour ham and sausages as treats during leisurely Sunday breakfasts, but there it stopped. Beef was never a part of the culinary discourse. So I don't really know if my parents had strong views on the subject. It was unspoken but understood—we were a 'no beef' family.

Since food preferences were largely determined by what my mother cooked, I tasted a beefsteak much later in life. I must have been in my thirties when I walked into Gourdon restaurant near Churchgate station, and my friend ordered a beefsteak with pepper sauce—buffalo or cow, I don't know. One bite and I was converted! I don't think I 'confessed' to my parents—the question never came up! Today, when I see what is happening across India in the name of the cow, it pains me deeply. I continue to enjoy my steaks, but these days I have become acutely conscious of the fact I am eating beef—even when I am travelling overseas. It is not a religious dilemma at all. I know my beliefs and those have nothing to do with the consumption or non-consumption of beef. I am not less of an Indian for eating beef. I am not a bigger patriot for shunning it. I respect the sentiments of those who choose vegetarianism. I equally respect those who don't. The politics of food across the world is far too complex and comprehensive an issue for anybody to convincingly decode or comprehend. But for me, the question 'Where's the beef' has always had a singularly challenging meaning. Does anybody really know where it is?

~

Thank you, media friends . . .

It was just another weekday, and I almost didn't take her call. Her number was saved in my phone book under 'TV journo'. I had seen the number flash persistently. Five calls. I figured some story must have broken and the young girl was calling for a sound bite or two. When she called again, I answered and was ready to tell her I was unable to provide the bite, when she said, 'There is a big morcha coming to your home. The political party has informed the press. We will all be there by 2.30 p.m. It is looking rough. They are sounding very angry and have told us they were going to "teach Shobhaa Dé a lesson she won't forget".' I groaned inwardly and thought, 'Not again!' She asked worriedly, 'Are you okay? These people can be very aggressive. Should I inform the police and organize a bandobast?' I thanked her for the information and said, 'Nice of you to warn me!' She replied, 'Please don't thank me. It is because you have always been nice to me . . . and to all of us from news channels. Unlike others, you are always good to us, greet us, thank us, offer water or tea, treat us as professionals. You show us respect.' That set me wondering. I had done very little to earn her affection. I looked back on our many meetings over the years, and nothing special jumped out at me. Of course, I greeted her and her colleagues from other channels. Come on, that's basic courtesy, surely? These are hard-working people, caught in a highly competitive world, chasing absurd stories and meeting crazy deadlines. This one reporter always stood out from the pack. She was quick, clever, enterprising and on the ball. Our encounters were brief but mutually useful. I had extended no special favours to her and her small team. And yet, she was being so very kind and caring. It said a lot about her.

Thanks to her timely warning, I was prepped when the mobs and throngs arrived. It was an ugly encounter. But it could have been a lot worse. Ditto on another occasion when another friendly journo called to inform me a nasty crowd armed with black paint was waiting for me at a bookshop where I was scheduled to launch a senior journalist's book. I was stupid enough at the time not to pay attention to the tip-off . . . till the author himself called to tell me to turn around and head to an undisclosed destination. 'This mob is baying for your blood . . . it could turn violent. If you turn up, they will break the glass doors of the bookshop and wreck parked cars. Please lie low for a few hours . . . avoid going home. They are determined to find you tonight.' Both were close calls of the most unsavoury kind. I wasn't scared to face the mob. But I didn't want those crazy people to destroy the property of strangers who had nothing to do with the issue. For months after this incident, neighbours stared suspiciously at me—like I was the terrorist in their midst! Strange. Me? A woman who had faced sedition charges and survived (1991)? Hello! Sedition . . . treason . . . are you kidding me? But it happened. I know it in my memory as the notorious

Simranjit Singh Mann case. He was the IPS officer on the run after the assassination of Indira Gandhi. And I was the idiot journo who had interviewed him before he went underground.

Had the government of the time not fallen and had Chandra Shekhar not become India's eighth—and most short-lived—prime minister (seven months), I might have delivered Anandita in a filthy jail in Bhagalpur, where the trial was about to begin (Chandra Shekhar dismissed all those silly cases when he took office). I discovered the authorities make no concessions for 'traitors' in advanced stages of pregnancy, as I was at the time. The magistrate in the Bombay court told me tersely, 'You should have thought about your unborn baby before you indulged in all this.' Ha ha ha! 'All this'! I love it.

Unfortunately, ever since then, I show up as a 'fiery activist' in police records and on global computer screens. Which means I have trouble at most international airports, and a few domestic ones too. I am the woman who is invariably picked out and told to step aside, searched, body-scanned and more. I have had overzealous immigration cops saying, 'Keep your hands in the air while I go under your waistband.' I have also had them say loudly, 'I am going into your hair, do not reach for anything.' And 'Do you have anything sharp on you?' Yes, I wanted to shout, my brain! My tongue! But I uttered a glum, 'No,' and went along. What are these women looking for? 'Explosives,' informed a Mumbai cop knowledgeably. Okie!

Yet, this is the same woman who has been offered tickets on a silver platter to contest the Lok Sabha elections! Amusing when I look back at the irony of that! Me? Playing ball with a political party? Any political party? The first time it happened, I thought the mega industrialist making this offer was joking. I laughed it off, but he persisted. 'All you have to say is "yes" . . . the rest will be taken care of,' he said conspiratorially. I smiled broadly and drawled deliberately. 'I am saying "noooooo".' 'No? But why?' he couldn't believe his ears. 'Because I don't have the stomach for this dirty game,' I answered frankly. The man was aghast! He wasn't used to being turned down. By anyone! He kept quiet for a minute or two, and then said, 'Let me talk to your husband. I am sure he will agree with me. He is a sensible man.' I smiled, 'Go ahead. Ask him.' He walked across the room confidently and went into a huddle with Dilip. Remember, Dilip and I had not had the chance to discuss this at all. Guess what? It took Dilip all of two seconds to decline the Big Daddy's magnanimous offer! To Big Daddy's credit, he took the rejection on the chin. He shrugged, turned to me and grinned with a thumbs down sign. I have to say, he pleasantly surprised me. And we remain on good terms. 'You are too much to handle,' he tells me these days. That's funny. Really? Too much to handle by whom? In what way? I don't want to be 'handled'! Happy to handle myself.

Ditto for 'offers' to become the sheriff of Mumbai. Various 'agents' would come up with the proposal and say, 'But you will have to come with us and meet the chief minister and convince him before we propose your name officially.' Um. I think I'll pass! I told the astonished emissary. She was stumped, 'But . . . but . . . why not? Anybody would give an arm and a leg for this high-profile position!' Well, I put a much higher value on my arm and leg, so thanks, but no thanks. What glory was she talking about? A sheriff's role has zero attraction for me. It is an empty, meaningless post designed to boost the appointee's vanity. It requires the appointed person to receive and see off visiting dignitaries at unearthly hours. And host tea parties at one's own expense. Big deal. That too without a holster and a gun! Ridiculous.

Goodwill has always played a huge role in diffusing potentially dangerous situations. I remind my children of these occasions only for them to realize the importance of behaving courteously at all times. Those young reporters are professionals doing a job. They must be treated with respect and consideration. That's the least one can do. Meeting these enthusiastic kids, I am reminded of my own rookie days when it was often hard to get a toehold inside a crowded room full of senior journos. Being consistently polite to one and all should become an intrinsic part of one's nature. Put-on politeness is easy to spot. Especially the smarmy, exaggerated, gushy variety. Politeness costs nothing. But it pays rich dividends when you need it the most. People are entities with feelings, they must never be treated as 'invisibles'. It is a matter of training, I tell my children. Even if you cannot remember the person's name, but he/she looks familiar, smile and exchange a greeting. I run into young catering college graduates who are now in top, managerial jobs at hotels across the world; some are working for posh cruise ships. It's a lovely feeling when they come to the table to say, 'We had met you eighteen/twenty years ago . . .' The power of goodwill cannot be underestimated . . . I say this through experience and with gratitude.

~

When the rowdies came to my door baying for my blood, I was alone at home. As I mentioned, a well-meaning reporter had tipped me off about the aggressive morcha. The police, of course, knew in advance and were there in full force. A lady with a beautiful voice called me and introduced herself as the local head of the SPG (Special Protection Group). She said she had sent some cops over on hearing about the proposed morcha and there was nothing to worry about.

I was not worried, but curious. So is this how it works? Within minutes there were twenty cops inside our home. I looked out from the balcony and saw police vans blocking the entrance to our building. A few minutes later, 'they' turned up. I call them 'they' because they don't deserve to be identified. These are hired goons who will protest against anything and anyone if they are paid enough. They had come with a generous 'gift' for me—two gigantic trays of vada pav (a local snack that I actually love!), threatening to stuff it down my throat in front of television cameras.

By that time, there was a huge press contingent waiting for the tamasha to begin. The slogan-shouting started to get louder and louder as the goons performed for the cameras and hurled abuse at me. I watched it all like it was happening to someone else. I was not afraid in the least. Just baffled! So much fuss over an innocuous tweet! Surely, these political parties should have had something better to protest against. 'Popcorn vs vada pav' is hardly a national debate endangering Maharashtra's security. Why the touchiness? Is the Maharashtrian identity only embedded inside the soft, delicious potato vada? Is it that fragile? I love being Maharashtrian. But mercifully, my version of being a Maharashtrian differs radically from the virulent, militant, ugly and aggressive form that was being thrust on me with a vada pav loyalty test.

I had to make a split-second decision—to go down and face the music (vada pav) or stay upstairs in the safety of my well-fortified home, and wait for the hooligans to disperse. My real anxiety was not about personal safety. What if these miscreants pelted stones at my neighbours driving home from work, or damaged their cars? I decided to go down and go eyeball to eyeball with them. It was a good decision. This way, I also got the chance to interact directly with the media, instead of avoiding presswallas who were sending out incomplete details about the fracas. A few arrests had taken place and the protesters were stepping up their demands for an immediate, public and contrite apology from me for 'hurting the sentiments of the Maharashtrian people'. The hell I was going to offer one.

It should have ended there but it didn't. What followed was a messy saga with a contempt notice slapped on me. I was asked to appear before the members of the Legislative Assembly in Mumbai and 'explain' my tweet. But there was an absurd catch—even if I did appear and 'explain' those 140 characters, the Speaker had the right not to accept my explanation. This attracted a jail term of ninety days. It was to be a modern-day version of a Draupadi trial conducted mainly by boorish leering men, out to strip me of my dignity and pride. I preferred to take them on and fight the contempt charges in the Supreme Court. I was not just fighting for my personal freedom but for the fundamental rights of all citizens of India—for the freedom of speech, which is enshrined in our Constitution.

I could never ever have undertaken this arduous and extremely stressful exercise, had it not been for the phenomenal support I received from Mr Dé. He was magnificent! There is no other word for what he accomplished. Looking back, I find the amount of effort and time he invested in the case extraordinarily touching and awe-inspiring. I watched awestruck as he worked tirelessly to put the relevant papers together and send them on to our friend, the top senior legal counsel Aryama Sundaram, in Delhi. Not only is Aryama brilliant, he is also a loyal and true friend.

When we called Aryama to ask whether he would represent me, he didn't hesitate for a microsecond—'Of course,' he replied, adding, 'let's start the paperwork immediately. Send me everything you can find on the case.' Suddenly, we both felt a tremendous boost of energy and confidence surging through us. I was crying and so was my husband. This was the right decision, the only decision. We had faith in the judiciary. We believed we had a strong case and we would win. It was a tense, touch-and-go Tuesday morning for us in Mumbai. The appeal was heard by a two-member bench headed by Justice Dipak Misra, the current chief justice of India. I was granted a permanent stay! It was a great moment for not just me, but for every citizen. I felt vindicated on several levels. No law had been broken by me at any stage. There had never been any intention on my part to insult or cause hurt to anybody. The question of disrupting the proceedings of the house did not arise.

When the MLA who had slapped contempt charges against me in the assembly read the Supreme Court directive, he arrogantly issued a press statement asking, 'But who is the Supreme Court?' Buddy, you got your answer. Why not just shut up and accept it?

On Aryama's advice I had decided to stay put and not rush to Delhi. It was good advice. Fortunately, the case did come up as scheduled (it was number nine on the board), and we managed to get a stay. The ball was now in the Speaker's court. The battle was short and savagely fought. But I am happy to report the story ended well. And I started relishing vada pav once more—the spicier the better. There is an added thrill to the vada pav snack break these days. But hey—popcorn is still sold at the movies.

~

It was a nasty time, but not without an upside. My nerves were jangled beyond belief. I was dealing with a media onslaught that involved countless interviews—print, radio and television. There were times I couldn't even grab a few minutes for a meal. Most of the policewomen assigned to my home were young and in touch with what was going on. They would urge me to drink water and bite into an apple between all those sound bites. I found that most endearing. Woman to woman, they understood my plight. I was not alone in this fight.

I am happy to state I received unprecedented and enormous support from the press and citizens across the country. The state assembly's resolve to suppress and silence an individual was seen for what it was—plain bullying. Even as uncouth legislators spewed abuse and used the most despicable language to put me down, it was a different story in the streets of Mumbai, and in streets across India, people would approach me spontaneously—women to give me a wordless hug, men to say 'salute'. They empathized perfectly with what I was going through. They too were experiencing similar sinking feelings—of being 'dabao-ed', browbeaten by authorities. We were being treated like ants being trampled on by oppressors, drunk on their own power. The climate in India had altered dramatically and it was getting harder for citizens to speak up. They too knew it was likely to get tougher. They were as afraid for themselves as they were for me. 'Please continue to speak your mind,' they would urge. And that, more than anything else, was really what kept me going.

Friends were a little more cautious, understandably so. Some phoned, adopting the same irritating clichés: 'Hey Shobhaa, are you okay?' I wanted to yell, 'No, you twits. I am definitely *not* okay!' But I would answer tiredly, 'Yes, yes, yes, I am fine. Mr Dé is on top of it.' He most certainly was! Hours and hours were spent by him to prepare the all-important 'paper book' (generally prepared by a solicitor's firm), to pass on to Aryama Sundaram's superb legal team. It was Mr Dé who tracked and clipped every press clipping, television reportage, previous judgments and researched the technical implications of the contempt charge. What he produced (a weighty volume) was monumental, comprehensive, invaluable and complete. A true labour of love that overwhelmed me completely. His commitment! His focus! His hard work! His pyaar! It's a debt I can never repay. He will, no doubt, recoil at that word (debt). But I want to place my deepest gratitude on record.

The few friends who stood by must be acknowledged too. Like the loyal couple, for example, my close and loving friends of thirty years. The husband was all set to lead a citizens' march to Azad Maidan, protesting against the harassment. 'We will all be there to march in solidarity,' he said staunchly, adding, 'not sure it will help you, given my beard and Muslim identity. You don't need a *daadhiwalla mulla* leading the protest!' That's what it has come to.

Some 'friends' stopped calling, since they knew my phones were tapped. Hardly any of them turned up at home—they didn't want to be identified by the cops guarding my door. I failed to understand their cowardice. What were they afraid of? Getting on to some goons' hit list for being my 'friends'? I don't need such gutless people in my life. Two of my siblings occasionally made the mandatory calls to check on me. I guess they too didn't want to get 'involved'. Or am I being unfair? In any case, my life was never on a parallel track with theirs. It has always been far removed from the world they occupy. For them, perhaps I remain a brash, outspoken younger sister bringing trouble upon herself. Even though Mandakini repeatedly assures me these days that she has always been proud of me, Ashok used to say the same. But never to my face! I'd hear it from others. Maybe I am wrong. It's possible they were most concerned and didn't know how to express it. In any case, I don't hold grudges.

And then there was Sunita, a warm, generous and wonderful friend of forty years. Sunita, this time you are in my book 'officially'. From the day we met, we knew we would be friends forever. Sunita used to joke each time a new novel of mine was published—'I am a character in all her books and stories. Try to guess which one?' And it's true. Well, now is the right time for Sunita to play herself. At one point when the heat was getting to me, and I was physically and emotionally drained, I called her spontaneously to ask, 'Where are you?' Sunita lives between four cities. 'I am in Delhi. Come! Don't think. Just get on to the next plane and come here. I leave for Ranikhet in a day or so. Let's go together. Get on that flight.'

I did exactly that. Nobody was to know my plan or location except my immediate family. That was the advice I was given by Aryama Sundaram, after assessing the situation. It was pretty hairy and tense, with new and filthy abuses being hurled at me on a daily basis. 'We want to teach this woman a lesson once and for all,' thundered an MLA with a criminal record and a couple of murder charges to his name. I followed Sunita's advice. I didn't think. I flew to Delhi. Once I landed, Sunita took over my life seamlessly, just as she had thirty-five years ago, when I had faced another major personal crisis. She asked for no details, no explanations. Quietly and efficiently, she took me grocery shopping to a sprawling food store, and we stocked up for our trip to Ranikhet. I had no idea how long I would stay there, and she didn't ask.

We drove up chatting and laughing, snacking and singing. The Mumbai goons and my problems receded into nothingness by the time we arrived at her beautiful home. 'Stay with me in my room,' she urged, 'I don't want you to be alone.' And that's where I healed. Felt energized. I watched Sunita cook, cut vegetables, feed her dogs, knit sweaters, tend to her garden, meet her friends, have her feet massaged three times a day, smoke in bed (horror!), chase away stray leopards from her compound wall, flirt with retired army men, laugh a lot, and nothing more was needed but her silent support and loving understanding.

She drove me around the rugged terrain tirelessly, pointing out various peaks, as we waited for the range to emerge from the clouds. She took me to the only Mrityunjaya temple in the region, where I had a strange experience with a tantric who was meditating in one of the caves near the temple complex. He had just roasted a sweet potato on his *trishul* when I barged in, not knowing he was inside. He looked up like he was expecting me and gave me half the potato to eat. He said slowly and clearly, 'There are forces working against you. The winds are strong. But you are stronger. They can't touch you.' How did he know what I was going through? He just knew. After that short exchange, I was dismissed. I told him I would find him at the *kumbh*. He laughed, 'A sadhu cannot be found by anyone—a sadhu finds you!' Sunita and I were stunned.

Driving back, I told her what the pujari of my favourite Shiva temple in Mumbai had said when I had gone there during the *aarti*, at the height of the trouble. He had signalled to me to wait till he finished conducting the aarti. My heart was pounding, wondering what he wanted to say. The temple bells were clanging and he was blowing into the conch as the flames from the camphor on the puja thali lit up the space. Once the other devotees had left, he lowered his voice and said very sombrely, *'Aap ki jaan khatrey mein hai. Aap apne parivar ke baarey mein sochiye.'* I asked him what he was talking about, and he placed his finger on his mouth and said, 'You don't know these people. They are dangerous. And you have angered them.' I understood later that the same goons who had organized the morcha to my home were regulars at his temple and he had overheard their plans. It was a disturbing conversation. As I recounted it to Sunita, the hairs on her forearms stood on end. We drove back in silence. That night, she was extra caring over dinner, as we chatted at the dining table, and heard the howls of wild dogs in the distance. I can never forget this special time with this very special woman.

There is a lovely Tamil word that sort of sums up my feelings towards all those who stood by me and said, 'You know what? You'll be fine! We love you. Who cares about those rotters?' That Tamil word is *nanri*. So yes, I am filled with nanri when I look back at that black period. The overused word 'gratitude' really doesn't describe the essence of this delicate emotion as evocatively.

~

'So what can I do for you, madam?'

Politicians are bad news. In Bollywood parlance: *Mujhey unn sabse se nafrat hai*. I really detest the breed. The breed detests me in return. It's almost pathological. In all these years of neta-watching, I have yet to come across a single politician who has touched my heart. A lot of them have touched my mind—that's not tough. They are super smart, articulate, cunning, even witty. Their job is to deploy words and the better ones do that effortlessly. But to win someone over, to earn respect—that takes much more than manipulating words and emotions. I am not even intrigued by politicians! If anything they bore me. Those devious games they play. The clever moves they make. It's all so depressingly programmed and predictable.

The older breed—here I am talking Morarji Desai and his generation—represented our future. India was young then, and so was I. India was filled with hope. As was I. But even at that age, the pomposity of office made the man appear puny. I felt exactly the same way when I was part of a delegation invited to meet the former President of India, Pranab Mukherjee, in the Yellow Room of the magnificent Rashtrapati Bhavan in Delhi. I can understand tight security and protocol. What I don't get is the exaggerated air of grandeur and ceremony. India is a democracy. Every individual occupying that lofty position is there because the people of the country want him/her to be there. He/she is the first citizen. The most important word is 'citizen'. Equal to every other citizen. It is not an elected-by-the-*janta* position, in that sense. Our President has no real executive powers. But is supposed to inspire citizens by being a non-partisan head of the republic. A symbol of over a billion aspirations.

The Rashtrapati Bhavan is indeed magnificent. But it has become an embarrassing anachronism. Getting an audience with the great man/woman still rates as a memorable experience. But it is only after you have made it inside the staggeringly impressive building and gone through the immense and absurd theatrics of the all-important face time with the President of India, which lasts less than sixty seconds, that you wonder—do we need this? The Raj era lives on in a ludicrous manner inside that impressive edifice. My 'meeting' took place bang in the middle of the searing Delhi heat—a motley group of twenty-odd people were asked to 'rehearse'. We were herded around for this comical rehearsal before the President showed up. Rehearsal? For what? To be seated in the right order, to stand forming a perfect 'U'. To take our fixed places in the glare of the harsh mid-afternoon sun for the official portrait. Oh yes . . . none of us could wear sunglasses even though we were all facing the sun—that was the sole prerogative of the President of India. I was sorely disappointed. I turned to a European ambassador to see his reaction. He smiled, 'This place is much grander than the Élysée Palace.' Take that, Napoleon!

Whether it's someone in that genuinely exalted position, or a *maamuli* MLA throwing his weight around on a flight, something awful happens to people when they taste power. They lose perspective totally. Even the educated, supposedly sophisticated, intelligent ones who start off well. In an astonishingly short period of time, they turn into insufferable idiots. Everything changes—their body language and their language. Sometimes, the dramatic transformation happens on a very public platform—television. Fumbling, uncertain, crude 'netas', barely able to express a single coherent thought, display a drastic 'work in progress' during subsequent television appearances. It starts with personal grooming—the first thing to change is the hair. From unruly and unkempt, hair undergoes noticeable alteration. It gets darkened if it's grey. Shortened if it's long. The facial expression alters with more control over muscles. The eyes don't dart all over the place and teeth are rarely displayed. Overdue dental work gets fixed overnight. Women start colour-coordinating their outfits, and focus on matt make-up, so as to look less sweaty and more 'fashionable'. So do the men, ever since Prime Minister Narendra Modi brought sartorial flair into Parliament, his partymen seem to have engaged clones of his personal stylist and designer to create vivid colour mixes for them—pale yellow sleeveless jackets over mint-green kurtas. Both sexes learn to preen for the cameras. It's so much fun to look at old clips of some of the prominent politicians on the national scene. Vanity is what shouts out the most. If they appear unlikeable on television, they are much worse in person.

What gets me the most is the presumptuousness of politicians. Most assume you are dying to meet them. They really do believe in their own lies. The reason they think people want to hobnob with them is because they have such a low opinion of everyone else. To them, the world is divided into favour-seekers and bigger favour-seekers. They stare incredulously if the response to their standard question, 'So what can I do for you, madam?' is met with a cold stare and a curt, 'Nothing at all! Thank you very much!' So used are they to all sorts of people lining up for favours big and small, it is simply beyond their limited comprehension that there are loads of self-respecting citizens who would never stoop to ask for anything from their ilk. One such person was so angered when I gave him the freeze treatment that he followed me into the elevator and said snarkily, 'You have your nose in the air. You are too uppity.'

What gets me the most is the presumptuousness of politicians. Most assume you are dying to meet them. They really do believe in their own lies. The reason they think people want to hobnob with them is because they have such a low opinion of everyone else. To them, the world is divided into favour-seekers and bigger favour-seekers.

There have been several such encounters, including one with Narendra Modi, who on being introduced to me by an industrialist, just after becoming the prime minister, said sarcastically, 'Who doesn't know her? For years and years I have been at the receiving end of her criticism!' For once, I was stumped. On that sardonic note, I felt emboldened enough to ask for a selfie. He readily agreed. I tried and flopped (I am still hopeless at clicking selfies). When I confessed my attempts had flopped, he gathered a few people around and said gleefully, '*Dekha?* For the first time in her life, Shobhaa Dé has failed at something.' Touché! Not for nothing is he called one of the shrewdest, toughest, most ambitious men alive. A man who can think on his feet, fix adversaries, win over foes. And go for the kill.

I have been a declared, vocal and very public critic. That comes with a price tag. I have paid it happily. And will continue to do so. Taking our democratic privileges and fundamental rights for granted is something I am not willing to relinquish. I am not a political activist by any description. But I am an involved and engaged citizen of a great country, who, like all other citizens, believes in the freedoms guaranteed to us in our Constitution. Till the day the Constitution remains in its present form, I will continue to fight for what I have been promised and deeply believe in—all our precious freedoms as Indians.

~

Living dangerously is not such a bad thing

Friends ask what it was like living with cops outside our door, and on the front seat of the car, for close to two years. Frankly, it was funny! And a bit of a joke. Though their duties rotated, one or two of them became family. There wasn't a single aspect of my life they didn't know. Some people would find this a ghastly invasion of privacy, but it didn't bother me at all. I really don't have anything to hide. My daily routine is pretty mundane. I didn't care if they overheard all my conversations while travelling in the car, or witnessed me arguing with my husband, squabbling with my children, haggling with shopkeepers. They were just there, doing their jobs the best way they could.

Initially, I used to get bothered seeing how casually they dealt with their guns—tucking them into their waistbands, or leaving them on the table in front of them while they ate their meals. The sight of loaded weapons would rattle visitors, some of whom would refuse to enter our home or sit in the same car. My children didn't like the idea of cops being present at every family function—our daughter Arundhati's wedding included. Maybe the kids were embarrassed? Perhaps their friends made them feel this was 'not normal'. How many moms were under police protection? Surely, their mom must have done something wrong?

The cops assigned to protect me were earnest and happy to hang around. Since I barely leave my home during the day, their duty was pretty easy. They'd relax, wait for their meals, watch movies on the phone, listen to music, chat with the staff. When they accompanied me, they seemed to enjoy the outings, especially if those included a glamorous evening at a posh hotel, with the odd chance of running into a Bollywood star. Not that they ever forgot what they were there to do. I often wondered why they never stared at the road ahead when we were driving to some venue, but kept looking at the side mirror almost fixedly. Finally, I asked. 'Madam, we are trained to look out for motorcycle killers at traffic lights. Our guns are in our shoes when we get into the car. Hitmen generally approach from the back. Don't worry! Our aim is good.' We laughed. I did so uneasily. All the recent killings of journalists had happened in exactly the way it had been explained. These days, I look at any helmet-wearing, backpack-carrying motorcyclist who comes too close to the car with utmost suspicion and dread. Bang! Bang! And I'll be dead. It is that easy.

Over months, we became friends, and I got to understand more about their lives. One particular chap endeared himself to me so much, I started caring about his off-duty life and obvious concerns. We remain in touch and I am so proud of his progress. While he used to spend hours outside the front door, I would find him solving what looked like examination papers. He would be at it diligently, barely looking up, unless the visitor seemed 'unusual' (cops have a sixth sense about such matters). I asked him what he was studying so hard for, and he said it was to get into the Railway Police after clearing an online, competitive exam. Well, recently he sent me a cheerful WhatsApp image with the good news—he did it!

But it's his backstory that touched me the most. Born into a desperately poor family of bricklayers, he spent his childhood helping his father with masonry work in the village. Their family was shunned by upper-caste villagers who would refuse to serve them water during the scorching summer months. There were times when he and his two siblings didn't have even salt to eat with dry, burnt rotis prepared by their undernourished, sickly mother. When his father decided the boy should go to school, it was a major shock to the other villagers. The boy not only went to school, he excelled! When I met him, he told me proudly he had a master's degree. 'Which subject?' I asked. He blushed, 'English literature!' I said, 'Wow! I have lots of wonderful books I'll be happy to give them to you.' He looked crestfallen. 'But . . . I won't be able to read them!' I was puzzled and asked, 'Why not?' He kept silent. Then he confessed, that though he had a legitimate degree, he could neither speak English nor read it! Not even the headlines in the English newspapers I used to pass on to him. I was shocked. 'So how did you get that degree? Is it fake?' He told me how the quota system works in reality. Since he was the first boy from his village to pass out of school with reasonably good grades, he was encouraged to enrol in a local college. Once in, he was pushed ahead, year after year, till he graduated and applied for his master's programme. 'But didn't you have to attend classes and write papers?' He said he wrote in the Devanagari script, since he took notes the same way, and the teachers 'understood'. Since it was a matter of pride to have the first graduate from the village, nobody objected. When he got into the police force, armed with his degrees, his family's stock went up considerably. Now, whenever he returns to meet his parents, he is shown respect by the very same neighbours who had despised and humiliated all of them earlier. The best part of his story was his deep love for his parents. He sacrificed and toiled, because he had vowed to accomplish three things: get his sister married, educate his younger brother, build a pukka home for his parents. When I met him last, work had started on that promised home, his sister had been married off and his brother had passed his board exams with flying colours. 'What about you and your life now that you have fulfilled all your duties?' I teased him, 'When are you inviting me to your wedding?' He grinned, 'I am looking for a good girl who will look after my parents . . .'

The other cop was older, seasoned and cynical. For him this assignment was perfect. Though the two of them were supposed to take turns and be with me 24/7, I never ever kept them hanging around or insisted on night duty. After their afternoon *chai paani*, I would pack them off, saying, 'Nobody is going to kill me . . . run along . . . be with your family.' Their duty hours were so flexible, and their work so light, it was like a paid vacation for them. I rarely let them work on weekends, though they were assigned to it. People who visited felt uncomfortable to see burly black-belted cops at the door. It was funnier still if I was travelling to some event and had an armed guy occupying the front seat. I insisted they stuck to plain clothes and avoided uniforms. From time to time, their seniors would drop by to review the 'threat perception'. We would chat in the living room, sip tea, enjoy snacks and crime-beat gossip. Sometimes they would make strange requests. One of these officers came armed with a file filled with certificates and photographs of his eligible daughters. He said to me (ingratiating smile in place), 'Madam, you know big-big people in hi-fi society . . . please find a suitable match for my daughters . . . see, see . . . they are educated, fair-complexioned and good-looking . . . we are prepared to give dowry also.' I was caught off guard. Finally, I joked, 'I have an unmarried daughter myself. I am also looking for a groom.' At another 'review' meeting, the man brought his attractive wife along and said, 'My missus is a fashion designer . . . can you please help her to find good clients from your circle?' This is so us. So typical of India. And I love the informality of such peculiar requests during 'official' meetings ostensibly being conducted to assess whether I was on someone's hit list!

My last visit to the nearest police station was priceless. It was yet another 'review' meeting. I walked in with the older, beefier cynical cop, who was asked by a senior, 'How many rounds are you carrying to protect Madam in case she is attacked?' He answered carefully, 'Sir . . . thirty.' The senior scratched his head thoughtfully and said, 'Not enough. I think that can be upgraded to ninety!' My jaw dropped. But my bodyguard was cool, 'Okay, sir, so, I will need a carbine from tomorrow . . .' It was comical. There I was in an overcrowded cop station, with a sprawling slum across the road and several unsavoury drunks who had been picked up for a nasty brawl involving knives sitting on the floor next to me and squabbling noisily. Their womenfolk were yelling from a few feet away, '*Maaro saalon ko . . . andar hi rakkho, saala madarchud . . .*' And here we were discussing a carbine-wielding bodyguard for me! What had I done? Tweeted! About *dahi misal* and vada pav. About compulsory prime-time screening of Marathi films at multiplexes. That's it! Aaah—huge crime. How silly of me! I flatly refused and told the senior cop the old arrangement was just fine. He shrugged, 'Madam, it is up to you. If you think there is less threat perception than we think there is, that is your decision. Don't blame us if something happens . . .' If something happens, my dearest fellow, I'll be dead. I won't be around to pin blame. But thank you very much for your concern.

A couple of months later, I signed off on this crazy protection. And got my life back!

We are still in touch, my 'boys' and I. They had become a part of our family, and a certain attachment developed over time. We knew which cop liked sugary, milky tea and which preferred strong coffee. We kept track of their fasting days and made sure we cooked *upwaas* food (*sabudana* khichdi or upma—no onions, no garlic, no masalas). When Arundhati got married, they were right there at all the ceremonies. One of them even chased a press photographer who had managed to sneak in through an unguarded entrance at the back of the venue, and politely asked him to delete all the pictures he had clicked surreptitiously (he didn't!). They were there when we rushed to the hospital for Arundhati's delivery, and they were there when I broke down and fought back tears at an emotionally charged event. Both were good men assigned to perform a duty they may or may not have enjoyed. I like to think their time with my family was one they will look back on with fondness. As for us, out of sheer habit, we leave the house expecting to be greeted cheerfully by one of the men!

For me, being protected by cops was just another interesting experience. I still don't know what exactly the threat perception was, nor do I want to find out. All I do know is that no less than four senior diplomats from Europe generously offered me 'asylum' in their countries. Perhaps they were in the know about something I wasn't aware of. Remember, this was when writers, bloggers and rationalists were being cold-bloodedly murdered. I had appeared on countless panel discussions on television, talking about the alarming rise in intolerance, about 'award *wapsi*' and other troubling developments. I had stuck my neck out over and over again. And the political dummies were at it, doing what they do best—abusing and threatening.

Some of us at that time were viciously targeted by trolls and politicians, and dubbed 'presstitutes', 'sicularists' and 'libtards'. I recall responding with a couldn't-care-less 'proud to be a presstitute' on Twitter, which led to more trolling. But it had to be said. Many things had to be said. Now I am wondering—what difference did it make? There is zero room left for any sort of logical discourse with those in authority. The state has appropriated total power. The state is everything. The state is bigger than anybody. The state can fix any citizen, any time. When I realized my phones were tapped (it is so clumsily done, I feel like interrupting and saying something provocative just to wake up the interceptors), I didn't feel alarmed. Being monitored and eavesdropped on by Big Brother is now a part of life. I am told I am watched and followed as well. I must be doing something right! Watch and follow, snoop away. And if you do find something interesting, share it with me.

The state has appropriated total power. The state is everything. The state is bigger than anybody. The state can fix any citizen, any time.

I guess there are some individuals who attract trouble. I am one of them. People stupidly ask whether I consciously 'court controversy'. What rubbish! Who does that? Perhaps a few desperadoes with a great deal of time on their hands and nothing to lose. I have no use for controversy. It's expensive, pointless and pretty unaffordable in the long run. It serves no purpose and can be tedious and tiresome as hell. Is compliance the opposite of controversy? If so, then you could say I am anything but compliant and passive. 'Complicit' is a dirty word. 'Complicit' is worse than 'compromised'. I remain my own person. Is that a crime these days? This can lead to situations that my children call 'highly avoidable'. They admonish me far more than my husband. I guess it has to do with experience. 'Mama—why can't you stay shut for a change?' they scold me if I speak out on an issue. 'Is it going to make the slightest difference what you state? No! Just stay out of all this nonsense and mind your own business.' Sensible advice. But who says I am sensible? Or that I even like sensible?

I really don't know who I am fooling when I vow to behave after I have annoyed my family greatly and been in the news for all the 'wrong' reasons. I tell myself to keep mum, lie low, not react, stop tweeting, get off social media, show more restraint. These resolutions don't last for even a day. The thing is, our lives throw up so much rich material! How can we not respond to stimuli? What's the point of being 'in it' and yet staying 'out of it', if you can't or don't participate? Soon, my grandchildren will be of an age when they can figure their naani is somewhat 'off'. As in, odd. Different. They might compare me to the other naanis of their friends and shudder. Well, this is the naani they have and they'd better get used to her. I can't change and have no desire to. I hope they can see beyond the oddities ('a tattoo-wali naani—how funny!'), and accept their naani just the way she is. Like I accept them—those monster poppets capable of effortlessly breaking my heart.

Living dangerously is a very attractive option.

I feel like a complete fraud when strangers walk up to me to shake hands and declare admiringly, 'Ma'am, you are so bold, so brave, so courageous.' I swiftly correct them. I am nothing of the sort. If I am brave, so are we all. I have not faced bullets nor been in a seriously life-threatening situation so far. If I have not tested myself in those contexts, what is 'brave'? Standing up to bullies? Of course I have done that and will continue to. My husband calls me an overgrown 'teenage rebel' and points out all the incidents from my past when as a schoolgirl, I rashly bucked the system and behaved with the sort of useless defiance that only silly little girls indulge in when they loathe discipline and their teachers. That sort of defiance achieves nothing in the long run. I lost out on a hell of a lot at school because I was impetuous and defiant. 'It's in your DNA,' my husband says to make me feel less bad.

My siblings were model students—high achievers who never disobeyed their teachers. Look at me. Getting into one mess after another—at seventy! My children think it's daft. So do I. But I can't help myself. Who would have imagined a tweet about a grossly overweight policeman would have stirred a national debate and led to so much trolling? It was a win–win situation for everyone but me. The cop received free treatment from a surgeon who made headlines. And a media-savvy nutritionist milked the moment to get hired as a consultant to the police force. When the story broke, and I was accused of 'fat-shaming' a poor cop who was suffering from stones in his gall bladder (as I found out later through his interviews), I was thousands of miles away in Reykjavik, the capital of Iceland. Everything seemed surreal and absurd as my phone kept ringing. It was minus 8 degrees, Reykjavik had experienced a record snowfall in four hours, and the city had come to a standstill, with mounds and mounds of snow burying cars, homes, bridges. Never had I seen such blinding whiteness. I wanted to take it all in. I knew we would never experience anything like this ever again. But calls from India kept interrupting my sense of wonder. And the subject was a cop from Madhya Pradesh who needed to lose weight drastically. I switched off my mobile phone. I hadn't come to Iceland to give sound bites about a poor man who needed a fat-reduction procedure but didn't have the money (after my tweet, he received generous funding, and subsequently thanked me publicly for saving him). I was there to live a dream. The one I had cherished since I was ten years old.

The first time I read *Heidi*, I wanted to know what it felt like to be with a grandfather. Both of mine were dead by the time I was born. I envied Heidi and her life in the mountains, surrounded by goats, sheep, cows, horses, enjoying the sight of snow-covered peaks and spending time with a loving old man—her grandfather. The Northern Lights were mentioned in the book. And all I dreamt of back then was to see these wonderful lights some day. I became a little obsessed with the aurora borealis, and stayed obsessed.

When the trip finally materialized, more than fifty years later, I couldn't believe we would be standing awestruck on a low hill in a tiny village called Hella, mesmerized by the dazzling show of ever-changing lights in the northern sky. Neon green, yellow, orange, purple and pink—the patterns kept whirling dizzily overhead as we tried to imprint them on our minds forever. It was the most significant trip of my life and I remain grateful to my husband for making it happen. At one point I did feel afraid, uncharacteristically so. As we stepped out for our first sighting, I experienced a panic attack. I didn't want to take one more step on that slippery ice. My fingers were numb with the cold. I was misjudging distances, feeling disoriented and sick. Even the sky didn't tempt me to look up and gaze at what we had travelled so many miles to see. I kept repeating, 'I don't like it, I don't like it, get me out of here. I don't want to see anything.' Around us, Japanese enthusiasts were aiming sophisticated cameras at the lights and capturing the celestial dance expertly. And there I was, refusing to look up at a long-cherished fantasy that had finally become a reality. What was wrong with me?

I still don't know what happened that night. Could have been the thin air, the biting cold, lack of acclimatization, dehydration. This behaviour was so odd for me, my husband was baffled. If he felt disappointed by my reaction, he didn't say it. It was a mind-boggling spectacle and he was there to enjoy every microsecond. I am glad I overcame my fear the next night and the night after. We were most fortunate to see the lights on three consecutive occasions. This is pretty rare, as some of our fellow travellers told us. A few of them had been chasing the lights for years and from different locations. A couple had spent ten days in Norway and gone home without a single sighting. Others had had a glimpse or two but with very faint lights that disappeared as quickly as they had appeared. So I feel blessed many times over. I will forever look back on this special trip and thank Heidi and Dilip for making it happen in the most wondrous and loving way!

Nearly a month later, I was still under a spell. I was literally seeing lights. But more than just the thrill of experiencing something as magical, I began searching for my own internal 'lights'—the elusive ones that were as capricious as the Northern Lights. We all have our personal lights glowing away within. We forget to switch them on most of the time! Or worse, even when they are blazing away, we focus on the darkness surrounding them. Experts say all of us are 'born' with characteristics that define us for life. Like, saturnine creatures remain saturnine till they die. Or night owls stay night owls, while nightingales are the happy, rise-and-shine, blessed ones making the most of daylight hours. I have always preferred the night for everything I enjoy—write, eat, relax, read, travel, listen to music, watch movies. Um. Sex. Give me a late-night flight over a dawn one any day. Just the thought of waking up early induces serious stress, and I can't fall asleep a week in advance just thinking about that damn flight!

The trip to Iceland gave me time and opportunity to think in an environment stripped of the familiar. Travelling abroad was once the ultimate thrill for me as a young girl with severely limited resources. Even today, it's that young girl whose eyes light up when a 'foreign' trip is scheduled. No matter how many times I have gone overseas, I still feel my heart pounding when I think of 'abroad'—especially that special 'abroad smell'. My children tell me the same thing. When we walk into a few destinations in India, we look at each other delightedly and trill, 'Abroad smell.' And what is this special smell? I'd say it's the smell of all things posh. Of luxuries that were unaffordable, completely out of reach years ago, or experiences we thought were impossibly exotic. It is the smell of money and possibility.

While I miss India's special 'smell' terribly after a week spent at a foreign destination, I still look out for that heady mix of freshly ground coffee beans, the aroma of buttery croissants straight out of the oven, a seductive bouquet of divine perfumes and aftershave lotions—it's a whole bunch of elements I find attractive. And I think, 'Well, my grandchildren will grow up taking these very aromas for granted. Urban India smells like 'abroad' more and more. And that's incredible! Confusing too. When I stroll into a glittering shopping mall in Mumbai these days, I could be anywhere in the world—it's equally soulless and impersonal. But it also exudes a level of reassurance. We are not all that 'poor' any more, even though we actually are. We are *amir log*! We have money and cars and cheese and wine. My grandkids may not know the meaning of deprivation ever, or perhaps their idea of deprivation will have changed radically. Though I never ever felt 'deprived' even when there wasn't any extra money to throw around on 'non-essentials'. I grew up with the fixed idea of any form of waste being a sin. I still feel the same way about it. I recycle whatever can be recycled. I reuse and reuse. I don't throw away what I call 'perfectly good stuff' even though it is about to fall apart.

I grew up in a different India, a different social environment. Everybody knew everybody else! By name. Our worlds were that small. Neighbours walked in and out of one another's homes without calling to check if it was okay. That was considered normal. People who chose to stay aloof were treated with suspicion ('What are they hiding?'). The genuinely reticent ones were dubbed 'eccentric'. The concept of being a loner by choice was alien ('Why would anybody want to be alone?'). Today, I barely know my neighbours.

There was a major fire in our high-rise residential complex recently. I was travelling, but two of my daughters were at home and fast asleep when the fire broke out in a flat right above our floor. They grabbed Gong Li, our Pekinese, and rushed down in their pyjamas . . . standing in the darkness, waiting for the fire brigade to arrive, they found several neighbours also in their nightclothes—more embarrassed about being 'caught' in such a dishevelled state by people they only met in the elevators than worried about the fire spreading to other floors! Women in nighties, stripped of their public faces (read: no make-up) and with their otherwise perfectly coiffed hair in a mess were miserable and awkward. Nobody spoke. Nobody hugged or reassured anybody else. The kids were busy taking selfies against the backdrop of the fire!

How alarmingly impersonal our lives have become! Here's another telling example: A plumber employed by the building society died suddenly after working in the complex for twenty-four long years. A kind office-bearer of the society decided to get members to contribute towards a fund for the man's family. Here's a person who had been visiting all our homes for over two decades, unclogging potties, fixing leaky taps, replacing showerheads. And yet, very few people could remember either the man's name or his face! Residents asked quizzically, 'Who died? The plumber? Which one was he? Short or tall?' Blank! Most people were blank! The man had simply not registered on their mind's screen! These people were not being arrogant or mean—they were just too preoccupied with their own lives to notice others who were not 'important' enough.

~

Why do I tweet? Am I nuts?

Nobody stays completely immune to criticism, even if the person claims indifference and detachment. Some people are hyper touchy. Others vindictive. I know friends who have waited for a decade or more to settle scores. I have zero energy to wage war. For the most part, I really couldn't care less for what some disgruntled person has said or written. Take social media—sure, it's a monster nobody can tame. Live with it at your own peril. It can devour and devastate anybody! In that sense it's a very democratic monster, and I respect this monster a lot, even when I have been chewed to pieces. Trolls are 'hidden people'. People in Iceland (the land of the original trolls) believe in these hidden people, like we in India believe in spirits and *bhoot-pret*. Trolls are an important part of Icelandic mythology. But for most of us who are visible on social media platforms, trolls are vicious, nameless people who stalk and target those who don't agree with their views. That is too generous a description! I think trolls on Twitter are just people with no *kaam dhanda* other than to heap abuse on strangers. The only reason I am not affected by trolls is because I never read nor respond to comments on my tweets. I say what I have to say, and that's where it ends. People are surprised when I tell them this. But I have found my attitude to be the least wasteful, most energy-saving way of hanging on to one's sanity. Of course, it's a nasty world out there! If you have a thin skin, don't get into the space. If you are already in the space and find it hard to stomach the daily abuse, jump out! Nobody will miss you! That's the fun of social media. Attention spans are ridiculously short and today's social media star can be taken apart and thrown into the dustbin within seconds. You are as relevant as your last tweet.

Why do I tweet?

Because I am an idiot! God knows why people follow me . . .

I enjoy tweeting. And I am not an immature, attention-seeking idiot tweeting recklessly about anything and everything. I know perfectly well what I want to say in 140 characters. If people find that fun, that's great. If not, so what? The reactions to my tweets are interesting. A charming compère at an award show introduced me by saying, 'One tweet from you shakes up Parliament!' I scratched my head and thought, 'Really?' That's not *why* I tweet, though. I want to shake myself up, first! How can one not react to the political and social environment? I have never been a passive bystander to life's moving circus. If what I tweet does cause reverberations, I figure I must be doing something right! My husband says I get a childish kick out of being provocative. Conversely, what I see as 'normal' is deemed provocative by others with a more conservative outlook. I find the idea of disruption very attractive. No wonder I like Arvind Kejriwal—India's Great Disrupter. It was always this way. Twitter suits this side of my personality perfectly. If a price has to be paid for outspokenness at a time when most lips are sealed, I am happy to stand up and be counted.

After a trip to Delhi, I was asked by a Dilliwalla if I had noticed a peculiar Delhi phenomenon. Which one, I wondered. 'Nobody is willing to open the mouth and say something—anything! People are so scared and wary. Notice how shifty-eyed everyone is . . . looking over the shoulder . . . just in case there is a sarkari snoop around.' Absurd! 'Why do you stick your neck out?' I was asked. Because I have a neck, I joked. 'But look at the level of personal attacks.' Yup. Go ahead. Look at them! Aren't they foolish? 'No—you are foolish.' That's what I am told by 'well-wishers' constantly. It's too late to stop being foolish.

I like being foolish. Criticism? I can take it in my stride. If that had not been so, I would have been dead . . . or silent . . . decades ago.

At a super lavish party in Delhi, a very successful but slightly drunk man kept repeating, 'Madam, I salute you. You are so gutsy, don't you feel scared?' Huh? I must have looked totally baffled! Initially, I thought, is he confusing me with someone else, perhaps a television anchor, an activist, a politician? My husband was seated between us on a large sofa in the garden, making it a little difficult for this gentleman to slither any closer. I asked, 'Scared? About what? Scared of whom?' He looked over his shoulder (people in Delhi do that a lot, it's almost a reflex action), and indicated with a hand gesture that I could be shot. I burst out laughing. 'Why would anybody waste a bullet on me?' He leant across my husband and said in a hoarse whisper, 'Many people, madam, many people.' This was months before Gauri Lankesh's murder rocked India. He then went on to narrate how 'dangerous' it was in the current political environment to open one's mouth and express views that did not echo those held by those in power. 'Madam, in Delhi it is like this—you keep your mouth shut, and your head low. You never know who might be listening and then taking action against you.' He pointed to his attractive wife, 'She keeps warning me not to say anything controversial to anyone. But after a few drinks, I start blabbing . . . can't stop myself. But, madam, you just say whatever comes to your mind . . . that is not allowed.' Allowed! I hate that word. I merely smiled and told him the option of keeping mum does not appeal to me. Never has. Never will. I reminded him (and myself!)

that I was not some giddy-headed, immature, irresponsible schoolgirl shooting my mouth off to attract attention. What I expressed in the public space was something I staunchly believed in. If that was unpalatable to a few, so be it. If the consequences of taking a stand were unpleasant—that's that! I also gave credit to my husband and children for standing by me when things got rough. They may not have agreed with my views. But they respected my right to express them. The man beamed and pumped my husband's hand. 'So you are the hero. Congratulations, Sir. Boss, *aap kamaal ke aadmi ho*.'

I was not some giddy-headed, immature, irresponsible schoolgirl shooting my mouth off to attract attention. What I expressed in the public space was something I staunchly believed in. If that was unpalatable to a few, so be it.

See what I mean? This was such a transparent and innocent response, I didn't feel in the least offended. The man ordered another drink and must have gone home a happy fellow thinking, 'No wonder she is gutsy! She has a strong man behind her!' Aaaah—the delicious ironies women deal with! Such an attitude does not bug me, because it is upfront and minus hypocrisy. Most men and women cling on to stereotypes, because any other kind of thinking demands too much effort.

I keep questioning myself about this whole 'gutsy', 'courageous' business. So many women—complete strangers—walk up to me at airports and other public places to pump my hand, hug me, take selfies and tell me they 'admire my courage'! Some go further and add, 'You are one of the few women in India with balls.' Sometimes, my chest puffs up with pride, and I turn to my children/husband and gloat, 'See? And all of you constantly criticize me.' They don't take offence, they just look exasperated! 'Oh please, Mother/wife . . . get over it! What does it cost anybody to say that? Nothing. You like flattery. It is your weakness. Would any of these people calling you *himmatwali* or Mardaani Bai ever switch positions with you? No, they won't! They are clever. They know how to protect their own interests and stay out of trouble. Look at you! You open your mouth constantly—and what do you get? Abuses! Threats. Even open death threats. For *what*? Are you an activist? No, you aren't. Are you a politician? A crusader? A martyr? Then why the hell are you sticking your neck out? There are zero benefits and far too much hostility out there. Just calm down and mind your own business. Look after your health. Enjoy your grandchildren. Chill! This is your time to put your feet up and do what other women your age do.' Are they right? Am I a childish, monumental, gullible, naive fool? I dare not look for the correct answer, if there is one, that is. What if my kids have provided it and I have pig-headedly rejected it? But I have to say this, I have never backed off from a fight or backed down when challenged. I don't see that happening in the future either.

If there is one card I have consistently refused to play, it's the victim card. As a woman, I find it insulting to trot out my gender and use it as a shield when attacked. I felt most disheartened to read Barbra Streisand's comments on being discriminated against as a woman director. She mentioned it was not just men who didn't want to be directed by a woman, but other women too. I have always admired

Streisand and her enormous talent. She is outspoken and articulate, politically informed and feisty. Why then the whining? Why now? Sometimes, I feel bad for women in privileged positions who pull out the 'I would have been far more acknowledged had I been a man' at the tail end of their careers. Get over it! Why not stand back and admit maybe you were not that amazing, after all? Seventy is the time to own up. Just be brave enough to admit at least to yourself that you have fucked up—not once, but multiple times. It's not easy, but at least it makes you feel lighter. You cut the flab the minute you say, 'Hey. You know what? I was wrong.' The pressure you place on yourself by claiming to be right all the time becomes unbearable and starts to give you—I don't know—migraines, wrinkles, constipation . . . some other horrible stuff.

I have started the process of discarding all sorts of baggage and garbage from my life. Frankly, I had launched the exercise years ago. Criticism used to sting in earlier times. I would read a spiteful review, or a nasty swipe somewhere, and lapse into bouts of self-doubt. Am I really such a yucky person? Are my books that terrible? Certain slights and malicious comments would corrode my insides . . . and I would stupidly wonder, 'But what did I do to that person to warrant this?' Quite forgetting that I had wounded countless people myself with my sharp remarks in print. Once I recognized this two-way process for what it is—part and parcel of being a public person—I stopped fretting. But that doesn't mean I stopped remembering! I forget very little—it's both a boon and a curse. Conversations, in particular, or certain incidents remain permanently stuck in my memory bank. Sometimes,

I get irritated by this 'total recall' and try to declutter my brain. But memories are like chewing gum—the more you struggle to get rid of them the more they stick.

~

The new breed spawned by Bollywood

Much has been written about Bollywood stars battling depression and other mental illnesses. Given the unreal worlds they occupy, and the pace at which they live, high levels of stress are a natural by-product. If far lesser beings like ourselves are forced to deal with unfair expectations at times, one can only imagine what movie stars go through. Having seen the film industry evolve into the movie factory it has become today, I have been both amused and alarmed. Since in the age of digital media, nothing is hidden and stars are happy to parade and peddle their insecurities to fans, one wonders what happens when the lights go off, and they are alone with themselves. I suspect they are rarely alone. And even if that does happen, I'm pretty certain they have coping mechanisms in place to help them deal with themselves, really.

The younger ones do not utter a word without consulting their managers. They are so closeted, they appear dazed if asked a direct question. Whether it's the commercial events they show up at, or press interactions, their every breath is accounted for. It costs! They refuse to make a single decision—something as minor as 'Do you want a coffee now or later?'—without looking at their minders for a correct response to the question. They are not dumb at all. Just dumbstruck when it comes to dealing with the real world, the one outside the studios. They like hanging with one another in such a claustrophobic way, one feels a little sorry for the bunch. Insular and insecure, they refuse to discuss anything outside the movie orbit. They live, breathe, eat and think movies. Not in a way that makes them appear passionate about cinema. Rather, they end up sounding passionate about themselves. It is the next film, the next song, the next shoot that is discussed obsessively. No wonder they rarely have friends outside the closed world they occupy. Watch them in public. Watch in particular when they look around and don't find anyone else from the film industry. Their eyes widen in panic, and their body language changes dramatically. They rush to the washroom and stay put for a really long time, till their minders walk in and persuade them to emerge as their fans are waiting. Once the photo op is over, they rush out into their waiting limos like their pants are on fire!

Another quirk. Stars love awards. Call them to any award function and they'll turn up, provided they are guaranteed an award. The category doesn't matter. An award is an award. It looks great gleaming away on the mantelpiece. This is the deal: Organizers concoct bizarre categories in order to ensure a great star turnout. No stars means no sponsors means no media coverage. Escorts are posted at the sprawling residences of top stars to make sure they leave home on time and show up for the function. Based on how many stars have been roped in, the camera crews take vantage positions. Advertisers start counting eyeballs as soon as the first star makes an appearance on the red carpet.

Once inside the venue, stars head for other stars and ignore everybody else, the chief guest included. They form a noisy, rowdy clique of their own and think nothing of disrupting the proceedings. The attitude is obvious: We are doing everybody a favour by showing up. We get paid to show up—not talk to anybody or even smile. Decibel levels keep rising from the star table, as more friends arrive. All of them huddle on this one table, even if it is a sit-down dinner with designated seating. Nobody dares to ask them to take their assigned seats. Once the awards get under way, the stars lustily cheer one another, but nobody else. Neither do they wait for other awardees to collect their trophies. The moment they get theirs, they coolly walk out with an entourage, no apologies, no goodbyes, not even a 'thank you'. If asked why they aren't staying for the dinner they have accepted, they trot out the same reason, 'We have a flight to catch!'

Rehab is no longer a bad word in Bollywood. Neither is depression. In fact, it's cool to talk about mental health issues. Or tell the world about an early bout with some deadly disease, since cured. AIDS and gay relationships still face taboos. But even those two last bastions are likely to be breached soon. Bollywood has stepped up, as it were, and outed several sensitive subjects in recent times. Young actresses talk about alcoholism, young actors proudly discuss their battle with drugs. This new openness is refreshing and welcome, as compared to the past when movie stars lived in a parallel universe in which there were only vestal virgins who sipped colas, while their male counterparts stuck to lassi and nothing more potent. Today's movie stars, perhaps taking their cues from Hollywood, are open about everything—from their relationships to their addictions. Does that tarnish their image? I'd say, to the contrary—it makes them less godlike, more human. Even if in their more 'human' avatars they can and do get away with murder.

I have always maintained a healthy distance from Bollywood. It is one of my better decisions. There is no such thing as 'friendship' in showbiz. And journalists who believe they have close friends who actually care for them in the mad whirl of movies are deluding themselves. Movie people only care about themselves and other movie people. So long as they have use for a person in the media, and the person becomes 'complicit', the relationship endures. Once the journalist steps down—finito. I have seen a lot of angry, disillusioned film magazine editors, television journalists and those handling social media expressing anger and hurt when they are struck off those all-important Bollywood lists, sometimes for writing a less-than-gushy piece about a star. It is a mutual state of suspended love–hate between media and movie folks across the world. A serious trust deficit both ways. I don't see that changing. We love our stars. We also hate them. They feel the same. So it's all good.

~

The great media bazaar

Sometimes I wonder how some of my contemporaries would have fared had they stuck to their jobs in Mumbai/Kolkata, and not moved to Delhi. I am talking about the ones who used to boast, 'I have fire in my belly and balls of steel.' Now, sadly, the very same chaps have malt in their bellies and rubber balls between their legs. Had they stayed back in the cities which nurtured their early journalism, I think most of them would have grown phenomenally as writers/journalists, but that may not have been their ambition. Almost without exception, every single editor who relocated to the capital gained clout, but lost credibility. There is something toxic about the air in Delhi. The pollution is not restricted to the foul atmosphere. There is moral pollution that pervades every inch of the capital and ends up destroying the very people who set off jauntily to 'clean the system'.

Editors who shaped opinion and influenced policy in the eighties are dead, dying or drunk. Drunk with their sense of entitlement and power, as they hobnob and get into bed with oily netas and boast they can bring down governments. Most have amassed fortunes in ten short years and live the lives of pampered nawabs, strutting around the corridors of power leering and sneering at lesser beings. The era of *jhola*-wallas ended long ago. But the Mumbai brigade that migrated to the capital, mercifully, did not pay the slightest attention to that pretentious dress code of Dilliwallas and brazenly took with them the Mumbai style of sharp suits and tailored kurtas to the salons of Prithviraj Road—a look that was more corporate honcho than hungry hack. These men knew their malts and molls, and impressed rustic politicos with their savoir faire. Coming from Mumbai, it was erroneously assumed they were on backslapping terms with Bollywood superstars. Media barons fell over backwards begging for 'intros' to starlets. Netas assumed these chaps could swing deals with fat-cat Mumbai industrialists and the fat-cat industrialists assumed the smart-talking journos would open sarkari doors. So many assumptions! Journalism itself became incidental. Cutting deals and peddling influence created the new generation of super hustlers, PR agents and—plainly put—media pimps. It was a huge sellout.

But then again, the ones who left knew exactly why they were leaving. They moved to Delhi to make money. Big money. They would visit Mumbai, stay in the best suites, throw their weight around and brag about their closeness to the biggest political personalities in the land. Soon Mumbaiwallas began to suffer from a major inferiority complex. Former colleagues turned into rivals and foes as they bitched out Dilliwalla editors and threw big numbers around to 'prove' their corruption. We heard stories about Swiss bank accounts and exotic foreign mistresses, lavish farmhouses and kids whose education had been underwritten at Oxford, Harvard, *vaghera*. Every neta had his coterie of pets, and the ex-Mumbai men no longer needed to crawl for acceptance. As one of them put it, 'We've all made money. What we need is fame.' Tra la—television bosses decided the best way to shut mouths and neutralize criticism was to give everybody a talk show. It was an inexpensive way to co-opt top journos and a win–win for both. I remember one of them telling me in thrilled tones how he gets mobbed at airports!

Today, of course, it hardly matters who edits a newspaper or magazine. Readers don't care. Nor do media *maalik*s. Papers are produced by the marketing guys who decide content. Every square centimetre is for sale—the front page, the sports pages and all else in between. The former Mumbai gang does not matter. But Bollywood does. Delhi bows to Bollywood and therefore to anybody in Mumbai who is connected to the movie world. I watch the charade from a distance and smile. Of course the media has changed. Of course it isn't what it used to be. But then—what is? Move over, journos—make way for bloggers. And what is sweetly called MOJO (mobile journalism). I am all for it. Everybody is a journalist today. It's far better than putting up with mediocrity parading as genius. Showbiz rules. Fake news sells better than the real stuff. Someone in Delhi, who once made a living out of ideas and words, now sits in the Rajya Sabha and peddles influence of a different kind. The masters have changed—from media maaliks to political patrons. Closeness to power corrupts. Cosiness with power corrupts absolutely. *Theek hai, bhai.* What the hell is 'truth', in journalism or outside it. Why point fingers at 'sold out' journos? Idealism in this business is about as useful as a fish that flies.

I have never been a people pleaser and I don't write to impress my peer group. I know what they think of me. 'Please, yaar, I can't take her seriously! So banal!' That's okay. I don't take any of you seriously either! Please don't take me seriously. I would be seriously worried if this lot thought well of me. Some time ago, I was asked to be 'in conversation' with a very successful journalist/author. I think he expected to chew me up during the session and made the singular mistake of arriving for the interaction without doing basic homework (arrogance!). We were introduced in the foyer by the organizer and the author looked me up and down rather insolently before adding, 'Oh . . . I saw you at the Jaipur Lit Fest last year. I was on stage with a prominent Pakistani writer who looked at you and said, "I want to meet her—she's such a hottie!" You were wearing black leather pants.' Mr Journalist, why the bullshit? So much for your journalistic eye and sense of observation. I don't wear pants. And leather? Never! I smiled. We went up on stage.

He tried a few more sexist cracks that were pathetically out of sync with today. I steadily kept up my part of the evening by sticking to his rather mixed-up book. He tripped over himself over and over again. How can I take such a man seriously, huh? Later, I had a good laugh when I overheard him commenting about me in incredulous tones to one of his grovelling, snivelling groupies: 'Man—she is something else! I am amazed—I mean, she's so intelligent!' No kidding, baby! Chew on that!

When *Socialite Evenings* was included by Juggernaut publisher Chiki Sarkar in her representative and very personal list of seventy books ('A Reading List to Beat All Others') for a special on India@70 (*Hindustan Times*, 12 August 2017), there was the expected sniping and bitching. But hey—I was thrilled! I got a huge kick out of the honour, just as I had when Penguin Random House picked the same book as a part of their tightly curated list of thirty classics when Penguin India turned thirty in 2016. I danced around the dining table with a copy of the book, singing a Bollywood song. 'I am a classic!' I told my family, flashing the book proudly. They smiled indulgently and asked, 'So have you ordered *chingri malai* for dinner or not?' Only my husband looked impressed and asked for a copy for his collection—God bless the man.

~

Making small talk, and big talk, can be fun

I enjoy people. I enjoy interviews. The idea is never to trip up or trap anybody with clever-clever trick questions (any idiot can do this). For me the best interviews take place in a comfort zone. It is up to the interviewer to create that zone. Even if the person you are interviewing is a known crook, swindler, murderer, rapist, gangster, drug lord—or a politician, who can be all of these—respect your subject. Good manners dictate that the person who has agreed to meet you is your *mehmaan* in a way. Follow a few basic rules—or don't put your foot into it. Establishing a quick rapport with the interviewee is key if you want the person to sing. Eye contact and a relaxed body language sets the mood, and a smile often disarms and takes the person in the hot seat off guard. Especially if the subject is deadly! Only an egotistical journalist will display attitude—we have no dearth of megalomaniacs ranting away in India.

But take a look at Oprah Winfrey—I consider her the best in the business. Oprah radiates energy and good humour. She smiles, she jokes, she touches. And the subject melts. I have to confess I found it hard to smile, joke or touch Mamata Banerjee when Aveek Sarkar, who was editor of the *Telegraph* at the time, asked me to spend a day with Didi on her campaign trail. I was surprised Mamata agreed. But there I was in the back seat of her Omni car (she preferred to sit next to the worshipful driver) as we hurtled through paddy fields and stopped several times for Didi to stick her neck out of the car window and greet half-naked, miserably thin villagers, emerging from their huts to see what was going on. It was obvious she would win—going by the rapturous reception she received once we got back to Kolkata, where a huge rally had been scheduled. She insisted on my being on stage with her and we clicked several pictures.

Throughout those long hours, she had not made eye contact with me. I noticed her taking frequent swigs from a tiny bottle placed within easy reach. She caught me staring and said shortly, 'Cough mixture. Bad throat.' Ah. Of course. Aveek gave my story huge front-page play. Not sure what Didi made of it, but soon after she became chief minister of West Bengal, feelers were sent out to ask whether I would be interested in a Rajya Sabha nomination, 'since you speak good English'. I politely declined. I guess Derek O'Brien passed the 'good English' test with flying colours.

Soon after Narendra Modi took office, I was an invitee to the Agra Lit Fest, and found myself chatting with an attractive, articulate, smart BJP spokeswoman (one of several). We hit it off and after a longish chat, she asked me whether I would be open to interviewing Narendra Modi. She said she was aware of my opinion of him, and that is precisely why she believed this was a good idea. I jumped at the chance and asked, 'When?' She said she would let me know. I was amused and curious. This would be a major coup given that the PM had not given any journo an exclusive interview at that point. After a couple of hours she sought me out to say it wasn't happening. No surprises! She added, 'It is because you have credibility that I thought it would be a good platform for Modiji. But his team said you wouldn't agree to screened questions and a controlled interview.' Chalo. At least they got something right!

Then came the infamous Raghuram Rajan piece I wrote for the *Economic Times*. Goodness! It created havoc! But why? Does nobody get a joke? I was in Goa when the deputy editor called and asked if I could dash off a piece on the brand-new mighty governor of the Reserve Bank of India. Rajan was all over the press and photographers couldn't get enough of the tall, lanky, well-spoken gentleman, more movie star than a federal bank chap. I didn't know him, had never met him. Just read all the media hype. I was most amused by the hoopla around the appointment and said so. A friend forwarded photographs of formal governors of the Reserve Bank. 'Take a look at the man's predecessors—now do you get it?' Um. Yes. He was dishy. I decided to have some fun with the piece—deconstruct the stuffy job, make a few irreverent comments on the guy's photogenic looks. Why not? Women in the banking sector have to deal with personal scrutiny constantly—their hair, sarees, make-up, appearance and jewellery interests one and all. Why the discrimination? Equal and level playing field, right? I decided to 'objectify' Raghuram Rajan in the same vein, while suggesting cheekily that he'd 'put sex back into the Sensex'! The reaction was immediate and insane. I was pilloried and slammed for 'trivializing' such an erudite economist. It became the most quoted piece about the new guy on the block. It is to Mr Rajan's credit that he took it sportingly in his long stride.

Mercifully for him, and more so for me, we didn't run into each other during his short but dramatic tenure. Till a few weeks before he packed his bags and went back to America, leaving his fans bereft. It was at a high-profile 'royal' reception for Prince William and Kate Middleton at the Taj Mahal Palace Hotel. I noticed him standing at a short distance and boldly walked up to him, encouraged by the twinkle in his eyes. He smiled, we clinked champagne flutes and my daughter Avantikka clicked a pic on my phone for posterity. It required a man of his maturity, stature, experience and exposure to 'get' the satire in the piece and not be outraged. Thank God for his sophistication and savoir faire, a lesser chap may have run in the opposite direction! No offence was meant—and happily, none was taken. But even today, when I run into corporate types, they look at me in 'that' (leering) way, and ask about just this one column. I stick to my stand. And these days I don't bother to hide my man crush. Who can forget the governor's unforgettable line, 'My name is Raghuram Rajan and I do what I do.' Ditto, darling! Different name. Different gender. Same attitude.

As for those idiots still referring to that *Economic Times* piece, listen up, you guys: Small minds and small dicks go together. Why are men so antagonistic towards women with attitude?

Talking of clinking glasses . . .

I used to be a bubbly fan. Over a relaxed evening, I could *aaram se* put away a bottle of Dom. Not any more. But who knows, one day I may return to my love for champagne with added fervour and raise a glass or two or three to moments that make life memorable. When I was honoured by champagne major Veuve Clicquot in 2012, little did I imagine how huge it was and what it meant, till I visited the vineyard at Reims (about 130 km east-north-east of Paris) to participate in this solemn and elegant ceremony. I had been chosen to be a part of the Veuve Clicquot tribute to women around the world, who reflect the spirit of Mme Clicquot, a woman ahead of her time, who boldly took charge of the family business after being widowed at twenty-seven. We are talking eighteenth century here! The tribute ceremony, which began in 1972, is held at an event loaded with glamour, prestige and significance. While I thoroughly enjoyed the stirring speeches made by women from different fields, who had flown in to share views and concerns, what took me totally by surprise was the 'baptism' at the scenic vineyard. The first thing I noticed was the Indian flag fluttering in the gentle breeze. I was so thrilled, I let out a small scream—like an overwhelmed schoolgirl. When I looked closely, I found a gleaming brass plaque, with my name and the year on it, delicately attached to the first vine of a long row, growing on a gentle slope, alongside other vines, also bearing plaques of famous women. Soon a distinguished gentleman appeared with a chilled bottle of the finest vintage, offered a glass, and requested me to step forward and 'baptize' the neat row of vines. 'Whenever grapes from this row of vines are harvested and bottled, a part of your literary and social legacy will be shared across the world.'

It was like a dream I didn't want to wake up from. Gaurav Bhatia, who was the marketing director for Veuve Clicquot India at the time, told the press I had been selected for this rare honour for being 'the perfect combination of boldness and elegance' and that the tribute was an 'ode to Shobhaa Dé's enterprising spirit, strong leadership, unapologetic audacity, serious creativity and zeste de folie. We celebrate the quintessential Mrs Dé—her candid, vociferous, brutally honest style of writing and opinions that have influenced many a point of view and the social fabric of India.' My! My! In all those generous words and gushy-mushy compliments, I loved 'zeste de folie' the most! Did I deserve to be thus honoured?

Had I earned it? I wasn't sure! But it sure felt fantastic! At that magical moment, I reminded myself of all the hugs I spontaneously receive from strangers, mainly women, who come up to say, '*Aap ko padh ke . . . aap ko dekh ke . . . humey bahut courage milta hai!*' Just for that, and in memory of the pioneering lady who revived the fine reputation of her dead husband's vineyard to make it one of the most recognized champagne brands globally, I shall stay loyal and stick to Clicquot whenever a bubbly mood takes hold of me.

~

What if?

There are days that spell 'wretchedness', for no explicable reason. Everything seems terribly wrong, even when everything is the same. That worries me. A lot. I ask myself: Have you just got used to this? Is that why you no longer notice how blah it is? Are you that passive? Placid? What happened to the woman of steel, the one with the balls? Why are you settling for less? Fight! Go on. This isn't the life you wanted. You are a born gypsy. Run away. Be rude. Listen to the songs your heart is singing. Before you know it, you will be eighty, or dead. And you won't have been to Argentina. On such days, I eat a lot. To forget, to overcompensate for the other hunger. I hear something on someone else's playlist, and suddenly, I reconnect with my younger self—listening to the same music. But reacting passionately, deeply.

I walk into an art gallery, and stare at a painting. I feel I have seen it before. In another life. Accompanied by some other companion. I start crying. For the painting. Me. The other companion. Around me, I watch people making social conversation. Most of it is meaningless. I make a lot of it myself. Why? It is that intensity of feeling that creeps up when I least expect it, and I hit a downer. I panic. I start questioning all my choices. Every decision I have ever made. What if? It's that bloody 'what if' that stealthily takes hold of my imagination when I try to still my mind, get some sleep. My dreams change from the standard escapist ones to much darker subjects. I wake up feeling alone, feeling scared. Some of the dreams are recurrent and common. They involve wicked, harsh people looking for me at my old home (my present home does not exist in my dreamscape). And I dream of that old home being targeted by low-flying aeroplanes buzzing just above treetops. I have never been able to fathom my war dreams, considering I have not lived through one. Just like I can't fathom 'wretchedness' when there is nothing tangible to be wretched about.

Just at this critical juncture, with dreams and thoughts bothering me, I watched a movie that was so morbid that I wondered why I sat through it. Around me were old folks like myself. Not a single youngster in sight. At the end of the film (about a man who decides he is ready to die but only in Varanasi!), I sense despondency all around me. Most of us are senior citizens. It is obvious from the shuffling, slow gait as we make our way carefully to the exit. We hang on to someone, temporarily lose balance, grab the nearest seat, straighten up and laboriously amble out. 'Did you like the movie?' we ask one another anxiously. Nobody knows what to answer. It is not a movie one 'likes'. Which is why we are so uncomfortable. We see us! We see our own death. We feel scared. Nervous laughter follows. We walk out into the darkness overwhelmed by a feeling of aloneness.

Age is a stealthy creature. It creeps up on you when you aren't looking. Haven't you noticed how people you've known all your life as youthful, vibrant, talkative types start appearing and acting like they are a hundred years old without a fair warning? One day they are their familiar selves, and the next, they are ancient. What happened? A tragedy? An accident? Or is it just that slippery villain called age claiming one more victim? I guess we all have a secret, dark side. Some of us are brave enough to expose it openly. Most hide. I play hide-and-seek. Even with myself. Besides, my family chases away dark clouds before they gather. My children are most uncomfortable with my dark, low periods. There is a preconceived idea shared even by close friends, of a person (me!), who is a positive energy field 24/7. If I slip even briefly and withdraw, there is a swift reaction: 'Snap out of it. Don't be dramatic. Stop it!' This applies to my appearance. Once, when Anandita took pictures of me at my worst—shabby, old, faded kaftan, tired, make-up-less face, slouchy body language—and shared it with the others, there was an immediate response, 'Delete immediately. We like our glam mom.' I agreed! 'Delete!' I almost screamed. But why? These are vanity traps we set up for ourselves. And anything that contradicts the fixed images constructed over time has to be shunned.

Age is a stealthy creature. It creeps up on you when you aren't looking.

My children's response forced me to think about the oppressive nature of stereotyping those we admire and love the most. Even strangers we don't know, may never meet, but who fascinate us. I was forwarded a really grim picture of a famous movie star on his deathbed. It was a horrific shot. The man, who was once the most handsome actor in Bollywood, was cruelly photographed, with a smiling wife and son on either side of him. His sunken eyes were shut, he was unshaven and gaunt. And most humiliating of all, he wasn't wearing a lower garment—the short hospital gown just about covered his modesty. When I saw the picture, I was sickened by the insensitivity of it all. Was his permission sought before clicking him? The once strapping, good-looking, dashing, broad-shouldered hero of countless hits? Why wasn't he allowed privacy, dignity, grace during his last hours?

Then I thought of another celebrity death that had occurred a few months before this one. She'd lived her entire life as a supreme diva, worshipped by admirers and lauded for her incredible style. When she was hospitalized and informed the end was near, she summoned her family and oversaw the minutest detail of her last journey, which she wanted to be conducted in utmost secrecy, away from prying, intrusive eyes. Mumbai woke up to the sad news that she had gone the previous night, and the cremation had been conducted within two hours of her death. Not a single picture was released, apart from the super-glamorous ones in circulation. No details of her last moments were shared. She went, the way she lived—privacy intact. Mythology intact. Image intact. She will always be remembered the way she wanted to be perceived—a beautiful, stylish, strong woman, impeccably groomed and dressed fabulously at all times, on all occasions.

'A life well lived—a death well died.'

~

I have been thinking about death a great deal after losing Ashok Rajadhyaksha, my beloved brother, this year. Those heartbreaking exchanges with him as he lay on his hospital cot, staring expressionlessly ahead, his mind ticking but his voice taken away, will always stay with me. Those exchanges—short, funny, occasionally emotional—will remain priceless for many reasons. He continued to call me 'baby sister' till the very end, as I stroked his damp forehead and tried to make 'light conversation' with a dying man who knew he had but a few short days ahead of him. I would force myself to crack silly jokes, remind him of his penchant for buxom ladies, discuss the 'good old days' at IIT Kharagpur, offer him a single malt or a martini, talk about his only child, Joya, remind him about his favourite songs, his incredible memory for lyrics, movie dialogues, his love for and knowledge of aeroplanes, his expertise with the harmonica—I wanted his last days to be somehow less morbid. I tried.

After he was gone, I sank into my own delayed morbidity. There never is a real acceptance of loss, is there? Ashok had uncharacteristically said, 'Kiss me before you leave,' one evening, and I had covered his forehead with little kisses as he tightly held on to my hand. I now wonder, 'Who will kiss me when I am dying?'

~

A new foe—memory

Memory starts playing wicked tricks after 'a certain age'. What is that awful age? I know for sure I am approaching it rapidly. But in a peculiar way. Experts say as one gets older, the first thing to get affected is short-term memory. One forgets conversations, people, events and objects. I am okay with forgetting names. I am okay not recognizing acquaintances. I am okay forgetting details of destinations I have enjoyed thoroughly. What drives me nuts is losing my spectacles. I have half a dozen pairs placed strategically all over our home. I have a couple in my car. An extra 'backup' pair in my travel kit. Despite all these efforts, I often end up frazzled and upset because I am spectacles-deprived at key moments. I talk to girlfriends who assure me I am not alone. But they have foolproof systems in place and are never caught squinting miserably at fine print, frustrated at not being able to send a WhatsApp message, or feeling stranded at an airport unable to call a driver whose number can't be located in the mobile phone book. I have missed flights because I have failed to read the correct departure time! It's that bad. Nothing works—not even stringing spectacles around my neck like an ugly garland. My rage against *chasma*s manifests itself in many ways. And the rejected chasmas strike back viciously by disappearing or breaking! I run through four to six pairs a month. Does that happen to all senior citizens? I see so many of my contemporaries staring blankly at people, but refusing to wear glasses. A gal pal asked me recently, 'No cataract?' I assured her my eyesight was okay for now. She shook her head, 'Lucky. My cataract is making it difficult for me to write these days.'

My siblings remember everything in minute detail. Mandakini's memory is spectacular. So was Ashok's. Mandakini remains the proud custodian of family memories.

She even remembers the colours, prices and textures of sarees purchased and worn forty-odd years ago! They think I am pretending when I can't recall an incident. But I am really not! My mind is blank when references are made to family occasions where someone said or did something terrible. If they remember it so vividly, how come I don't? I have asked myself the same question. Am I in denial? I don't think so. Does my childhood bore me to that extent? Possibly. Or could it be that I vastly prefer to stay firmly anchored in the present? Even as I write these words, I am trying to recall last night's lively dinner at home. I know the conversation had been particularly sparkling, and the company exceptional. But it's already over! And the slate has been wiped clean. I expressed this anxiety to a friend—a much younger woman—who told me to relax and not feel bad about forgetting. 'We are trying to process far too much information. Our brains are overloaded. We are doing too many things. Our bodies are exhausted. At some point, the system breaks down and everything blurs. It's fine.' I felt instantly better, and started making a conscious effort to let go. There was a time when reading five or six newspapers thoroughly was a big part of my daily regime. These days, I scan and pick up what I want to read. I have stopped watching television. My magazine-reading habits have changed. I no longer care if there are stories I have skipped. Books, too—terrible admission! But if the author fails to engage me in the first thirty pages, I discard the book instantly. No guilt. I feel lighter and more relaxed after getting rid of a few sticky habits. I used to go into withdrawal if I had bypassed a cover story or not reacted to breaking news. I no longer obsess over being on top of every major and minor news report. Since that liberation took place, I find I have more time to enjoy small treats—could be food or just playing with a grandchild. My children tell me they prefer this 'softer' person. And I laugh internally! What does that even mean? 'Softer' person? Ha! We are all composites of many persons. I like all my 'persons'. I offer a generous à la carte emotional menu—family and friends are free to make their choices. And I am equally free to pick from their menus.

Most times, people opt for straitjackets designed by society. I create my own jacket and change it frequently. That is the ultimate luxury—to be whatever and whoever you choose to be at that moment. I encourage my children to express themselves without fear and conditioning. The more you listen to that one compelling voice within, the easier you make things for yourself. Today, I choose to simplify. To uncomplicate. In so doing, I am being selfish. And being selfish has helped me to become far more accepting of other people's selfishness. I have understood that selfishness can be constructive and life-affirming, so long as it doesn't hurt the other. By placing myself first in a few situations, I am in fact being able to give of myself more intelligently, more efficiently. People talk endlessly about time management and meditation. Both are useful techniques if you know how to

Most times, people opt for straitjackets designed by society. I create my own jacket and change it frequently. That is the ultimate luxury—to be whatever and whoever you choose to be at that moment.

harness and employ them. My one short strategy when I meet people is to take a couple of minutes to read the dynamics of the shared space. It's not difficult to pick up signals and figure out equations, provided you tune in! Tune in to others. We spend far too much time tuning into our own selves and in the bargain, we fail to identify the true nature of the situation. Decoding the unspoken . . . figuring out body language . . . these are tools we possess but don't exploit. Close friends tell me I am exceptionally intuitive. That I have X-ray vision. That I can read people's thoughts. That their lives are magically known to me. One thing I can definitely boast about is my almost uncanny instinct when it comes to romantic liaisons. I can tell if the suitor is suitable/unsuitable in a second! I have foolishly warned young women in love to stay away from their boyfriends and been told I was wrong. Years later, the same women have come back to mourn, 'How I wish I had listened to you!'

Am I intuitive? Or is it just practised awareness that helps me better understand emotional equations? We can achieve this level of awareness quite easily by being honest with ourselves. If I dislike a person (and I dislike many!), I ask myself why that is so. If I can sense hostility towards me (I get a lot of it), I ask the same question. There is no logic involved. Just gut feelings. Step out of the war zone sometimes. Then again, is peace all that attractive?

Detachment is a desired state for most. But I also enjoy over-involvement! These are the contradictions that add zing to our lives. Uncertainty breeds tension. Tension triggers creativity. Tension is good! It's a question of how much tension you can take. These are relative and personal matters that can seriously impact one's mental and physical health. So what? So be it! I often joke with family that there is no such thing as 'control'. We delude ourselves when we believe we are in control. The only control one needs is over one's bladder and bowels. If age erodes that, I would rather not live. Definitely no adult diapers for this woman.

We delude ourselves when we believe we are in control. The only control one needs is over one's bladder and bowels. If age erodes that, I would rather not live. Definitely no adult diapers for this woman.

Sigh. Where are the damned spectacles? Oops. There they are! On my nose where I'd left them.

~

Double . . . and quadruple standards

I don't know of a family that does not live with double standards on some level or another. For all my professed liberalism, when it comes to my daughters—and now, granddaughters—all the stated positions on virtually every lifestyle issue get thrown out of the window, starting with 'inappropriate clothes'. As I keep stressing, my concern revolves around their safety. It is not about 'protecting a woman's modesty', but about avoiding trouble. They mock at my agitated 'advice' when they are all set to go out clad in trendy outfits that I find too short, too tight, too revealing. They ask me what happened to the views I frequently air on television channels, in which I emphatically endorse a woman's right to dress as she pleases. Frankly, I have no convincing answer. I look sheepish and say a trifle lamely, 'But you know what's going on these days? You are looking fabulous—I don't want you to attract the wrong kind of attention.' They laugh some more, sling their evening bags over their shoulders, greet me jauntily and leave.

This is but one small example of my personal double standards.

I catch myself applying different yardsticks for the same problem pretty often. One thing in theory, another in practice. I argue this is done in a practical spirit, to avoid conflict. That is partially true. Not being a confrontational person, I do bend a few cherished rules in order to avoid an argument. Most times, it's over pretty small stuff, but my own 'weakness' annoys me. Why can't I be like so-and-so, I ask myself? Why should I accommodate someone else's wishes and compromise on my own? Then I get philosophical and shrug, 'Life is about those irritating compromises.' Not everybody can be an Anna Hazare or a Mahatma Gandhi. I'm pretty sure even Mother Teresa had her tough tests (as she has admitted), when she made choices that were at a variance with what her heart was saying.

The one thing I do keep underlining when we discuss the vexing issue of double standards at the dining table is the intention behind every such instance. If the decision taken is in the larger interests of the family/community/country . . . there is no harm in being a little flexible. The trouble starts when one is not sensitive to another's point of view and those very double standards come back to bite. How flexible should one be in a crisis? Depends on the crisis! I would say, judge the situation quickly. If it's potentially dangerous, forget your rigid standards and get out of the danger zone fast.

How we react in an emergency is a great test of character. Here's a simple example of making a hasty, if dodgy, call during a crisis. Assume the train you are travelling in gets derailed and you are left stranded in an unknown town, unable to reach your family due to a lack of mobile signal. A stranger walks up and offers help—for a price, of course. A bribe is being demanded. You are vehemently opposed to the idea of giving bribes. But you desperately need to reach your family at any cost. The stranger knows how to get you to a spot from where you can call. What do you do? Stick to your guns or reach for your wallet? I'll confess what I would do—reach for my wallet. At that crucial moment, my good sense would override my principles about bribe-giving. I would succumb emotionally and pay up. I would justify it to myself, arguing it's better to grease a palm during an emergency than to drive loved ones crazy with anxiety wondering whether or not one is alive. Does that make me a dishonest person? I am not sure!

Second chances: We all deserve a shot at something we have flunked—even an exam. But I have preferred to invest that same time and energy in new challenges, without revisiting old wounds. Scars and scabs are not for me. I am intensely sensitive to someone else's gashes. But my own?

Second chances: We all deserve a shot at something we have flunked—even an exam. But I have preferred to invest that same time and energy in new challenges, without revisiting old wounds.

~

Jhoom barabar, jhoom sharabi

My children never use the word 'booze'—it's always 'beverages' ('bevy' for short). Just as they say 'tabac' and not ciggies. Most families have secret codes and a special language that is understood only by members. In our hybrid family, we have countless abbreviations that no outsider can possibly figure out. When it comes to alcohol, let's just say, we like our beverages. A lot. And we have our preferences. I don't drink spirits at all. But I sure like my vino! White vino. If at all I have a drink in the evenings, it is a chilled glass of white wine. There was a time I could effortlessly put away a bottle of champagne over a long evening. These days, champagne gives me a really nasty hangover (Damn! Age!). I started enjoying wine pretty late in life. I grew up in a home where *daaru* was a terrible word and anybody who drank was promptly labelled a 'drunkard'.

The thought of women consuming alcohol was so preposterous, it was never raised. Since I had not seen my father indulge in even a glass of cold beer during Delhi summers, I remained unexposed to the delights of drinking anything more intoxicating than *limbu paani*! It was when I hit my late thirties that I had my initiation into what is called 'social drinking'. For the past forty-odd years I have enjoyed innumerable glasses of wine and become pretty boisterous as a consequence. Boisterous. Not drunk. The only time I have had to be helped to walk straight was on the night of our twenty-fifth wedding anniversary, which we celebrated with a lovely party at our Alibag farmhouse. My wicked children persuaded me to do shots—I swear I had no idea what those 'shots' were (tequila, I was later informed). Since the mood was already a bit nuts, I went along with it and knocked back three or four shots in under ten minutes. I was soon flying! I regressed, and became a naughty schoolgirl, pushing some of our fully dressed guests into the pool. They looked like they were having so much fun, despite drenching their fabulous clothes, I decided to join them myself.

The music was fantastic and I felt invincible. I wanted to sing and dance and drink some more. Fortunately, my husband realized just in time that if he didn't fish me out of the water and march me upstairs to our bedroom, I would end up a sorry mess. He got hold of our family friend and soul sister, Judith Bidapa, and the two of them firmly took me out of the pool and into dry clothes before tucking me into bed. But not before I walked out on to the balcony and lustily belted out, 'Don't cry for me, Argentina . . .' My Evita moment remains precious and sweet. Absolutely no regrets, but a few valuable lessons quickly learnt.

There are two more infamous incidents worth sharing. Both are great examples of my foolishness and ignorance. Many moons ago, when the children were really, really young (pre-teens and teens), I planned what I thought was an exciting holiday with our fun-loving family friends, the Bidapas, whose children are around the same ages as my two youngest and have grown up together, even though we live in different cities—the Bidapas in Bengaluru, and all of us in Mumbai. I had vaguely heard of a global music event called 'Full Moon Rave', off the Thai island of Koh Samui. I imagined it was a sort of Woodstock equivalent with a different kind of music. I eagerly booked a package deal for all of us, and off we went. I must have been really dumb that even after getting there in James Bond style in sexy speedboats, I didn't get it. The music was thumping over the waves as we approached the island, and my heart was thumping too. The children were in a state of heightened excitement, squealing and giggling in anticipation. We were there! At this amazing venue! I found it all terribly heady. I carefully forked out very measly sums of money for all the bachchas to get snacks and cold drinks. Cold drinks! Not alcohol. I settled myself under gigantic speakers and told them I wouldn't move from that spot till it was time to leave. Hours later, they found me fast asleep on the sand next to the ear-shattering noise emanating from the speakers. I had not touched alcohol, mainly because it was so bad. And I don't drink lousy wine. Nor do I enjoy beer. But the kids had certainly consumed something much more potent than colas. We managed to get them on to the speedboats heading back to our island . . . and I was furious! 'What on earth did you drink with the limited money you had?' I thundered. One of them admitted sheepishly, 'Breezers!' Would you believe it—I didn't know what Breezers were! For all my worldliness and outward sophistication, I had been exposed as a hick by a bunch of kids who had effortlessly outsmarted me.

Then came my unfortunate experience with a cocktail the world loves—Long Island iced tea. I was with the family at a popular bar in a posh south Mumbai hotel. I forget what we were celebrating, but one of the kids teased me by saying, 'Come on, Ma . . . try something new . . . you will love it. Forget boring white wine for once.' Just to appear sporting and with it, I jauntily ordered the wretched Long Island iced tea—it was a hot, muggy night, and the tall drink looked most inviting. I took a few sips and loved it!

Refreshing, chilled, yummy. I glugged it down thinking it was indeed just iced tea with perhaps some white rum poured into it. Twenty minutes later, I was ready to take charge of the dance floor and perform an impromptu cabaret. I was dizzyingly high! Surprised to see me this far gone on a single cocktail, it was decided we'd make a quick and discreet exit. Since those two occasions, I have made a couple of key resolutions—never to listen to my wicked children while ordering a drink. And to bloody well *know* what the hell I am drinking if I am in an experimental mood!

One more confession: There was a wedding in the family. One of the daughters had cautioned me that her future in-laws were arch-conservatives. The family did not 'take' (Marathi slang for consuming alcohol—'he "takes", but she doesn't'), and it was going to be a really long, formal evening. How would I survive it? On just Darjeeling tea? Limbu paani? I decided to 'relax' a little, after the proceedings got under way. I went into the kitchen and poured myself a generous amount of white wine into a patterned water glass. It was assumed my throat was parched and I was sipping *thanda* paani. Only my vigilant daughter was smart enough to catch on! She marched me into the bedroom and gave me such a scolding, I felt like a really naughty schoolgirl being ticked off by a prefect. I apologized profusely and threw away the wine (good bloody white at that!). But I did vow to myself I would never ever sneak a drink. If I wanted one, I would go ahead and have it boldly. But no hiding wine in a coffee cup or patterned water glass!

Fortunately, I get extra talkative and garrulous when I am high, but never aggressive or nasty. I repeat myself in an annoying fashion (the kids tell me!), and yes, I do get pretty rowdy. I definitely feel like dancing—especially to Elvis Presley tracks. And I can spend hours listening to music that makes me go gooey—like Abida Parveen, Nusrat Fateh Ali, Andrea Bocelli . . . of so many others. Nothing beats bhangra remixes and Bollywood hits. One of my most enjoyable public 'performances' was at the Wagah Border last year. I jumped from the stands and joined college girls dancing uninhibitedly at the venue. Or the time I danced at home in the presence of Arundhati's friends during her pre-wedding chandan–haldi ceremony. The track? '*Malhari*' from *Bajirao Mastani*. I became Bajirao, aka Ranveer Singh, in drag. I prefer dancing solo, with my eyes shut, lost in another world. Dancing is meditation at its most enjoyable. I do hope everybody will sing and dance at my funeral, after consuming lots of wonderful wine.

There is something terribly sad about drunks. I know I am not being gender-neutral here, but there is something even sadder about female drunks. I have seen an astonishing number of female acquaintances throw it all away because they were unable to 'manage' their alcoholism. Loneliness is often cited as the biggest driver. So many of my much younger girlfriends, who work long hours, travel a lot and live on their own, tell me they can't wait to get home and pour themselves a drink. I worry when I hear that. They laugh. 'Imagine walking into an empty apartment and wondering what to do with your time. You are mentally and physically exhausted. You open the fridge—you find a chilled bottle of your favourite wine. You say, "What the hell," and start sipping. Sometimes you don't stop till the bottle is empty.' Dangerous. So to all you lovely ladies out there, who mistakenly think woes will magically disappear in a large glass of vodka–tonic ('I swear, what you see is loads of ice . . . swear!'), let me tell you that large glass becomes three large glasses . . . perhaps four. By the time you wake up and try getting out of your stupor, it's way too late.

Follow some basic rules: Never sip a glass of wine on your own, saying, 'Oh . . . I've had such a stressful day . . . I need to unwind . . . I have earned my wine.' Utter rubbish. Reach for the phone, not the bottle. Step out and go watch a movie—any movie. Go to the gym. Go for a walk. Distract yourself. Review the clothes in your wardrobe. Order the latest season of your favourite TV series.

Rule number one: Do not drink solo.

Rule number two: While at a boring party, avoid the temptation to perk up your spirits. If the crowd doesn't interest you—leave. An extra drink or two won't make those folks instantly interesting.

Rule number three: Enjoy that *last* drink only with people you know well and feel comfortable with. It's okay to talk stupid, be stupid, act stupid sometimes. But when it becomes a regular feature—stop!

Rule number four: Drink water between wines and snack before you start.

Rule number five: Don't mix drinks. If you are enjoying a heady cocktail, stick to it for the rest of the evening.

Rule number six: Make sure you head home with a trusted person. Do not be reckless and drive yourself.

Rule number seven: Remember the context. If you are dressed for a beach party and are tippling away merrily on the beach, do not wade into the sea 'because the waves look so inviting'. That could be the last swim of your life.

Rule number eight: Light-hearted flirting with strangers is a subtle art, best practised sober! There's nothing more pathetic than the sight of a tipsy lady coming on to random guys.

Rule number nine: Stop when your head starts swimming. It means you have reached the danger mark.

Rule number ten: This is the worst—don't pick up other people's discarded drinks and guzzle those thirstily. If that has happened to you on a regular basis, check into rehab. And yes, drinking yourself silly with total strangers is a huge no-no. That sweet person offering to hold your handbag while you pee could be a common thief at best, or a slasher at worst. Did you just say you vomited at your own farewell/birthday party? It's okay to pass out elegantly on a stuffed sofa. But vomit or pee in your pants? God forbid. To use Arundhati's favourite expression, 'I'd rather kill myself—slash my wrists!'

Parents who have to deal with serious drinking/drug issues, either their own or their children's, have the single biggest challenge to confront. These troublesome issues didn't exist on such a rampant basis earlier. But today, I see so many wrecked families around me, I wonder what compulsions have led to this tragedy. Too much money? Lack of a real education? Exposure to all the garbage the Internet throws up? Peer pressure? I watched a strong film titled *Udta Punjab*, and realized just how far the 'other' India has gone. It was a terrifying revelation and my thoughts went instantly to the many 'druggies' I have known . . . and the helplessness I felt watching them waste away. Parenting today requires nerves of steel—you never know what that late-night phone call from a stranger is all about. I see schoolkids who steal from their homes to pay for their 'fix'. I meet parents who have lived entirely different lives from those of their children—

they tell me they don't know what signs to look for—'Can you tell from your child's eyes whether or not there is an addiction issue?' What does one say? Parents don't want to be snoops and spies, but they don't want to see their kids die either! I have no real answers. I can only keep repeating (because I do believe it) that there is no substitute for love. A parent simply cannot—and must not—give up on a difficult child. It is hard. In the process, parents often suffer total meltdowns—I have witnessed a few. At such times, I have wanted to smack those irresponsible kids for piling on such pain . . . but stopped myself just in time. In that state they would probably have cracked a beer bottle on my head.

Parents need not torment themselves needlessly. If they find they are unable to cope or help the child, it's best to seek professional help. There is really no shame in this. You may actually save your child's life, along with your own. And remember—not everything is your fault. But at all times stick to a golden rule, hard as it is sometimes: Don't abandon your child emotionally and withdraw love. It's the worst abandonment on earth. Be there. Let the kid know you won't walk away from even the worst crisis faced by him/her. Sometimes, just that silent or stated assurance is enough. I have one simple method: During a tough situation, keep the angry questions for later. First things first: HELP!

~

Common sense: My magic mantra

I can sum up my magic mantra in two words: common sense! When in doubt, get real and consult your common sense—just that. Even in the most trying situation, it's best not to look for esoteric solutions, based on personal hare-brained theories or other people's experiences. Tap into your own life—remind yourself quickly how you did something, or avoided someone. Crisis management is nothing but common sense. Most of us lose touch with that basic something that saves our butts—it's called instinct. Often, we argue with ourselves—but how can it be this easy, this simple? There has to be a different route to solve this issue. Perhaps there is. There are always multiple routes to solve problems big and small. But which is the quickest and easiest? Sometimes, I feel I have taken unintelligent shortcuts in the name of practicality, when what was required at the time was a long-term strategy.

My attention span wavers dangerously, and if I am bored, I am prepared to do ridiculous things to escape boredom. Things that come at a steep price sometimes. This involves financial decisions too. I am a total dud when it comes to understanding money matters. I don't even try. To begin with, mercifully, I don't have too much of the stuff—just enough to cover my small indulgences. When I look back at a lifetime of writing (fifty years, for Chrissake!) and I ask my accountant how much I have in my bank account, it is he who laughs! But that's okay. What do I crave for which I can't buy for myself? Actually, nothing! My children tell me my tastes are very 'pedestrian' and modest. Modest, I agree. But pedestrian? I used to feel hurt in the old days. Today, I feel vindicated and smug, when I see my daughters raiding my closet and picking up those very same 'pedestrian' trinkets they once dismissed. I like it when they 'borrow' my clothes, with a grudging comment, 'So retro, Mom!' These are the sweet moments worth cherishing. As for the rest of the volumes of words we have exchanged over decades, well, hang on to the precious, positive ones and discard the rest.

I remember startling my husband with the loaded comment, 'Every single action in life is political, whether or not you are aware of its political subtext.' He didn't quite understand and I was sure it would lead to an argument. I hastily backed off, but I like to think I left him with something to chew on. These days whenever he makes a reference to that comment, I try to distract him. But I do spend a great deal of time thinking about the choices one makes. Every choice is a political act. But we don't always know it as that. Something pretty simple like eating this and not eating that also implies a political decision (being in a situation to reject or accept a particular food). Similarly, to make friends, marry, break up, sleep with, fight over . . . so many big and small decisions come with a political agenda that we don't instantly recognize. There is no such thing as an 'apolitical' person. Politics affects family dynamics the most. Social structures are created around political equations. Belief in God, or a rejection of belief, has its roots in a person's politics. We interpret that word—politics—in a very limited sense, which does not go beyond an organized political structure. But I guess it is hard for a wife to bluntly inform her loving husband, 'My decision to marry you was strictly political.' Sensing a negative response, I wisely keep my mouth shut!

Talking to a bunch of eager young women in a tier-two city, I once again cited common sense as being my guiding force. This time I illustrated my address with real-life situations they could identify with. When I mentioned mother-in-law issues, all the young wives perked up. They had murder in their eyes! I advised them to deal with those she-devils in a way that disarms them. 'Confuse the enemy', as Confucius said, I joked. And then they asked me innocently, 'Can you introduce us to Mr Confu . . . Mr Confi . . . whoever . . .' That was when a lot of things struck me all at once . . . these women were younger than my daughters. Their reference points were entirely different from mine. I was talking to India's millennials! And they occupied an entirely different headspace. Why was I assuming they would immediately decipher the subtext of what I was saying? Why would they even want to know anything about the past that didn't directly concern them? I instantly changed my tone and content. They didn't need me—I needed them! To stay tuned in, to remain relevant, one has to listen to the voices of the young. They are the future—accept that. The agenda is set by them—not you. For this generation, the only thing that matters is success—as defined by them. People like me are nobodies. We are puffs of smoke—here for the moment. Vapour the next. So what? Make the most of your time spent with the young. Learn from them. They have a lot to share, if you care to listen. Never talk down to them because they haven't experienced what you may have. Their experiences may be far richer! Treat them like equals. Show respect. The choices they make may shock you—but they are their choices! Driving to the airport in a luxury car belonging to one of the elegant ladies, I was filled with admiration. Their bright eyes and happy laughter stayed with me. Sure, they hadn't heard of Confucius. But was I familiar with Justin Bieber? Their 'ignorance' was as out there as my own. Despite that, so many of them remain in touch with me. We have a chat group, the name of which is 'Common Sense'.

Little things may not be as 'little' as you think . . .

Sorry, but there is no Big Picture. Life is merely a series of tiny frames played at a ridiculously rapid speed.

I used to read cheesy articles in weekend supplements and scoff at the treacly advice, dished out by God knows who, could be a computer, a robot, a bored person. There were times when I would resent the tone of the advice giver. Many years ago, I used to be an agony aunt myself. I know how tedious it is to churn out column after column filled with sanctimonious junk. I can recall my own words from way back when I ran a ghost 'advice column' for a famous star. I would tell some agonized soul to focus on the little things and the bigger ones would take care of themselves! Bullshit! Facetious and facile, fake and transparently phoney. I hated myself for doling out utterly meaningless, feel-good nuggets when my own sensibilities were so very different. That such columns find countless takers is no surprise. As a society, we remain pretty closeted and secretive. There really is no one around to talk freely to . . . or at all. Children feel pretty lost as they turn to peers for solutions, since they cannot approach their parents and they certainly don't want to approach their teachers.

Sorry, but there is no Big Picture. Life is merely a series of tiny frames played at a ridiculously rapid speed.

Today, so many summers later, I am once again thinking of the importance of those little things I used to airily dismiss as sentimentality in the past. Now, I value them. And try hard not to ignore a person who is sharing 'little things' without self-consciousness. I meet with a small set of girlfriends pretty regularly. I am proud to admit we listen keenly to one another's little things. And learn from them. These ladies are of a certain vintage, and we share many interests. But when we meet over wine and snacks there is an unspoken understanding between us. We don't talk shop. Well . . . we do! But that isn't all we discuss over three or four hours. Thank God!

The last time we met, we spent considerable time dissecting the many merits of cold cream. I am an addict. It's the only cream I trust. It's the only cream I use—regardless of the weather. If I grew up watching my mother carefully applying Hazeline Snow on her face after her bath, my children and grandchildren have observed my special relationship with cold cream with enormous amusement. 'Mother . . . you are acting mental . . . what do you do with so much cold cream?' they ask. I snap, 'Eat it!' Come on! They know what I do with the damn thing—why ask?

So it came to pass that a couple of years ago, I ran out of cold cream. Ran out! It was a major crisis in my head. No store seemed to stock it during summer, as research had established low sales during those four or five months. I sent out an SOS to friends in north India, south India, east India. One jar was found and couriered by someone who understood my condition. But what touched me the most was when my husband decided to make it his mission to track down as many jars of cold cream as he could physically locate and stockpile them for my future use. This exercise was undertaken on a war footing. An all-India hunt for cold cream followed. Today, I have backups for my backups! I see cold cream wherever my eyes travel in the bedroom. I have cold cream in all my kits and handbags. In the car too. Just in case! But my husband's involvement in this crazy enterprise was what touched me deeply. He had fully understood my 'little thing', not mocked me, and actually taken a great deal of trouble to make sure I had sufficient stock of gooey cream to keep this particular anxiety at bay. *Kaho na, pyaar hai!*

~

The other F-word

I don't like to be categorized as any kind of 'ist'. It's okay to be ambivalent about grand issues and movements. I strongly believe in myself. That is it. I was born female. I will die female. To be born female makes you a natural-born feminist. You know your destiny is female. And you live your life with that knowledge. You cope. You deal. You survive. You recognize your female identity as being the truest one—no politics. You accept it and yourself. Why give it another label? Your life becomes your own the minute you decide you want it that way. It can be painful. It can be beautiful. It can be both. But it is yours to claim, to own and be proud of, no matter what. I believe in absolute freedoms and absolute equality. That belief is enough for me. I will unhesitatingly stand up for the underdog first and only later identify the gender.

A person who is being oppressed is a person—not a man, not a woman, but an oppressed person who may need urgent help and intervention to survive. Don't think! Help! It's a reflex action we often forget, so busy are we in getting the context right. There are far too many 'isms' for me to deal with. So I just don't bother with any of them. The question I am frequently and annoyingly asked is: 'Are you a feminist?' And it bothers me. Aren't we all? Or rather, shouldn't we all be thinking equality? I don't know how to respond truthfully, for the young, eager, earnest women looking at me to provide a road map for their own lives don't really want to hear what I feel. They want an easy-to-digest capsule with the standard clichés thrown in. The word 'empowerment' also annoys me when it is thrown around during conferences. What does it even mean? Who is an 'empowered' woman? The one armed with an education? The one with enough money in the bank? The one who is single by choice and says she doesn't need a man to validate her existence? The one who is at the barricades fighting for her sisters? The one who is pushing for legislative reform? I don't know. I really don't.

We are all strugglers. Each one of us—men and women. We all deal with the same anxieties and cope with the same phobias. Basic fears are gender-neutral. Fear of death, pain, loss. All we want is to stay healthy and happy. That's it. Achieving that goal takes a lifetime of doubt and uncertainty. Even then the goal remains elusive. We talk about Wonder Women and Superwomen, and constantly repeat mantras about how transformative this era has been for women across the world. Every era feels that way. But every era didn't wear message tees or celebrate International Women's Day. I see young girls declaring their independence and defying social norms. They are sure they have changed the world. Back home, when they peel off those tee shirts with teasing, brave slogans saluting girl power, they become the same person—a little scared, a little unsure. And I want to hug these girls and say, 'It's okay. You are gorgeous. You will win.'

Sometimes, I find myself featured on lists of feminist writers, and I feel like an impostor. I am whosoever I am. With failings and doubts and troubling thoughts. I have compromised thousands of times when, as a woman, I have taken practical decisions in the overall interests of my family. I have played myself down, acted and pretended, hidden my true feelings, kept mum . . . yes, all of that. Real life does not support Wonder Women, unfortunately. We all find ways to hang on to our principles and survive the best we can. Yes, my fiction has focused on the lives of women. Yes, I choose to write about women. Yes, most of my friends are women. Yes, I vastly prefer to invest my energy trying to fathom what it means to be a woman. I find women far more complex, far more interesting than most men. I like working with women. In fact, there's hardly any area of a woman's life that does not engage me. None of this makes me a feminist. All it means is that my emotional investments are not equally distributed. I favour my own gender. I generously give a woman the benefit of the doubt . . . something I don't do with men. In fact, I wish men would leave me alone. Not that they are queuing up to grab my attention! Which suits me just fine. I find it a strain to communicate with men. The effort to break the ice with a male stranger doesn't seem worth it at all. With a strange woman, making eye contact and even starting a conversation seems like the most natural thing to do. People say I intimidate men. I really don't! Even intimidation requires effort—why bother? I deliberately chose to stay out of the #MeToo movement. It is important to stand together in solidarity. It is equally important to help other women in real terms that go beyond trending hashtags. I have never encountered gender discrimination. No groping, no inappropriate touching. I escaped! But I am solidly behind any woman who has been victimized. Her pain is my pain.

A relatively new woman friend told me disingenuously, 'We were discussing you the other day, and one woman said she found you very domineering and aggressive, which is why she hesitates to talk to you. And I told her you were anything but. In my eyes you are a soft and caring person. I also told her you are very simple.' Maybe, I said to her, I am both. In my heart of hearts, I was so relieved! What if this other woman, who had decided I was domineering without having met me, had actually liked me? I am sure most of us go through life battling stereotypes. There was a time I would feel the need to explain myself. I no longer bother. Call me feminist. Call me anti-feminist. Call me elitist. Call me stupid. Call me a cow. Call me whatever. Age has its advantages! At the age of seventy, people have already made up their minds about you. Those who know you and accept you the way you are stay in your life. The others? Do I care? There is only so much time left. I prefer to invest it in people I respect and love. Or people I have fun with. People I can talk to freely. Egotistical? Nope. Emotionally self-sufficient. Finally.

People you instinctively take to generally reciprocate your feelings. These are the people who grow into lifelong friends. You don't have to meet them frequently or have daily conversations. But when you do spend time together, that time has to be valued . . . for it is precious. Oh, and remember—if they need you during any sort of an emergency, and you let them down, you don't know the real definition of friendship. Once, a group of students in Manipal dedicated a song I love: 'Stand by me.' It was a girl band, and they invited me to join them on stage. I did. It was a unique occasion at which for those brief moments, five strangers found themselves perfectly in sync. I never saw those girls again. But I never forgot them either. And the song still brings tears to my eyes. If we don't stand by one another—what are we? I dare not provide an answer.

I used to wonder about the exact meaning of the word 'epiphany'. Not sure I know the dictionary version. But I experience it over and over again. It is a tingling feeling of recognition. All of a sudden, a person in front of you—a person you think you have decoded years ago and know so well—says or does something that opens your third eye, and right there in front of you is a stranger you don't recognize. This used to scare me in the past. It demonstrated my lack of judgement. Yes, mine! And I have always been told how shrewd and insightful I am. How accurately I read people and situations. Was I ever that smart? Hardly! I faked it pretty well, I must admit!

Time is the most expensive commodity. We don't put enough value on it. I used to fritter the hours away earlier, only because of my inability to articulate that simple two-letter word, 'no'. Resentfully, and fuming from within, I would attend functions I didn't want to, and meet people who meant nothing to me. Once I started using the word 'no', I also realized it comes at a big, fat price! People get accustomed to your saying 'yes'. 'Yes' is easier to take for granted. In relationships of the intimate kind, 'yes' becomes a habit. When that 'yes' becomes a 'no', problems start. Partners get bewildered. Children feel disoriented. Friends start suspecting your loyalty. 'But you always said yes to this . . .' they accuse. And you feel like screaming, 'I did! I was an idiot to do so. But from now on, I will be saying "no". Yup. To the very same things I mutely but often angrily went along with—okay? And even if it isn't okay, I don't care. And yes . . . I will not pick up your calls when I am writing. I may never pick up you calls. Okay?' Believe me, after the first few times, everybody falls into line. Because they know you mean it. Because they have no choice but to accept your stand. And if not, they can tell you to take a walk, and you can do the same. Try! It's worth it. You may find this very hard to believe, but I have been bullied and bulldozed for years and by the unlikeliest of people. When I say that, friends scoff, 'Rubbish! You? And bullied? Come on . . .' Sorry. What I am saying is 100 per cent true—and those bullies out there, who unfairly pressured me to go along and who may be reading this, know that.

Put a value on your time more than on anything else. Once gone, it can't be replaced, unlike other precious commodities. Your time is your time. Become possessive about it. Guard it. Share it only if you think it's worth sharing. I have always liked time with myself and I can honestly say I never ever feel bored when I am alone—whether it's at home, at work or in a foreign land. I don't understand boredom. What's that? How can life be boring? Is that even possible? *Kabhi nahin!*

These days I find myself saying 'no' a lot. I wish I had done that earlier. I wasted far too many valuable hours in situations and with people I loathed only because I was too polite to say, 'Sorry! You are not my type. I have absolutely nothing to say to you. We are losing precious time even at this very second as we try to engage. Goodbye!' Worse, I didn't permit myself to think, 'No!' My first reaction was to say yes to plans. And then fret. 'Why the hell did I put my foot into this?' I would ask myself. Sometimes, it was easy to make an excuse and get out. Sometimes, I was stuck. Today, I first say, 'No,' and then weigh the options. And I never pick up calls from unknown numbers. If they need to reach me, they can always text. Or send an email. Earlier, I felt people would judge me and say, 'What a bitch! Who does she think she is?' Soon, I figured, those sorts of people would say, 'What a bitch,' regardless! Even if I did turn up and was at my charming best. These days I get to the point very quickly. If the venue is too far (any event that requires more than thirty minutes of travel time is out), and the people inviting me are not blood relatives, the answer is 'Nyet.' Ditto for requests to address various social service organizations. It's a colossal waste of time and effort. All those earnest doctors, chartered accountants and corporate top dogs are good people doing good work. But I know their main plan is to network. And eat lavish meals. And get speakers for their five-star luncheons. Why they bother to invite me, I'll never know. Most have never read a book in their lives. Most are conformists and play-it-safe citizens incapable of saying 'boo' to the local municipal corporator. There is no common ground. I refuse to play performing flea, unless there's a fee attached. No free speeches! And so it goes, with social acquaintances who suddenly remember you when they need something done. Women and men who have not bothered to reach out to me for decades phone out of the blue, thinking foolishly and mistakenly that I possess enormous clout and power. I absolutely do not! So . . . to believe I can get their duffer child into a top college by talking to the principal is a fallacy. I wouldn't do it even if I did possess the required 'influence'. No, no, no. I am really fine being unpopular. I don't need more people in my life. I am not looking to make new 'friends' and am happy with the few I have. Saying 'no' comes easily to me these days. And I feel so liberated! The stupidest phrase is 'social obligations'. Really! There are none! Unless you want to play that meaningless game. I hear people saying, 'Oh . . . but if you don't attend their functions, they won't attend yours!' The point is, I neither want to attend those functions nor do I want to invite those folks to any of mine. We should all choose early and choose wisely. I remember with a sense of horror how I used to force myself to eat rubbish at parties 'out of politeness' ('Why hurt the hosts' feelings?'). Today, I generally eat at home before attending dinners. Or decline invitations altogether. I don't accept writing assignments if the topic doesn't interest me—regardless of which editor will feel cheesed off and snubbed. If your heart isn't in something 100 per cent, don't bother. The result will be mediocre.

That goes for the mistakes I made with some of my books too. I really didn't want to write them! But was talked into it by persuasive publishers more hell-bent on marketing a certain kind of book—and forget what I felt. Cash in while the author is 'hot'. That's how it works worldwide. Writing has always come easily to me. So the effort involved in crafting a story out of approximately 80,000 words, was never a daunting prospect. But here's the thing: Those 80,000 words can go into a book you have enjoyed writing, or a lousy one you have rolled out under duress. I look back at some of my books and think—left to myself, I would have written a different book. I am not saying a better book, nor am I saying a more saleable book. Just a very different book! Publishers know their markets. And they knew what they wanted to do with my early books—flog them as India's breakthrough 'sexy' novels written by a 'bold' woman. Someone who photographed well and was fun to interview. That disgusting tag of 'Jackie Collins of India' stuck! It will follow me to my grave. Nothing wrong with Jackie Collins. But I prefer to be me.

I enjoyed writing about sex. That is fine, not complaining. The reactions were tedious. Making me more and more determined to raise the sex bar as it were with each successive novel. I tried strictly no-sex books too. And focused on chaste non-fiction for years. But no! That tag of being a 'porno writer' (if you please) refused to go away. Hmm, I said to myself tiredly. Damned if I do and damned if I don't. So . . . why not just bang them out and have fun? I am determined to write even sexier books in future. What will our puritanical 'samaj' say? *'Yeh buddhiya badi badmash hai.'* What fun! That's it? I can handle that. Besides, if you are a buddhiya, better to be badmash than a bore!

I look back at some of my books and think—left to myself, I would have written a different book. I am not saying a better book, nor am I saying a more saleable book. Just a very different book!

~

Write with your heart . . . not just your head

I am a little cross with myself for going along with the 'written to order' books, even if the stories, characters and all else were mine. Some of the novels were mangled during the editing process. I thought I would offend the star editor by not agreeing with editorial tweaking. A lot of it was invaluable, I readily concede. But most of it was just meaningless interference. I watched mutely as a total mess was made of the manuscript. I kept quiet and accepted the mangling passively. Why did I keep silent? Because I didn't want to offend the know-alls who were butchering the original by arbitrarily reshuffling sequences. I wanted them to 'like' me and not think I was throwing my weight around as a 'senior bestselling author' and being egotistical or a bully. They meant well, I am sure. They were just not competent. And I bloody well should have yelled, 'Noooooo! Leave my book alone. It's my book and my ass on the line. It may be the worst, most unreadable piece of tripe. But it is mine. My words belong to me! Let readers decide.'

A good editor nudges, never shoves. Suggests, never imposes. Nurtures, never demoralizes. Tightens, never twists. A good editor is the author's most trusted ally. There aren't that many good editors around!

Young writers are so much smarter. I was headed to yet another lit fest. Seated next to me was a hugely successful author—a former banker (how come there are so many bankers-turned-authors suddenly?). This gentleman was my son's age. We started chatting. He was being a bit too deferential and I began feeling like a 'mataji' straight out of a television serial. He wanted to talk books. Nothing but books. Okay, I said to myself, let's talk books. I asked about his latest ones. And he shared so many wonderful details about the making of the book—how long it took him to research and design the intricate cover, how each tiny symbol came with a deep philosophical meaning and why he preferred to write a certain kind of book, after consulting his wife who heads his publicity team. At no point did he discuss writing! It was more a marketing presentation and less a conversation about creativity. He was generous enough to share a great deal of relevant sales information with me. He knew most major booksellers by their first names and stayed in daily contact with the top few. He travelled extensively to network with book agents and distributors across India, on whom he lavished gifts and sweetmeats. 'If you invest in these guys, they make sure your book gets a prominent display. If you ignore them, they can kill your book by shoving it to the last shelf,' he confided innocently. He also admitted he bought back thousands of his own books in order to stay on bestseller lists. Why did he need to do all this? He said earnestly, 'It is very, very important to stay at number one! Writing a book is only a small part of it. Marketing is everything.'

Of course, the ball game has changed. And it is authors like this person who have altered the rules. This is the new generation of writers, who first strategize with a smart, savvy team and then write a book. They have the pulse and they don't feel at all embarrassed to go out and hire a top PR company to project them across media platforms. Most young novelists have their eyes on cracking a Bollywood deal. They write primarily with that goal in mind. Bollywood is the ultimate dream, and they waste no time pursuing it, via agents and 'contacts'. Once in, they work the system and do whatever it takes to stay in that orbit. In essence, they are scriptwriters in search of a producer. I admire their focused, single-minded agenda. They are there to make money, period. They go about writing a book like they are filling a ledger. They don't read. Have never been readers. But that does not mean they lack imagination. Somehow, conducting a market survey first, and then deciding on the theme of the next novel, seems a pretty mechanical way of writing to me. But it works! I call them the canny 'spreadsheet' authors. First—a business plan. Then the book. No wonder so many successful authors are former money managers. I enjoy talking to them when we meet at lit fests. And marvel at their confidence. 'You are such a rock star!' I teased one, who had a bunch of teenage girls trailing him across the lawns. He smiled smugly, shrugged and said, 'I know! Just look at my fans!' Okaaay! Impressed!

Sometimes I wonder, if I had asserted myself thirty years ago, and not participated in the circus, would I have written any differently? Why did I go along with those over-the-top photo shoots? Why did I constantly play myself down by making self-deprecatory comments? Why was I so apologetic about my 'glamorous' appearance, or the 'elite' lifestyle that obsessed critics? So many books and years later, nothing much has changed. I still have people come up to me to ask angrily, 'But why do you have so much sex in your books? Why can't you write about

Sometimes I wonder, if I had asserted myself thirty years ago, and not participated in the circus, would I have written any differently?

ordinary people? Do you know what it feels like to be poor? You are so hi-fi!' I plead guilty! Had I been shrewder and put my foot down the first time I was asked to go along with the marketing strategy that 'positioned' me forever, I would not have had to put up with crass, ignorant, idiotic 'assessments' of either me or my work. I laughed at myself a lot (I still do!), and it was a licence given to strangers to do the same! Self-deprecatory humour is not for everyone. It certainly didn't work for me. Young writers are clever—they laugh all the way to the bank.

I am awestruck by young writers who are so full of themselves after publishing one piddly little nothing of a novel. They strut around like they have changed the world through their words and ideas. Nobody laughs at them. Their pompous pronouncements in interviews are taken at face value. They hire stylists and PR outfits to project them in the right light. They brag and hustle non-stop. Suck up to lit fest organizers. Brazenly manipulate each and every aspect of the publishing world. Nobody laughs. They employ touts to buy back their own books. Some have mini godowns stacked with copies of their titles. Nobody laughs.

My fate was sealed the day I agreed to pose for a glamour photo spread, lounging on a tiger skin for *Time* magazine. And it was that profile which created the nauseating 'Jackie Collins of India' nonsense. (Damn you, Anthony Spaeth!) Why did I go along? Sheer stupidity! I was flattered. I fell for the spiel. Even on that tiger skin, dressed in an antique rani-pink lehenga—I was laughing at the absurdity of what I was willingly participating in. But, unfortunately, the joke was on me.

It is important to value yourself from the word go. Don't get talked into publicity campaigns that may sell more books, but may cause you immeasurable damage in the long run. Of course, publishers are greedy beasts. They want to milk you for all you have to sell. But nobody can force you on to that tiger skin! I was not forced. I did it voluntarily as a bit of a lark—to have some entertainment. It was an extension of my modelling past, that's all. I was sending myself up! But that is not how it works! As a model, you are participating in a fantasy. All those crazy shoots I had done over decades were just that—someone else's fantasy. But this was me playing me in reality! How come I didn't recognize the difference? Once stuck with that ridiculous image, I was branded for evermore. With each subsequent book and the ensuing publicity blitz, the stereotyping got further entrenched. I had asked for it! Nobody complained . . . least of all, my publishers.

But—aha—there is an upside to all this *golmaal* as well. Over time, I had become a part of the Penguin India family. These days I joke, 'I am the designated grandmother of the group.' It is a position of enormous privilege and I deeply value it. What better then than to have been offered an honour of a lifetime when I was asked whether I would like to head an imprint of my own, under the Penguin umbrella? I nearly fell off my chair. We were at Mumbai's iconic Sea Lounge, in the Taj Mahal Hotel. Three of us—two top dogs from Penguin and moi. I wasn't sure I had heard right. The offer was repeated. I still didn't take it seriously. I mean, the only other woman with an imprint to call her own that I had heard of was Jacqueline Kennedy. I asked what the offer actually meant. 'It means you get to create your own publishing list, and the books carry your name as publisher,' a representative of Penguin explained solemnly as David Davidar grinned broadly. I can be really immature at moments like this. I needed to pee. But I stayed put and let it sink in. Done! It was that easy!

I have enjoyed every book and every author published under the SDé Books imprint. With each new title, I have learnt something invaluable. We do a limited number of non-fiction titles a year. But I get to read several fascinating manuscripts. Sitting in the publisher's chair after being an author has made me far more sensitive to other writers. There are lots of wonderful voices out there, and several hugely talented people waiting for that book contract that often transforms their lives and starts an exciting adventure. It gives me as big a thrill to hold the advance copy of 'my' author's book as it does when my own arrives. Goosebumps and all.

Today, I feel like I am ready to face just about anything. 'Cut the crap' has always been my attitude. It has served me well. 'Cut to the chase' is another. I have an overdeveloped sense of the ridiculous. And irreverence is a religious belief. I meet many pompous asses who take themselves far too seriously and declare without a trace of embarrassment, 'I am an intellectual.' Get over it, friend! No, you are not! You are just another smug person with a highly exaggerated sense of worth. Climb down from that high horse and look around you. What do you see? Far more talented people! Look at yourself now—what do you see if you are honest? A mediocre individual

'Cut the crap' has always been my attitude. It has served me well. 'Cut to the chase' is another.

who has read a few books, watched a few films, attended a few concerts, and can brag about it. That's all!

I read an article with the headline 'Men Write Erotica. Women Write Pornography.' It was written by a woman whose books contain sexually explicit passages. Like a few of mine. I know what it feels like! People are obsessed with the sex lives of women. I still get asked that irritating question, 'Madam . . . so much sex-vex in your books, na? Is it about your own experiences, hai na?' I feel like yelling, 'Yes, of course! *Bilkul, ji!* Aren't I one hell of a lucky bitch?' I mean, come on! Nobody asked Khushwant Singh that question! Then there are the young girls who come up to whisper, 'I love your novels, yaar. You write amazing soft porn, ma'am! It's too good! I was not allowed to read your books when I was in school. My mother used to hide them after wrapping the covers in brown paper. She wouldn't let me touch them. So mean! Still . . . I managed somehow. You are too cool, ma'am . . . all those hot bits!' Yeah . . . right . . . all those 'hot bits'. Young men sidle up to say (heavy breathing at this point), 'Madamji, *aap toh India ki Lady Kamasutra ho!* Can we click a selfie?' I feel like saying, '*Gadhey! Aur kuch nahi padha zindagi mein?* Just the "hot bits"?' But I figure, why waste my breath? I also feel like yelling, 'Yes! Haan, haan! *Yeh sab mere hi experiences hai. Bas*, you dirty little fellow with the broken, stained teeth.' Instead, I shrug. I smile a crooked smile. Next time, I am going to tell these kids to address me as 'Your Royal Hotness', just to see the expressions on their faces. Maybe they will squeal, 'Sooooooo cute, yaar!' Yup. I get that too. Or they'll turn away, thinking, 'What is this woman thinking?'

Then come the ignorant foreigners who react with arched eyebrows and a sideways smile when I am introduced to them as a writer. 'Oh really? So, dearie, what do you write? Romance? Cookbooks?' I reply with my straightest face, 'I write hardcore pornography disguised as cookbooks. Devouring orgasmic food is the ultimate pornographic experience, don't you agree?' Some of them get the joke. Others look startled, stare at my 'native costume' (saree) and move away swiftly.

~

Nanga–bhooka India

I am not one of Midnight's Children. Rather, I am a Child of the Republic (1948). Technically, I was born into a 'nanga–bhooka' India. Except India never looked nanga–bhooka to me. India always looked beautiful. Still does. I don't care if I am accused of over-romanticizing India. I can deal with that. What bugs me is the other idiotic charge, 'Madamji, you are so elite! What do you know about the "other" India? How the majority lives?' True to an extent. And not true, as well. Do you have to be the man on the moon to figure out a lunar eclipse? And yet, India's image in the world continues to be defined by a begging bowl. Not too long ago, my husband and I were on a cruise along the many stunningly beautiful islands of Croatia. There were around thirty other people on board the midsized yacht. All of them were affluent and educated, and from different parts of the world. Nobody was interested in India. Nobody had heard of Narendra Modi. Even those smug Americans and Canadians on board weren't aware that India was, in fact, the world's largest democracy! Nobody knew India is considered one of the fastest-emerging global superpowers. Everybody was aware of China and its place in the international pecking order. I could read a few of their thoughts: How come these two have the money to take such a cruise? They did say they are from India—right? Isn't there a famine going on there?' Just like my generation associated the word 'famine' with Ethiopia. Same ignorance. Same prejudice. My husband was offended and outraged and delivered thundering lectures at the breakfast table, complete with statistics and published reports on the Great India Story. He was disturbed by their indifference. He wanted to change their perspective and set the record straight by bombarding them with information. No wonder they started avoiding us!

Yes, it hurts. It hurts deeply when foreigners continue to think of India as the land of snake charmers, sadhus, elephants and tigers.

Today, they add with a wink and a horrible snigger, 'Oh yes, we heard about that terrible rape in a moving bus [Nirbhaya]! Women are treated very badly in your country. Rape capital of the world, eh?' The English are happy to discuss cricket and Sachin Tendulkar before adding, 'But the Pakistanis are bloody good . . . perhaps better!' Most goras have never heard of Bollywood, even though more than 1500 movies are made here annually. Indian cuisine is reduced to: 'Spicy! Yes, we have sampled your curries!' Which bloody curry, you idiots? There is no such thing as a generic Indian 'curry'! They have no idea about India's IT whizzes, even those heading prominent American corporate giants, they haven't heard of the number of billionaires who make it to the top of global rich lists. Ask about our Davos-walla industrialists and you get blank stares. People know next to nothing about this gigantic land mass with more than 1.4 billion people! They look dumbstruck when one discusses India's position at the high table—there is disbelief when they learn India is a part of the G20. All they know or wish to talk about is our starving masses. Not even our staggering corruption! I thought the stratospheric numbers involved in cases of corruption, plus some of the prominent personalities, would make an 'impact'. I was that desperate! I still wonder: How can such a vast seventy-year-old nation, a country as diverse, as culturally inspiring as India, leave the rest of the world this cold? And here we were, my husband and I, discussing the cultural and political contours of every country on the map, with casual acquaintances we weren't likely to meet again. We knew more about their history than they knew about India's present.

That cruise became an eye-opener of sorts. To our co-passengers we must have looked like aliens from another galaxy. Brown people. One or two of them were foolish enough to state incredulously, 'But you speak English! And you don't look Indian.' What did that even mean? That we were not representative enough of the nanga–bhooka India? We didn't look poverty-stricken? We drank wine and used knives and forks? I was asked the standard stupid questions: 'Was yours an arranged marriage?' To which I would answer with a straight face, 'Not just arranged by an evil uncle . . . it was also a child marriage.' Most didn't get the irony of that comment. I was also asked if I was South American, since my looks were not 'Indian' enough. I asked them to describe what they meant by 'typical Indian looks'. And they would talk vaguely about a National Geographic documentary they'd once seen, in which 'dark-skinned women wore brightly coloured garments and covered their faces with a veil'. Over and over again, the conversation kept coming back to poverty. No amount of kiddish 'boasting' about our burgeoning middle class with enough spending power to keep Croatia afloat, no amount of talking about our satellites and space programmes, or India's nuclear capability, could distract them from the nanga–bhooka narrative. Did they not have poor people in their own countries? And rape and violence and disease? I didn't like the feeling of having to 'explain' India. Why are we made to behave in such an apologetic, defensive way, when we should be able to thrust our chests out with pride? Not all our men can boast of having a fifty-six-inch chest like Narendra Modi. But, come on . . . I sincerely think we are pretty terrific! I like the brashness of India. Yes, there are huge issues. But somehow, when we are celebrating any one of our outrageously colourful festivals, India appears perfect in the glow of all those diyas. My heart soars along with the cheeky kites during Sankranti. Or as I giddily swirl with the garba raas dancers and imagine I am Deepika Padukone singing, '*Dhol baaje* . . .' I don't enjoy playing Holi, but when I see the expression in the eyes of revellers smeared with myriad colours, it makes me happy.

Right now, I am stuck! Happy to admit my dilemma. I love my India. I loathe the politicians in control of our collective destiny. Unless there is some dramatic and unforeseen development, I believe the BJP will be the main party dominating the political scenario for the next twenty years. I have uneasily made my peace with that forecast. There is little choice. Though Rahul Gandhi's Berkeley address may turn the tide for the Congress party. Day by day, I watch with a growing sense of alarm, dread and concern as various freedoms are trampled and critical voices get silenced. Making the singing of Vande Mataram compulsory in schools? Tick. Monitoring social media accounts and actively spying on citizens? Tick. Rewriting history books and wiping out any positive reference to Mughal history? Tick. Appointing RSS-approved personalities to some of the most coveted administrative/ceremonial positions? Tick. Jailing, hounding, prosecuting and persecuting dissidents and free thinkers? Tick. The state is creeping up on citizens in obvious and insidious ways. We are told it is being done 'for our good'. Inch by inch, we are surrendering priceless personal ground, precious territory. The next generation may not even know the existence of our fundamental rights. The process to infiltrate and indoctrinate every aspect of our lives has started. India being declared a Hindu nation seems a certainty. Which automatically means Muslims beware—behave or else.

Today, we are being dictated to at multiple levels—told what we can eat, drink, watch, wear, think. The protests against these diktats have been feeble at best. Hamid Ansari, a soft-spoken, erudite scholar, spoke for many when he stated on television, soon after his term as the vice president of India ended, 'This propensity to be asked to assert your nationalism day in and day out is unnecessary. I am an Indian and that is that.' That really should be that. But is it? Ansari candidly referred to a sense of unease among Muslims, and he said 'a sense of insecurity is creeping in'—can anybody deny this? His stinging critique must have upset the prime minister enough to rebuke Ansari publicly in words one can only describe as unfortunate and undignified ('You can now follow your basic ideology and instinct . . .').

Despite all these dreadful and discouraging signs, my faith in the Constitution and in the basic decency, even goodness, of our people never deserts me. Indians possess enormous reserves of common sense that has saved them over centuries. It will save them again, even if the present regime ups its game. It may take a generation to set things right. A huge price may be extracted. Even so, I don't feel discouraged or defeated about India's future. Along with the dream of greater prosperity and more jobs, there are other equally compelling dreams. Dreams of equality and safety. Dreams of free speech and the right to dissent. Dreams of privacy and progress. Why should any citizen back down in the face of dadagiri? Take on the bullies! Protest with all your might. A free India is the only India. Fight and reclaim what is rightfully yours—it is our Bharat *mahaan*. Yours and mine. It belongs to us. Remember, we have not handed it over like a yummy chocolate cake to any political party, at any time in our history. The BJP has the people's overwhelming mandate for now. And that mandate must be respected as long as the BJP serves the people. It is our job as citizens to make sure they deliver as promised. I am not an economist, I don't understand GST and demonetization—but nor do 99 per cent of Indians. Like them, all I know is I am paying more and more and getting less and less for working harder and harder. Makes no sense to me. If I am feeling conned and angry, so are millions of others.

Yet, we cling on desperately to the few and far between lollipops we receive—mainly from our judiciary, which seems to have taken over the running of the country, simply because there is nobody else willing to do a good and honourable job of it. To those men and women, who protect the Constitution and provide hope to millions of citizens—a big salaam. The landmark judgement which was hailed by all gave privacy back to us as a fundamental right. In an atmosphere defined by fear and repression—this was a major victory signalling an era of justice and equality in the years ahead. This vital ruling enshrined the right of every citizen to 'dissent and critique'. Nothing beats this!

> Yet, we cling on desperately to the few and far between lollipops we receive—mainly from our judiciary, which seems to have taken over the running of the country, simply because there is nobody else willing to do a good and honourable job of it.

The past four years have added new words to our everyday vocabulary that make me uncomfortable. We have gone smoothly from Donald Trump's 'post-truth' to our very own 'post-guilt'. These are phrases that generate pain and unease of an unfamiliar kind. I voice my anguish. As do thousands of others. The rather foolish response to any of our concerns is: 'Go to Pakistan.' The first time this happened, I wrote a column which ended with the line, 'My bags are packed. I am ready to go to Pakistan.' Agreed it was an impulsive outburst, and I really don't want to go to Pakistan. Or live in any other country. But this silly refrain—'Go to Pakistan'—has not stopped. The level of public discourse is shamefully low. Name-calling is not a cogent argument. I ignore abuse. But what about all the writers across India who have been physically targeted? Abducted? Murdered? Yes . . . things have changed. The slide has been dramatic and too sudden. We no longer react with horror and shame—as we should—to casteist slurs, for example. Words like divisive, Dalit, lynchings, *gau rakshaks*, rape, *ghar wapsi*, to name just a few, are so liberally strewn in the media, they no longer generate a response—no shock, no outrage, no anger. The present regime believes we have been successfully inoculated into accepting the restructuring of India along dangerous and narrow religious lines. No, we have not. Like dengue, there is no inoculation in the world that can succeed here. Speak up—and be damned. Keep mum—and also be damned! So what? Speak up, you must. India is yours. Fight for it!

~

While I was driving through a surprisingly green and lush part of Rajasthan with Arundhati, she drew my attention to young boys playing cricket in the clearing near a village. There were at least ten teams playing side by side. Some of the boys wore only tattered shorts. Nobody was wearing shoes. From these very fields, so many of our most talented cricketers have played for India and brought glory to the country. Maybe I am consoling myself. Maybe I don't want to face grim realities. That's my call. It's like a child looking trustingly at the mother who is less than perfect. Does the child notice her flaws? I think not. My emotional relationship with India is something similar. I feel protective when India is criticized by people who are not stakeholders. I am a stakeholder. I have earned the right to feel possessive. And the right to criticize. For nothing in the world will I walk away from the land of my birth. The land of my forefathers. India is my DNA. Nanga or clothed. Bhooka or well fed. Boss—*yeh mera* India, okay? *Jaisey bhi! Kaisa bhi!* Don't mess *hamarey saath*—mind it!

~

Mere apne

My kids drive me nuts. I am sure I drive them nuts. Perhaps they can imagine a life without me. I dare not ask—what if they cheerfully chorus, 'Yes! We can!' But I certainly cannot endure a day without them. Modern-day mothering is something else. I shudder when I hear about the countless daily challenges faced by parents today. And how ironical it is that someone like me has to be constantly tutored on what is 'cool' and what isn't. There are life-threatening situations out there that nobody prepared my generation for. I remain cautiously optimistic about the future and blow kisses heavenwards that so far I have not had to deal with a) a child getting arrested for something trivial/not so trivial, b) a drug bust, c) OD-ing, d) run-ins with the law, e) drunken driving, f) gang wars or f) public or private brawls. If, in reality, their lives have in fact been far wilder or more colourful than I am aware of, *and* they haven't got into a serious mess, well then, good for them. I don't necessarily want to know anything or everything in an overwrought, paranoid mommy way. I think I know as much as I need to know. And that's already too much!

We are in constant touch no matter where we may be, in India or overseas. WhatsApp has been one of the greatest tech boons in my life for this sole reason. I can chat non-stop on our group, aptly called The Brood. If my incessant chatter bugs them, they haven't said so. I know how obsessively I keep checking for messages from them. I joke I can read not just their hearts, but their kidneys and gall bladders too. Today, three of them, Radhika, Avantikka and Arundhati, have children of their own. I see them as exemplary mothers—hands-on and well informed. They have their priorities in place. And are married to caring, loving partners. The other three? Vagabonds! Lovable vagabonds. They will decide when they decide, and I will accept their choices unconditionally. They know as much. Rana and Aditya—the 'boys' are men now. Rana is in his own Zen-like zone in Singapore. Aditya likes his cave equally. The ladies love both of them. As for Anandita—she is the 'baby' we hope will stay our baby for ever, even after she has her own. Their dissimilarities intrigue me. Sometimes, I step back and watch us when we are together and ask myself in wonder, 'Did I really have something deep and wonderful to do with all of them that goes beyond biology?' When I shut my eyes, just after switching off the lights at night, I first say a small prayer expressing gratitude for one more fulfilling/maddening day on earth. I remember my mother . . . and imagine she has just stroked my forehead . . . held me. Then I smile. That smile is only for my children. They never see it. I wish they could. For they will see a contented, peaceful mother . . . not smug, not uncritical, not all-forgiving . . . oh no! But a woman who cherishes their presence with every breath she takes. If this narrative does not have enough mentions, memories and anecdotes about each one of them individually, it is because I find it the toughest writing assignment of all! Children are competitive. They count words and lines. They note omissions and commissions. It is impossible to please your own. I was touched when Arundhati asked for her 'birthday letter' this year. It used to be a tradition for me to write these letters to the birthday child . . . and I am not sure when or even why I stopped. Perhaps I thought my over-sentimental words no longer interested my children. And that was hurtful. The only reaction I'd get was, 'Ma . . . you have made me cry again!' Was that praise? Or an accusation? I wasn't sure. I did not ask. And then Arundhati made her request . . . my heart soared! After writing the letter, I searched for words that captured my emotions adequately. I was at a loss. Suddenly, the miracle happened. I found them! Those two little words: 'Mere apne', so evocatively put together by our great poet Gulzar, express my feelings towards my babies better than any tome. The words are all embracing and complete. My children are my entire universe and beyond—they are my precious 'mere apne'. And I love making them cry! Because that gives me an excuse to cry too!

~

Once a 'kaarti', always a 'kaarti'

I am talking about more than just this book. Why did I even write it? Or, on a more abstract, philosophical, perhaps even loony level—I believe this book was meant to be written. And sort of wrote itself. All I needed was a nudge—no, a shove. I had started to think the era of books had ended a decade ago. And I may even be spot on. Sure, thousands of titles make it to the bookshelves even today, but who is reading all these wonderful and not-so-wonderful books? I know I no longer have the patience to force myself to read a book that doesn't captivate me in the first five pages. I give up! Toss it aside and look for something else to read . . . or do. Despite all these reservations, I still decided to go ahead and commit. Yes, a book is a commitment. Once committed, I am in. I have been writing professionally for close to fifty years. Writing is what I love more than any other activity. I write every day of my life. Today, I write four columns a week—all of them distinct and different, given the profile and demographic of the readers of the various publications. It is thrilling and unbelievably challenging to reach out to anonymous readers and wonder how they might react. On an average I write between 1500 and 2000 words a day. This has been my pace for decades. I don't wish to compute the number of words this adds up to. But I am pretty pleased I have been able to achieve my targets day in and day out for five decades. There are also the twenty-odd books that, over thirty years, have carried my name as author. Despite the industry and plain slog involved, my family still thinks I don't have a 'proper' job! I mean, come on! Give me a break, you heartless people!

In a way, it's good to be taken for granted. Everybody takes me for granted, I swear—family, friends, even my publishers! My children watch me hunched over the laptop, with a look of intense involvement, and say half-irritatedly, 'Oh God! What is she busy with?' Um . . . you still don't know? My right wrist gave up on me (tendonitis), my right hand developed what is called a 'trigger finger'—a pretty painful condition. I required medical intervention for both! And they still wondered what caused it? It annoys me sometimes. I see how others react to writers who are family members. They are treated with respect! Reverence! Their time at the desk is considered precious. Nobody disturbs them. They are allowed to shut themselves off for months and years on end, while people around them whisper in awed tones, 'He is writing a book. He needs his peace . . .' Yes, it's always a 'he'. And sure, he needs his peace. What about me? And other women who write from home? Do we possess a magic button? Are there goblins and elves writing on our behalf while the family sleeps? Are we supposed to turn invisible while we soldier away? Just so the others don't get bugged? I choose to write from my dining table. No locking myself in a study. I guess the thinking is, 'If she is writing in a shared space, then she's asking to be interrupted. Sorry! We need to eat too!' Yes. And chat loudly over the cell phone . . . and play music at an ear-splitting level. Of course, I have 'asked for it'. Go ahead—punish me!

~

I thought about this and more on a vacation I took this year. It was a break I was taking from writing and much else, with many reservations. This was to be one of my longest trips (twenty days) away from home. And it was going to be just me and my husband, adventurously opting for a Croatian cruise. I was apprehensive and voiced it. I even joked, 'What if only one of us comes back alive to tell the tale? So much intimacy . . . so much proximity . . . we aren't love-struck honeymooners any more. What if we argue and fight? Sulk and storm? Imagine being stuck in a yacht's cabin for seven days and nights! What if I feel suicidal or even homicidal?

Jumping into the Adriatic is worse than slashing my wrists.' The children laughed at my anxieties. 'It will be just fine. When in doubt, have a glass of wine.'

My husband, on the other hand, was like an excited schoolboy, planning what we'd do at each port. I felt cynical and low. Journeys are no longer as easy as they used to be twenty years ago. Age! Everything reflects the cruel passage of time. As we packed, telling one another to keep it light ('Remember, there are no porters these days, and we'll have to lug our bags all over the place on our own!'), I smiled inwardly. We were carefully sorting out our assorted tablets and emergency medicines, I was making sure I had at least three extra pairs of reading glasses, he was taking his armband to support a sensitive elbow. In the past, I would enthusiastically buy new bikinis and fun kaftans. This time I was carrying sensible capri pants and sturdy footwear. Both of us were concerned about slipping on uneven cobblestones, or missing a step while exploring some ancient ruins. We were discussing digestive issues and ensuring we had muscle relaxants in the kit. Where was the old don't-care-a-damn spirit?

At the airport, we resembled two oldies, checking and rechecking our boarding cards and fussing with shawls, cardigans, socks. We had decided to be careful and not touch a drink on the flight ('Dehydration—let's stick to lots of water'). This was nuts! No champagne before take-off . . . no Bordeaux with the meal. What sort of a holiday was this going to be? Two old people behaving themselves and being model tourists getting their fill of history and culture? Hell, no! We looked at each other and without saying a thing, it was decided all those great rules we had made for ourselves would be instantly discarded. Thank God! Immediately, as the new connection and understanding kicked in wordlessly, we knew it was going to be a memorable trip. Which it most certainly was. And here's just one example of why it turned out to be so much fun. We both grabbed the vivid memories and images of our much younger selves and decided to stay in that magical zone. Everything came back! Our reckless, naughty moments included. Late one evening, just before stepping out for dinner in Split (what a destination!), I got into a shortish black dress. Not a mini—oh, definitely not! But the hemline was defiantly and unambiguously above my knees. I thought Mr Dé would look at me sharply and suggest I change, or wear leggings. Instead, he beamed with delight. 'You are looking hot! Let's go. But before that, I want to shoot some pictures . . . the evening light is so good.' I was unsure, but went along with it, thinking he'd stop after five. But no, he kept on shooting! And I kept on posing! Some of the pics were pretty damn good! And some were rotten. I focused on the rotten. 'Just look at my legs here—oh God! Please delete!' He was surprised by my reaction. 'I think these pictures are great! Of course, your legs look different now—but they are your legs! And I love them.' I was incredibly touched. And as always, when I feel sentimental, I deal with the emotion awkwardly and immediately change the subject. We set off happily, with me thinking, 'What the hell—nobody knows me here . . .' But is there any place on earth we Indians have not discovered? Sure enough, a largish group from Gujarat walked up to me, asked for selfies and started a conversation. I noticed most eyes were fixed on my bare legs. I wanted to hide . . .

cover up! I was only too happy when the group moved away. 'I felt so embarrassed . . . did you see the way they were staring? And that too mainly at my legs!' I cribbed. My husband took my arm, smiled and said, 'We should have kissed . . .'

~

Mainu ki?

I came across *mainu ki* rather late in life. Trust the Punjabis to have the apt phrase handy when they want to say, 'Get lost! Just eff off!' Today, I have made it a motto of sorts. 'Mainu ki . . . ?' can be used in countless ways and in countless situations. It also depends on who you are saying it to. It sort of translates to 'Who cares?' Or a cruder interpretation which is deliciously colloquial: 'What goes of your father?' But 'Mainu ki . . . !' is so much sweeter. It's lovely to arrive at that stage in your life when you really don't give a rat's ass about most things and people.

I came across *mainu ki* rather late in life. Trust the Punjabis to have the apt phrase handy when they want to say, 'Get lost! Just eff off!'

You reach a certain point—clumsily, shakily, only when old wounds have healed. And you know you have made your peace with battle scars. There is no looking back in anger. In my case, there is hardly any looking back at all. The time for that walk back into the forest is upon you, and you start seeing the forest with different eyes. You notice things you had missed earlier in your hurry to reach the end of the forest. You look down as much as you look up. You catch patches of bright blue sky, and also enjoy the shadows. You stare at tiny wild flowers growing under the shade of tall trees. The light is mellow—always mellow. And pale gold. You stand bathed in it—feeling golden yourself. The glow you admired outside is now a part of you. You feel its warmth within.

Those who knew the much younger you are surprised and say so. 'Didn't think you would ever be this . . . this . . .' Often the word is left unsaid. I like to provide it—sometimes just to myself. Could it be 'tender'? Decades earlier, I would have recoiled at the mere suggestion and retorted: 'What? Me and tender?' Now, I cherish those special moments. Especially the ones I share with my family. And even more strongly, with my husband. I feel protective and far less confrontational. I admire his gung-ho spirit. I admire his taking a huge leap at the age of seventy-five and declaring himself an artist. Not just declaring it, but putting his art and reputation on the line, exhibiting it and taking the chance he could be rejected and laughed at. That takes guts. That's one thing he certainly has never lacked! When I watch him painting on his smartphone with a stylus (the first person to do so in the world), I feel a surge of tenderness. There he sits, a picture of utmost concentration, painstakingly filling in minute details, constantly reviewing and rejecting . . . then starting over with one image after another. He is so fortunate to have discovered a brand-new passion at seventy-five. A passion for creating art—not just admiring and acquiring it.

These days he paints versions of me obsessively. I find it a bit of a pain. When he is done with an image, he shows it to me proudly and waits for a reaction. I can be pretty horrid. Sometimes I express my delight. But most times I am hypercritical. He stares at the image for a long time, his eyes looking for the flaws I have spotted, and then he sighs, 'Have you seen Picasso's vision of his wife?' Uff! Such heartbreaking, disarming innocence!

There is something so comforting about familiarity and habit. Today, we know each other well—my husband and I. Truly know. Finally know. There are zero filters. We fight and argue on a daily basis. Over three decades of being together has led to enormous transformations. During the Croatian trip, we caught up with ourselves—our lives as individuals and as a unit. He said to me thoughtfully, 'You and I have spent more years together than as single people. You have spent more years with me than in your parents' home. We have our differences. But what we share, love and enjoy together . . . now, that's what counts. I would rather be with you than with anybody else. Ours is a good fit—physically, mentally and emotionally.' It was stated quietly, more to himself than to me. I thought about it later. And my own conclusion surprised me! I too would rather be with this unpredictable, impassioned, frequently infuriating man than anybody else! He is my 'breaking news'. He can't wait to provide headlines he has just read with his cuppa. I value the service—but not at the crack of dawn! Not before I have enjoyed my first cup of chai. Not late at night either. I definitely don't want to engage in a heated political debate at odd moments, when my mind is on more mundane matters—like, should I add *lal mirchi ka tadka* to the masala khichdi, and throw in a generous pinch of *hing*?

Sure, these are important matters. The state, the nation. But hey—the world can wait!

I thought of the many times I had contemplated throwing in the towel, out of anger and exasperation. I am pretty sure he must have felt equally aggravated by me and my moods. Yet, through all that volatility and those emotional storms, we hung in there. And not because we didn't want to 'rock the boat', or were worried about what anybody would say. Then why? It wasn't because of the children. We are both pretty individualistic to let such concerns dictate our decisions. I still don't know why. Nor how! But am I glad we did. We are here today . . . together, yes, but still our own impossible selves. I recall his words, spoken early in our life together, 'There is no place for an ego in marriage.' True. If only the ego would listen . . . and disappear! I also remember him saying, 'I keep searching for the horizon. Remember, after a low tide, there's always a high tide.'

This chapter is over. The 'turning seventy' one. Maybe there are many more chapters still left to chronicle. Maybe not! But, if at the end of this book, you still want to ask, 'Tell us, madam . . . how do you maintain yourself?' you've obviously read the wrong book by the wrong woman.

On the other hand, it's one thing to jauntily declare: 'Seventy . . . and to hell with it!' You, dear reader, are entirely entitled to retort, 'And to hell with you too!'

Toh bhi . . . you are warned: *Likhna abhi baaki hai, yaaron.*

See what I mean? Once a 'kaarti' always a 'kaarti'.

There's today . . . there's maybe a tomorrow. About the day after . . . who knows? Today is all that counts.

~

Acknowledgements

Kiran Nagarkar, I owe you a big one. A couple of years ago, we ran into each other at a literary event and I lightly joked about something or someone. Kiran stared at me with a look of undisguised amusement and declared, 'You are such a "kaarti"!' I had forgotten that delicious word, and more importantly, I had forgotten the 'kaarti' in me. It was one of 'those' moments—of recognition and terror! Me? 'A kaarti'? At this age? Disgraceful!

Kiran and I converse in Marathi. I do so hungrily, since I don't get the chance often. It's difficult to translate 'kaarti'. But let me try. A 'kaarti' has to be female. And a bit of a rebellious, annoying brat. A kaarti generally exasperates people in her orbit. The last person to call me a kaarti had been my maternal grandmother. And she had not meant it affectionately. So when I heard it more than sixty years later, I was thrilled! Yesss! I am still that 'kaarti'. Thank you, Kiran, for providing the trigger and tone for the book. I consider Kiran one of my best girlfriends. Kiran's an honorary woman—and I mean that as a supreme compliment.

Here's a big shout-out to my Penguin family for all the encouragement and indulgence generously extended over thirty years. To Meru Gokhale, for commenting, 'This is not a "coming to terms with age" book. It is more a "coming of age" book.' Her observation came at a time when I was hopelessly stuck and despairing. I needed her clarity to prod me. Hemali Sodhi, steadfast and true, contained and efficient. An affectionate and caring friend. And above all, a simpatico marketing whizz who understands the madness of writers. Exuberant, gorgeous Milee with the infectious laugh, who nudged me at the right time to just do it—write the book! Swati Chopra, my editor, elegant and reassuring at all times. A soft, perceptive and gentle presence with sharp instincts. Gunjan Ahlawat, bubbly, hip, enthusiastic and creative, ready to experiment with cover ideas without groaning. My daughter Avantikka Kilachand Raju for styling the cover shoot. Of course, it's Photoshopped! But not too much. I wanted to keep all the grey at the temples. She put her foot down: 'No, Ma! It will make you look old!' I said firmly, 'Honey, I am old!'

And . . . and . . . and . . . finally, my most precious ones—my family. My husband, Dilip, and all our bachchas, who had no clue I was writing this book and kept asking irritatedly, 'What the hell are you doing?'

Now they know!

~

Someday, somewhere—anywhere, unfailingly,
you'll find yourself, and that and only that can be
the happiest or bitterest hour of your life . . .

—Pablo Neruda

Something, somewhere—anywhere, that allows
you to find yourself, and that and only that can be
the happiest and [illegible] thing of your life.

—Pablo [illegible]